AMERICAN TELEVISION DRAMA

William Hawes

American Television Drama

The Experimental Years

THE UNIVERSITY OF
ALABAMA PRESS

LIBRARY OF CONGRESS CATALOGING-IN-PUBLICATION DATA

Hawes, William, 1931–
    The American television drama.

    Bibliography: p.
    Includes index.
    1. Television broadcasting—United States—History.
2. Television plays—History and criticism. I. Title.
PN1992.3.U5H38   1986   812′.02′09   85–8549
ISBN 0–8173–0276–X (alk. paper)

In loving memory of my mother and father

Contents

Photographs

Acknowledgments

Fortunately, this history of television drama covers a recent enough period that it need not depend solely on the indispensable records of *The Billboard*, the British Broadcasting Corporation, Columbia Broadcasting System, Inc., the National Broadcasting Company, *The New York Times,* and *Variety.* For recollections of the past by its participants and curators, the author is indebted to many contributors and organizations that have generously shared their knowledge and facilities:

NBC, New York: Aaron M. Cohen, Marilyn Dean, Norma Garner.
CBS, New York: Fred Rappoport, Marjorie Holyoak, John Behrens, Marc D'Alleyrand, Jeanne Dembroski, Laura Kapnick, Carole Parnes.
CBS Television City, Los Angeles: Charles Cappleman, Robert L. Davis, Jr.
Walt Disney Productions, Burbank: Hilary Clark.
Television Information Office, New York: Roy Danish, Bert Briller, James B. Poteat, Leslie Slocum.
Museum of Broadcasting, New York: Ronald C. Simon.
General Electric, Schenectady: Arthur R. Garland.
Broadcast Pioneer Library, Washington, D.C.: Catharine Heinz.
Directors Guild of America, New York: Ernest Ricca, George Wallach; Hollywood: David Shepard.
Academy of Television Arts and Sciences, Los Angeles: Robert E. Lewine.
BBC Written Archives Centre, Reading, England: Jacqueline Kavanagh, Gwyniver Jones.

Also greatly appreciated is the assistance provided by the librarians at the Performing Arts Library of Lincoln Center; the New York Public Library; the American Film Institute, Los Angeles; the University of California at Los Angeles Television Archives; the M. D. Anderson Library of the University of Houston—University Park; the British Theatre Association Library; and the Victoria and Albert Museum Theatre Collection, London.

For interviews of insight and length, the author is grateful to participants of the period, such as Arthur Hungerford, Robert J. Landry, Florence Monroe, and Edward Stasheff; to such distinguished producers and directors of television and film as Herbert Brodkin, Marc Daniels, Delbert Mann, J. Paul Nickell, Gene Reynolds, George Schaefer, Franklin J.

Schaffner, and David Victor; and to writers John Furia, Jr., Tad Mosel, and Malvin Wald. Brief conversations with Charlton Heston, Mercedes McCambridge, Agnes Nixon, Lela Swift, and Shelley Winters were also helpful.

Special recognition is given to Worthington C. Miner for a long, enlightening interview the summer before he died and to his family—Peter Miner, Margaret Miner Rawson, Mary Miner, and William Fuller—for access to his personal papers.

For the unfailing support of my good friends in the industry, deep appreciation is extended to Yvette Romero and Terry Benczik, in New York; Walter Coblenz, Dick Block, Terry Jastrow, and John Tracy, in Los Angeles; Earl and Rhoda Wynn, in Chapel Hill, North Carolina; and Alvin Guggenheim, in Houston.

I am indebted to James Pipkin, associate dean of the College of Humanities and Fine Arts, and to Myrta Owens and Paul Mott for their assistance in obtaining two grants from the Office of Sponsored Programs of the University of Houston.

For three years or more Malcolm M. MacDonald, director of The University of Alabama Press, has given much encouragement; he also found two excellent readers who enhanced the manuscript. My appreciation extends to the staff of the University Press and to Robert G. Ferris for editorial care.

Most of all, my gratitude goes to my wife, Ella, and my sons, Kent and Rob, for their patience, understanding, and love.

WILLIAM HAWES

Preface

The 1920s were a period of transition in the entertainment industries. Theater enjoyed a revival after World War I. The 1928–29 season was a peak one on Broadway, despite the imminent demise of vaudeville. Silent motion pictures were transformed forever when they gained a voice in the 1927 motion picture *The Jazz Singer*. Numerous radio stations moved out of the experimental stage to begin significant local programming. The National Broadcasting Company (NBC) and the Columbia Broadcasting System (CBS) formed networks. The music recording business, which had refined its 78 r.p.m. wax disc, improved its quality. And engineers laid the foundation for an electronic rather than a mechanical method of scanning a television picture.

Even the Great Depression, which had hit the United States by 1929, did not immediately affect some of the entertainment industries. Emerging financial giants in entertainment were monopolizing production, distribution, and exhibition by owning theater chains, motion picture studios, recording companies, and broadcasting stations. To illustrate, the Radio Corporation of America (RCA), an equipment manufacturing company, formed a nationwide radio network, NBC (1926), and merged with a vaudeville theater circuit, Keith-Albee-Orpheum (1928), a motion picture company, Radio-Keith-Orpheum (RKO) (1928), and a recording company, Victor (1929).

Visionaries developing one medium often applied their imagination and optimism to other media. The public was enthusiastic about sound motion pictures, "free" advertisement-supported radio, attending the theater (Broadway seats were $3.40), and seeing blurred images on a small screen receiver called a "televiser." Although television was born in a period of national prosperity, its early evolution occurred during a period of national depression. The powerful figures who were already established in competitive media would be responsible for television drama. These pioneers were business executives and engineers, and later, producers, directors, actors, writers, and craftsmen. The radio and television industries drew artists and technicians from theater, motion pictures, and the recording businesses to expand their programming. That television drama made steady progress despite bleak financial times and serious instability in the entertainment industry is a tribute to the persistent vision of its pioneers and the spirit of stimulating competition. Of the many types of broadcast programs, radio and television executives considered drama to be the most complex and the most expensive.

Drama is a crystallization of human emotion displayed in dialogue, action, and scenes that reveal the best and the worst qualities of human beings. A conflict of human wills, circumstances, or actions are challenged until the conflict is resolved. The greater the magnitude of the challenge, such as a human being in conflict with the gods, nature, the environment, society or oneself, the greater the dramatic form. Polishing a drama requires money, time, dedication, and the consummate skills of many artists and craftsmen. Forms of drama include tragedy, comedy, melodrama, opera, operetta, farce, pantomime, monologue, and puppetry. Of these dramatic forms, comedy is the most popular, but light romance and crime are the most frequent.

A fascination for drama is intrinsic in everyone, and the roots of its growth on television will probably be of interest to the general reader of this volume. The principal objective, however, is to detail, as never before, the initial two decades of television drama for serious patrons, scholars, and students of the human arts. From a historical perspective, this study is an effort to show what trends in American culture led to a drama for the mass public as well as the nature of the impact of new technologies and changing entertainment industries on these television dramas.

In brief, during the 1920s technology made television drama possible; the 1930s saw the development of dramatic program content and production techniques; and the 1940s brought advertising revenue to support the rising costs of television dramas and captured sufficient public attention to make the previous decades of experimentation artistically worthwhile, and eventually, profitable. This history records the first twenty years: 1928, the year of the first television drama, through 1947, the year of the first dramatic anthology series.

This study includes a list of all of the known efforts in drama—feeble though some may be—at CBS and NBC, and many dramas at other principal experimental companies: WRGB, WABD, WOR, ABC, WPTZ, KTSL, KTLA, and WBKB. The narrative tells who produced these plays and why, and tries to create an understanding of what television drama was really like at a time when the term "television" was almost unheard of, when employment in this medium was day-to-day or voluntary, when no television networks existed, and when a few hundred viewers were a large audience.

AMERICAN TELEVISION DRAMA

1

The Heritage

Through the centuries, dramatic expression has become inseparable from human experience. Whether stories and plays were performed in huge amphitheaters, church pageants, traveling sideshows, or local repertory companies, the drama has become a staple of existence. It has preserved the meaning of life—its sorrows, frustrations, and joys—even during history's darkest periods.

These dramas have been presented mainly in a live forum. The shape of that forum or theater has varied, but the stories themselves remain amazingly fundamental in describing human intellectual and emotional nature as well as human desires and challenges. The dramas of Western culture that emerged in the eastern Mediterranean, evolved throughout Europe, and found their way eventually to America were adapted to scientific ingenuity during the industrial revolution. Live theatrical productions were no longer sufficient in variety of content, public exhibition hall capacity, or cost effectiveness to satisfy increasing public demand for dramatic entertainment. Thus, the inventions of film, recording, radio, and television during the late nineteenth and early twentieth centuries were timely.

From a technical standpoint, the movements in Impressionistic painting, film, and television—the visual arts—depended upon a similar basis for their pictorial displays: particles of color or black and white arranged in a mosaic maximizing the subtleties of diffuse light. The beauty of a still picture such as an original painting could be more widely shared by the public in reproductions made possible through photography. However, capturing the silent image was not totally satisfying. Moving and speaking images made possible by means of film and recording came closer to satisfying the audience, but such progress was still not enough. Television would eventually enable the public to capture and to keep images that it could display on demand, particularly favorite dramas stored on film and videotape.

The narrative that follows is largely a chronicle of transference and adaptation of existing dramatic material to the new media: the rather simple use of what was in the decades of the mid-twentieth century then new technology to meet the demands of a mass audience. Old wine, if you please, in newly shaped bottles was being sold or given away "free" in previously unheard of quantities.

Like a poor relative, television drama borrowed from art, literature, theater, film, and radio to form an eclectic entertainment, information, and eventually, advertising medium. At the outset, television was a melting pot for media. Artistically, the form and content of television dramas came from the theater, which had been similarly influenced by novels, short stories, and the art world; then from radio; and lastly from film. Gradually, film would become the dominant influence.

Television drama at CBS was guided mainly by financial stringencies; at NBC, principally by improving technology. Both of these companies were local operations until the mid-1940s. Local stations elsewhere in the nation largely repeated dramas that had been presented in the New York area. Adaptations prevailed; original dramas were rare. In America, television drama, despite complaints from critics, was based on its potential as an advertising or promotional medium or as an engineering experiment. In Great Britain, the British Broadcasting Corporation (BBC), operating under government authorization, presented a widely varied artistic schedule of television dramas that reaffirmed traditional cultural and social values, but likewise produced few original dramas.

An Impressionistic Image

Theatrical stage design, moving pictures, and later television utilized Impressionistic techniques to create a luminous, romantic, diffuse image. A video picture consists of many horizontal lines composed of thousands of dots; the film image depends on thousands of granules of silver laminated to a clear celluloid base. Television in its earliest days centered on a number of experiments in light and shadow. These experiments in the electronic medium parallel the experiments that had been conducted previously by Impressionist painters, who used light and color on linear canvas surfaces to produce a shimmering quality in their compositions.

The Impressionist movement, which began with Claude Monet's *Impression: Sunrise* in 1872, initiated attempts at showing the effect of light on objects at different times of day. Brilliant colors or light from behind or juxtaposed with other colors created an overall luminescence. Georges Seurat's *Sunday Afternoon on the Island of La Grande Jatte*

introduced pointillism in 1886, a technique employing tiny specks of paint to produce soft, fragile images when viewed from a distance. At the time, Impressionism was deplored in art circles of France, but the technique was soon applied to theater design. Adolphe Appia, staging Wagnerian operas, produced movement with light by changing intensity levels during a performance, and he created an illusion of depth by placing pools of light in various locations on stage. Joseph Urban, designing for Florenz Ziegfeld's revues, decorated flat surfaces with dabs of brilliant color that, when lighted from the front, cast a new intensity.

Besides their experiments in light and shadow, artists sought new subjects. Instead of painting gods and goddesses of mythology, rulers of kingdoms, and biblical subjects, the Impressionists attempted to describe ordinary human beings and to endow them with a radiance previously taken for granted. Television drama would inherit electronic Impressionism, including a romantic perspective on the lives of ordinary people. Decades would pass before computerized television, foreshadowed by the Impressionists ninety years earlier, would influence experiments in painting with light.

Theatrical Origins

A brief history of the principal theatrical contributions—mainly vaudeville, the musical stage, and plays—will suggest a background for the television dramas that followed, for both in the United States and England they were primarily forms of theater on the electronic stage. Adaptations of vaudeville sketches, musical shows, and stage plays based on literary works formed television drama's content.

Major concepts transferred from theater to television were the philosophy of repeating success, the dominance of character over plot (this yields to plot/action over character from the 1960s to the 1980s and swings back to character dominance after the mid-1980s); the persistence of reproducing the familiar; the emphasis on upbeat, optimistic, happy endings reinforced by feature films; and dependency on a series of acts, initially of irregular lengths, each of which rises to a secondary climax, or "tag," involving sufficient suspense to carry through the intermission, and later, commercials.

In television, nothing succeeds like success. The formula for success was an inexpensive production of an adaptation or excerpt of a hit Broadway play, based on a popular novel or short story, promoted in a recent movie, written by a famous author, staged by an experienced radio or film director, and starring a well-known performer. Because of televi-

sion's short time frame, usually ten to thirty minutes, vaudeville material was especially suitable. These sketches were short as well as inexpensive to produce and had already been pretested on theater audiences for laughs and good taste. At the advent of television drama, vaudeville had faded from view, and therefore, its material, used successfully for more than seventy years, was available.

Vaudeville

Vaudeville was a form of variety in that it consisted of a multitude of novelty acts: singers, dancers, magicians, comics, animal acts, light dramas, and comedy sketches. A "single" act often played in the front of the stage (downstage) while the big production numbers were being built behind drapes that concealed the upstage. Performers and writers, many of whom were uneducated and poor, had come from circuses, honky-tonks, and traveling medicine shows. They were willing to take a chance on show business.

Anyone could try out for the vaudeville stage. A multitude of different ideas were presented to the public, so long as they were within the guidelines of wholesome entertainment. The public wanted to be titillated and thrilled. The performers, writers, directors, and assorted theatrical talents perfected their abilities in this popular form of entertainment. In 1883 Benjamin F. Keith, a farm boy from New Hampshire joined the circus at age eleven, learned the management business, and twenty years later opened a theater in Boston. It presented vaudeville acts, including Thomas A. Edison's first movie, and in 1885 introduced a policy of "continuous performance," meaning that instead of consisting of one or two plays a day the program lasted from eleven in the morning until eleven at night. This concept was absorbed by broadcasting and film.

Keith and F. F. Proctor formed the Keith and Proctor Amusement Company, which at the time of Keith's death (1914) consisted of more than 400 theaters. This chain became a vital link in the Radio-Keith-Orpheum (RKO) circuit. Martin Beck ran the Orpheum circuit, which controlled vaudeville in the Midwest. Oscar Hammerstein, E. F. Albee, and Marcus Loew, who later headed Loew's Inc., of which MGM was a subsidiary, were other prominent figures in vaudeville. Through the efforts of Beck, the Palace Theatre was opened on Times Square in 1913, and it flourished as the citadel of vaudeville entertainment until after the stock market crash in 1929. To play the Palace was the dream of every vaudeville entertainer.

MUSICALS

Likewise, even the showboat, referred to as "The Floating Theater" when it started sailing the Ohio and Mississippi rivers in 1831, turned to vaudeville and musical presentations after it was revived following the Civil War. The Floating Theater would find its way to early television at NBC in dramatic and musical forms.

It might be said that the recording business started on the musical and vaudeville stages, for that is where Thomas Rice's song "Jim Crow" was introduced between acts of a play and later became the first international hit. Exploiting the vogue for Negro songs, Edwin P. Christy founded the Christy Minstrels in 1842 by putting black cork makeup on white actors and giving them banjos. The Christy Minstrels moved to Mechanic's Hall, on Broadway, in 1847 for a ten-year run, singing such songs as Stephen Foster's "O' Susanna" (1848) and "Jeannie with the Light Brown Hair" (1854). Receiving popular attention on the stage before the distribution of records were such Civil War favorites as Julia Ward Howe's "The Battle Hymn of the Republic," 1862, and Thomas Bishop's "When Johnny Comes Marching Home," 1863; Scott Joplin's "Maple Leaf Rag," 1899; George M. Cohan's "Give My Regards To Broadway," 1904, and "Mary's a Grand Old Name," 1906; and Irving Berlin's "Alexander's Ragtime Band," 1911.

LITERARY ADAPTATIONS

For plot and characters, legitimate theater produced some original material, but depended heavily upon a substantial American and European literary heritage. When possible, stage adaptations of literary works were rewritten, meaning largely reedited, for television. An abundance of stage plays based on novels or other prose works offered the path of least resistance for television producers provided that permission could be obtained inexpensively, that parameters for rewriting were flexible, and that the cast and scenic requirements were modest. The number and quality of famous literary works attempted as television dramas during the experimental years are impressive. Adaptations of Poe, Stowe, Boucicault, Alcott, O. Henry, Wharton, Ripley, O'Neill, Connelly, Kaufman, and Wilder are only a few of the works that were presented before the end of World War II, but if the list were extended another decade, or through the "live" period from New York, television's indebtedness to its literary heritage is overwhelming.

Drawing upon a hundred-year literary legacy that predated the first

television drama, the principal trend luring the mass television audience was reflected in the works of American and European writers who were chosen for television adaptation. The principal category was escapism, roughly divided into adventure, romance, and fantasy. Adventure was represented by Mark Twain's *The Adventures of Tom Sawyer* (1876), *The Prince and the Pauper* (1881), *The Adventures of Huckleberry Finn* (1884), and *A Connecticut Yankee in King Arthur's Court* (1889); Howard Pyles's *The Merry Adventures of Robin Hood* (1883); Owen Wister's *The Virginian* (1902); Edward Stratemeyer's *The Hardy Boys* (1906) and *Nancy Drew* (1930); and Edgar Rice Burroughs's *Tarzan and the Apes* (1914). So strong was the interest in adventure that some of these stories have become continuing series during recent decades.

For romance, no one was more appealing before and after World War II than Louisa May Alcott, especially *Little Women* (1869) and *Little Men* (1871), though the Brontë sisters were her rivals among European writers. Later, when television drama gained momentum after the war, Clyde Fitch's *Beau Brummel* (1890), Kate Douglas Wiggins's *Rebecca of Sunnybrook Farm* (1903), O. Henry's "The Gift of the Magi" (1906), Eugene O'Neill's *Desire under the Elms* (1924), and Ernest Hemingway's *The Sun Also Rises* (1926) were among those added as major telecasts. Edna Ferber's 1926 hit, *Showboat,* reawakened interest in "The Floating Theater."

Fantasy designed for both children and adults was prominent. Aside from Poe, Joel Chandler Harris's *Uncle Remus: His Songs and His Sayings* (1890), L. Frank Baum's *The Wonderful Wizard of Oz* (1900), and Robert L. Ripley's "Believe It Or Not" (1918) are among the outstanding American contributions, though the works of several Europeans are of equal importance: Carroll, Stevenson, Wells, Verne, Stoker, and, of course, the enduring story that precedes them all, Mary Wollstonecraft Shelley's *Frankenstein.*

The significant influences on American television drama that came from Europe were the works of Shakespeare and the impact of the Romantic movement, beginning with Victor Hugo's dramas *Cromwell* (1827) and *Hernani* (1830); composer Hector Berlioz' *Symphonie fantastique* (1830); and Filippo Taglioni's ballet *La Sylphide* (1832). The Romantic movement's idealization of love, magnification of personality, desire for adventure, and emphasis on exotic locations prompted an atmosphere that enthralled the predominantly bourgeois audiences attending American theaters, and soon the greater mixture of economic classes attending the movies. To this day, Hugo's *The Hunchback of Notre Dame* (1831) and Lytton's *The Last Days of Pompeii* (1834), both popular romantic novels, are adapted for film and television.

Despite the social ramifications of the Great Depression, American television took little interest in controversy until recent years. Injustice expressed a hundred years earlier by Charles Dickens in *Oliver Twist* (1837), *Nicholas Nickleby* (1838), *A Christmas Carol* (1843), and *A Tale of Two Cities* (1859), as well as perhaps by Hugo in *Les Miserables* (1862), were sufficiently far removed not in theme but in setting to be "safe" for production. Escapism ran counter to the social realities of crime, hypocrisy, and vice in such novels as Gustave Flaubert's *Madame Bovary* (1857), Émile Zola's *Nana* (1880), and George Bernard Shaw's *Mrs. Warren's Profession* (1893), a stage play frequently banned. Leo Tolstoy's *War and Peace* and *Anna Karenina*, Fyodor Dostoevski's *Crime and Punishment*, and Henrik Ibsen's *A Doll's House, An Enemy of the People*, and *Hedda Gabler*—all dealing with individual and public reform—failed to receive much attention. The BBC did little better than the Americans in showing controversial dramas to viewers prior to 1947, though it did telecast four Eugene O'Neill plays: *Ah, Wilderness!*, his only comedy, *The Emperor Jones, All God's Chillun Got Wings*, and *In the Zone*.

Although television drama drew upon its theater heritage in vaudeville, the musical stage, and plays adapted from the literature of previous decades, it looked to the moving picture for aesthetic and technical standards. When television dramas were finally ready for public viewing, they should compare favorably with the movies. Television marketing experts figured that the public would expect a high standard of audio and visual perfection at the outset, and television engineers worked laboriously toward that objective, frequently using short dramas as experimental vehicles.

THE SILENT PICTURE ENDOWMENT

The impact of the movie industry on television drama was gradual. During the experimental years, its contribution to television drama was, first, as a standard of technical quality, second, as a provider of production techniques, and third, as a bequeather of the "star" system.

It might be said that television inherited the star system from the movies. Actually, silent films borrowed the system from the theater. Charles Frohman, a theatrical producer from 1896 to 1906, deliberately set out to promote attractive and talented personalities in order to enhance their box-office draw while touring the country. By putting their names on elevated electric marquees, he marketed performers as much as plays. Florence Lawrence was perhaps the first film actress who was presented to the public as a "star." She was originally known as the

"Biograph girl" because she made films for Biograph, a pioneer studio, which like other early studios refused to give screen credits to performers. Public demand to know her name was so strong that the British made one up: "Muriel Fortescue."[1] When the "Biograph girl" moved to Imp studios in 1908, their head, Carl Laemmle, planted a story of her death and then resurrected her in the press as the "Imp girl." Public attention to film stars was inescapable thereafter. Television drama sought them whenever it could obtain them, but during the early years they always came from the stage or radio.

No aspect of television drama is more fascinating than its aesthetic heritage: the motion picture standard of perfection. Like an accomplished older child, television drama could not escape comparison with its motion picture counterpart. The history of the motion picture standard arose from its antecedents in photography, which had evolved over the centuries. The year 1826 is a benchmark, for Joseph Niepce then photographed a country scene, still preserved, using a wooden camera. The 1830s and 1840s brought the stunning work of William Fox-Talbot, who used sensitized paper prints, and Louis Daguerre, who invented the daguerreotype, a method of producing an image on a copper plate with mercury vapor and silver. The calotype portraits of the Robert Adamson and David Hill team ("Picnic at Bonaly" and "Miss Monro") and Hippolyte Bayard ("Windmills at Montmartre") featured subjects that were delicately defined in soft tones and a subtle range of hues.

During the 1860s, continuity in photographs emerged as Mathew Brady told the story of the American Civil War. These still photographs are antecedents of and contemporary with Impressionism and pointillism in the 1870s and 1880s as well as moving pictures in the 1880s and 1890s. These photographs are works of art in their own right, though they were largely unrecognized at the time. Composition, chiaroscuro, timeless subjects, depth of portraiture, and conflict of situation are some of the characteristics that have captured the eternal beauty and arresting qualities enjoyed by succeeding generations.

Still photographs took on the challenge of movement when roll film was introduced in 1888, linked with a projection system, and viewed in 1895. A simple study in movement was then given continuity, grace, effortless interplay, and the direction of viewer attention to meaning, eventually through designed messages and stories. Photography, cinematography, and Impressionist art were similar in that common subjects assumed timeless attributes: a man's sneeze (Dickson), the flight of a bird (Marey), the gallop of a horse (Muybridge), the movement of a train (Lumière), and a close-up of a man firing a pistol (Porter) took on a new sense of artistic immortality. Once moving pictures were introduced, the

bulk of public attention turned to that industry; photography faded into the background and was not revitalized until Alfred Stieglitz touted its merits years later (1902).

As public enthusiasm and ticket sales at the box offices increased, ten- to thirty-minute filmed dramas lengthened to an hour or more. In 1912 Paramount's Adolph Zukor introduced the first four-reel feature in America, *Queen Elizabeth,* a filmed stage play starring the aging Sarah Bernhardt. Secretly, meanwhile, the silent screen's most noteworthy director, David Wark Griffith, filmed *Judith of Bethulia* (1913), a biblical story. This four-reeler tells about a young woman who enters the camp of a general beseiging her city and beheads him.

Disappointed that the film did not receive the attention Griffith thought it deserved, he combined a version of Thomas Dixon's novel *The Clansman,* a reconstruction of Mathew Brady's historic photographs, and his own southern perspective on the events of the American Civil War into his silent-screen masterpiece, *The Birth of a Nation* (1915). It tells how two families—one from the North, one from the South—survive the Civil War. In a rousing climax, the southern heroine is saved from an unscrupulous mulatto (the villain) by the Ku Klux Klan (the heroes). Controversy and even riots accompanied the showing of the film wherever it played, yet it remains a classic.

The list of silent feature films grew. The voiceless images concentrated on the visual element: the expression of meaning with little or no dependency on words. In shades of gray, sometimes sepia, and modified by hand-tinted or colored filters, the moving images possessed the timeless dimensions of fine still photographs. The great artists of moving pictures, demonstrating remarkable skill, managed to allow characters to flow in and out of the limitations of the film frame and to yield action, composition, beauty, grace, style, and enchantment.

By 1927 the silent film had found a voice that sounded its death knell. The concentration shifted from the timeless succession of beautiful still photographs, creating an illusion of monochrome movement with minimum continuity, to the complex addition of speech, noise, and music. Sound would rule the studios of the future. The following year, the troubled movie industry was in a confused state of transition, converting silent to sound studios at huge expense and trepidation, and it was therefore not ready to absorb television.

The silent-film industry, however, had consolidated the small pioneer companies and was well on the way to emerging as eight large corporations: Paramount, Metro-Goldwyn-Mayer, Universal, Columbia, 20th Century Fox, RKO, Warner Bros., and United Artists, which was mainly a distributor of independent feature films. These companies proceeded to

monopolize the principal aspects of production, distribution, and exhibition. Opinion on the potential impact and value of television was divided. Producers of films (the "product") saw the advantages of providing additional filmed dramas for television; by contrast, exhibitors and distributors were fearful that this medium would replace movie houses, in which millions of dollars were already invested. Because the business side dominated the film industry, the marketable items—the scripts, the stars, and the films themselves, even though in libraries and not in circulation—were withheld from television. Movie moguls did what they could to impede the progress of early television dramas by urging unions, for example, to demand scale wages for the profitless fledgling medium.

The major impact of the film industry would be delayed so long as the principal film companies monopolized the industry. This lasted until the 1950s, when, after more than a decade of litigation, the U.S. Justice Department forced the separation of production from distribution-exhibition interests (1952).

Television's inheritance from the movies other than its quality standard and certain operational techniques that were foreign to radio was passed on as a later endowment, a delayed collection of benefits that would influence television when videotape became available. As to aesthetics, the look of a television drama in the experimental days was different from a movie, as the look of a sound-on-film drama differed from a silent film or a photograph from an Impressionistic painting. Yet, the great works in these media are similar in refinement, eternal remembrance, and the richness they bring to human life.

Speculation on what influence film might have exerted on television drama if attitudes had been different is worthwhile. All television drama might have been on film; there might not have been a live period and never a transfer of stage-oriented dramas to television. Consequently, directing and production techniques might never have been infused from radio. If movies had filled the screen from the beginning, residual financial benefits in reruns and syndication might have become apparent, and the wealth might have accrued to the movie industry. The major film companies might have survived governmental concern over embracing the new industry, and the golden era of the American studio film might have extended to this very day. If television dramas had depended on film, the search for electronic substitutes—videotape—might have been less diligent. As it turned out, the reluctance of film moguls to embrace television drama during the experimental years produced a positive impact on television: it eventually made television and television drama self-sufficient. For this reason, television drama established technical ca-

pabilities, stories, stars, editing techniques, aesthetics, financing, and its own public.

The Influence of Radio

The early histories of radio and television are parallel in time. However, radio technology, which was simpler to devise, was ready for the marketplace sooner than that of television. Because theater and the silent films required ticket sales at the box office, public access to these media was limited. Radio, on the other hand, was advertisement-supported, used the public airwaves, and came into homes without charge. Accessible to anyone who had a receiver, it became a truly *mass* medium. As a result, it experienced many constraints, and these would be passed on to television drama. They fall into two categories: administrative limitations, including distribution, program scheduling, and financing; and production restrictions, including types of programming, the concept of live origination, sources of talent, censorship, and facilities.

RADIO'S EARLY HISTORY

Reginald Fressenden's broadcast of the first radio program consisting of voice and music in 1906 was made possible by the inventions of James Maxwell, who theorized on the nature of electromagnetic waves; Heinrich Hertz, who transmitted and received the first radio waves; Guglielmo Marconi, who developed a commercially successful spark coil transmitter; John Ambrose Fleming, who invented the superheterodyne radio circuit; and many others.

As World War I approached, radio looked promising for military purposes because it allowed a signal to be sent vast distances over inaccessible terrain and water. Shipping on the high seas was safer as the result of the Wireless Ship Act of 1910, requiring ships to operate ship-to-shore radios. In 1912 the licensing of radio stations in the United States was established through the secretaries of commerce and labor. Radio's usefulness proved itself to those serving in the First World War, and its values were expanded from point-to-point communication to a general distribution of informal conversation and music.

Businessmen, working with clever inventors in the laboratories of the major manufacturers of communication equipment—American Telephone and Telegraph (AT&T), Westinghouse, and General Electric (GE)—saw even broader potential for radio. To these companies, a

fourth was added in 1919: the Radio Corporation of America (RCA). It was organized specifically to operate radio stations and sell receivers. The boards of directors of these companies tended to be the same individuals, and they collaborated in establishing agreements that allowed each of the businesses to share in the development and ultimately the enormous profits of the new industries. The expense was substantial and speculative. No single company possessed enough patents to deliver sound at a significant level of quality for public acceptance. They therefore pooled their patents in cross-licensing agreements, which were substantially in place by the early 1920s. Meanwhile, these same companies conducted experiments in television.

If the corporate sector were to invest huge sums of money, it needed regulation. Public use of the airways could no longer be casual; action was necessary to improve the exclusivity and clarity of the broadcast signal. A series of conferences resulted in the Radio Act of 1927, establishing the Federal Radio Commission (FRC). The FRC determined engineering standards, assigned frequencies for operation, and began to establish formal guidelines for the industry. Once engineering requirements were formalized, stations concentrated on programming. RCA set up a subsidiary, the National Broadcasting Company (NBC), consisting of two networks that were linked through the leasing of AT&T lines and cables: the Red Network (1926) and the Blue Network (1927). NBC's chief rival in programming, the Columbia Broadcasting System (CBS), forming somewhat later in 1927, did not manufacture sets. The other major manufacturers—GE and Westinghouse—developed or sponsored programming only in limited ways as the result of an antitrust action.

For programming concepts, radio turned to the theater, specifically to vaudeville. By measuring the variety concept over a broadcast day in systematic periods of five-, fifteen-, thirty-, and sixty-minute programs, punctuated by briefer commercial inserts, radio scheduling was established. Its program log, resembling a vaudeville bill, grew to a $250 million business within a decade. Among radio's first dramas were *Henry Adams and His Book,* a serial prototype produced at WHT, Chicago, in 1925, and *First Nighter,* a theater anthology, heard on the Blue Network in 1929. An R. G. Dun and Company survey reported that the amount of money spent on radio entertainment in 1931 was $35 million; in 1932, $40 million. This boom in radio made possible the building of large studios and the purchasing of future sites, where eventually television dramas would be produced.

While radio progressed rapidly, television experiments were conducted in secret because whenever it was announced, as was often the case, that television was nearly ready for sale to the public, radio sales declined

sharply. The most prevalent explanation for delaying television was engineering difficulties. However, M. H. Aylesworth, president of RKO and NBC, speculated in 1933 that, even though RCA-Victor television was fit for the marketplace, it would be delayed for two or three years because of the depression.[2] Dr. Vladimir Zworykin agreed: "Television is ready now. The electrical problems are solved. It now remains for the financial and merchandising experts to do their job."[3] If it had not been for the nation's financial crisis, the public might have had television by 1933, and radio might not have become as prominent as it did. Radio's commercial program growth might have been stunted, and the dramatic programming and techniques television received from radio might have developed elsewhere and differently.

RADIO'S ADMINISTRATIVE CONSTRAINTS

Television drama came under the influence of the procedures of established radio networks and local stations. The networks presented major dramas that originated in New York, Los Angeles, Chicago, Detroit, and a few other local stations. To coordinate the scheduling of programs from diverse points of origin, a precise schedule, or "log," listing all the programs and commercials evolved; and it became the cornerstone of program decision-making, placement, continuity, airtime availability, pricing, research, and analysis. Television drama complied with the radio logging schedule. Scheduling is inherent in the American theater, where one or two plays begin at announced times; it is more apparent in movies, where a continuous schedule lasts most of the day and night; and it is imperative in radio, where shorter programs are offered throughout a twenty-four-hour day. Television drama followed radio in this rigid administrative decision; in contrast, varied program lengths are allowed in some foreign countries. During the experimental years, the lengths of television dramas ranged from a few minutes to more than one and a half hours. After television became commercial, an "hour" drama would actually run about forty-five minutes. Frequent interruptions became acceptable to the public.

Besides distribution and scheduling, radio passed along its system of financing programs mainly through the purchase of entire programs and/or spot announcements within program periods by advertising agencies representing major business interests, who usually sold products and services directly to a broad and diverse mass public. Television dramas sponsored by such clients provided prestige and product exposure. Shaping the public's perception of a corporation, that is, its "image," has always been a foremost buying consideration.

Public response has been measured virtually since radio became a viable commercial enterprise. The Crossley and C. E. Hooper rating services, beginning in the 1930s, advised radio advertisers of public preferences in programming. Unlike theater and film, which depend on box-office ticket sales for financing and recognition of public acceptance, television drama would rely on a rating system that had been devised for radio and was improved for television. The larger the audience, the greater the sponsor's demand to reach a major share of it. Cost per thousand (CPM) would eventually grow to cost per million viewers. Consistency in high ratings for nighttime programs would in future decades spell doom for live television drama.

RADIO'S PRODUCTION CONSTRAINTS

The principal constraints imposed on radio program content were program classifications, live programming, censorship, and limited facilities.

Program Classifications. Radio programming involved all kinds of formats. In drama, the classifications had been established by the silent films: romance, comedy, westerns, horror, crime, and so forth. Radio dramas came from theater adaptations, movies, and original scripts. The sound medium was not much of a competitor for theater or feature films; in fact, radio tended to stimulate them. The *Lux Radio Theatre* originated on the Blue Network in 1934, when it presented adaptations of Broadway plays starring Broadway actors. In 1936, however, it moved to Hollywood, where Cecil B. DeMille took over as host and director. From then on, it featured radio adaptations of famous motion pictures using film stars.[4]

Radio could not really duplicate theater or the movies. Radio drama was theater of the imagination. It stimulated the listener's imagination, an area in which constraint rested with the listener, not with the medium. Mystery, horror, and fantasy were especially popular. The fantasy that played upon the mind, because of the nature of the sound medium, was nontransferable to television. Programs like *Let's Pretend,* a children's series on CBS beginning in 1934, have never been equaled on television on account of the visual limitations imposed on one's imagination. Another special dramatic concept—the docu-drama—was transferred to television. The reenactment of historical events and biographies of famous persons, such as Zola, Juarez, Disraeli, Ziegfeld, and Pasteur, was also popular in the movies. The docu-drama includes actuality reconstruction; reenacted real events; semifactual stories; mainly fictional dramas "based on" or inspired by real events that use actual names and

places; and, recently, extemporized dramatic situations. A fine line has been drawn between truth and fiction. The NBC Blue Network and the CBS *Columbia Workshop* originated many of radio's finest experimental dramas and program series.

Radio recognized and expanded the categories of series dramas: miniseries, specials, anthologies of theatrical adaptations, original workshop dramas, serials, and soap operas. The gamut of programming that appeared as television drama during the experimental period was borrowed in principal from radio, which had taken it from the movies. Relatively few specific programs or series originating on radio were attempted on television during the early days because they were not considered adaptable to the visual medium.

Live Programming. Each medium offers something unique to the public. The stage was live. After the advent of sound films, live production engaged in a battle with feature pictures. During the early 1930s, a campaign to return live acts to theater bills, now dominated by the movies, was an attempt by managers to encourage public attendance. This move furnished temporary relief for unemployed vaudeville performers, improved ticket sales, and fostered the notion that live acts were superior to or better box office than motion pictures. In 1931 *The Billboard* announced that "it is absolutely impossible for any one publication to honestly serve both the film interests and the 'flesh.' . . . The Billboard prefers to be 'flesh.'"[5] Many show-business observers believed that, even if television were live and did not use film, theater would never die because the public would demand live performers.[6] The concept of living theater deeply infiltrated radio and early television. As Gilbert Seldes stated, "Everything in the movies exists in the past tense; in radio and television everything is in the present."[7]

Maintaining live programs proved to be a struggle. Radio aired many electrical transcriptions, then discs, wire recordings, and audiotapes. Television, from its inception, used much film, and eventually, videotape. *The Billboard* reported: "In 1930 World Broadcasting brought out the first $33\frac{1}{3}$ recording, using Western Electric equipment and benefiting from the research experience of the Bell Telephone Laboratories."[8] Six years later, it was expected that advertisers, then using recordings circulated by large electrical transcription libraries, would buy more than $10 million worth of electrical transcription time. Radio could have been engulfed by electrical transcriptions, but CBS and NBC held to the policy that "a network listener should always have the assurance he was listening to a program *now going on.* For this reason they early banned from their network facilities recorded music and recorded intelligible speech."[9] Not until

television threatened to ruin radio completely did network radio rely on largely recorded programs, though "the ban on the use of their network facilities began to be eased during World War II when eyewitness descriptions of battles, recorded by the new portable wire and tape recorders, began to be available."[10]

In regard to the radio performers themselves, the transition to television resembled that of silent film actors attempting to survive in the talkies. Some made it; most did not. Visual charisma, acting techniques, and public expectations were among the considerations.

Censorship. A threat of censorship has consistently pervaded the media, but they have thrived on it. They use it as a tool for promoting their services. In American culture, sex-related entertainment is probably the most powerful enticement the media can offer the public. Innuendo and double entrendre in dialogue, suggested and actual nudity on stage, and themes of promiscuity and prostitution date back to the earliest forms of theater. Censorship accompanied the movies from the first flickers. When Fatima danced in the Chicago World's Fair (1896), certain hip movements were blocked out of the film by horizontal bars.[11] The famous "kiss" between May Irwin and John Rice seemed infinitely more daring in a screen close-up (1896) than it did in their stage play.

The concern of the public was aroused when the images of its heroes and heroines on screen were confused with its perception of the off-screen behavior of the human beings who played them. This confusion manifested itself in a rash of adverse criticism and sensational reporting on the personal lives of major film stars during the 1920s. Such favorites as comedians Fatty Arbuckle and Mabel Normand as well as handsome hero Wallace Reid were involved in various scandals related to sex and drugs. As a result, the movies formed in 1922 a self-policing group, the Motion Picture Producers and Distributors of America, headed by a Presbyterian elder and former U.S. postmaster general, Will Hays. Dictates from the Hays office prohibited scenes of horizontal lovemaking and themes that tended to proclaim to America's youth that sin was attractive and worthwhile. Radio inherited these restrictive notions and added a number of its own, including the banning of unfavorable references to ethnic, racial, and religious groups that it served every day.

As the 1930s progressed, the media industries felt the impact of the depression (1933) and returned to an old standby, sex. Many stars specialized in the display of sexual prowess, but none personified its benefits better than stage star Mae West, whose income in the third year of the Great Depression was reported to be $480,833. Although until this time she had made few talkies, they usually showed the life of a worldly

woman who was intimate with handsome men, possessed untold wealth, enjoyed her allegedly wicked life, and, significantly, anticipated no retribution. Miss West never appeared nude in her movies nor did she perform any obscene acts. Surrounded by a good-looking entourage and often bedecked in an ostentatious display of diamonds, she delivered her lines of relative innocence ("It's not the men in my life what counts, it's the life in my men"; "Diamonds are mah hobby"; "Come up and see me") with sultry innuendo and good humor. Her distinctive nasal voice was a natural for radio; and in the mid-thirties she acted in an "Adam and Eve" sketch on an extremely popular radio series starring Edgar Bergen and Charlie McCarthy. Her sexual inferences were brought right into the homes of radio listeners, who had come to trust the medium as family entertainment. Many of them thought the sketch was hilarious, but others were offended. Miss West was virtually banned from broadcasting for many years.

Some of America's foremost playwrights generated public ire because their stage plays were presented on radio virtually intact. When a radio version of Eugene O'Neill's Pulitzer-prize-winning tragedy, *Beyond the Horizon,* was broadcast, a public outcry was heard again. The most memorable objection to a radio program did not involve language or sex. It was a last-minute adaptation of H. G. Wells's *War of the Worlds,* presented by the Mercury Theatre under the direction of Orson Welles on Halloween 1938. This one-hour broadcast, innocent in its intent, described an "invasion" of the East Coast by Martians as though it were reporting an actual news event. This was an early docu-drama. The public reacted *with belief*—to the surprise of everyone on the program—and horror. Many tuned in late because the highly rated competition, Edgar Bergen and Charlie McCarthy, was off the air that night. The latecomers thought the Martians were really bringing death and destruction. Complaints flooded in from all over the country; and, whenever the drama was subsequently presented, such as in South America, the same public outcry occurred. Claims in commercial messages as well as the programming of astrology, medical advice, and games of chance also came under scrutiny.

Religious organizations rushed in to establish guidelines in regard to moral judgments and the suitability of material for families and children. The Catholic National Legion of Decency took a leadership role in the 1930s that rated films as "Passed," "Objectionable in Part," or "Condemned." Encouraged by the Hays office, Catholics revised and enforced the Motion Picture Code under the supervision of Joseph I. Breen, who observed every aspect of production. Besides the filmmakers, the National Association of Broadcasters (NAB) published pamphlets that of-

fered suggestions to producers. Although these suggestions were not strictly enforceable like laws, they had the effect of law in many program decisions. Thus, an aura of content restrictions emerged. Continuity acceptance departments sprang up at the networks, and every script was read with an eye to its acceptablity.

The Federal Communications Commission (FCC), formed by the Communications Act of 1934 as a permanent body to replace the FRC, did not want to face the knotty problem of censoring broadcast content because the legislation did not include that responsibility and such action might be unconstitutional. But in 1937 the FCC did list fourteen kinds of program material it deemed to be unsuitable or against the public interest: defamation, racial or religious intolerance, favorable references to hard liquor, obscenity, torture, excessive suspense in children's programs, false advertising, and interruptions in artistic programming. Several years later, another guideline, not a law, was issued by the FCC entitled the *Blue Book* (1946), in which a more definitive position was provided for broadcasters. The powerful influence of public opinion, the FCC, and the historical experience of the media in regard to objectionable material distributed over public airways furnished a conscience for early television dramas, which were, above all else, seeking to please everyone.

Production.   Radio imposed production limitations. Its big studios were designed for audience participation programs, such as talk and game shows, musical variety, dramas, and comedies, where applause and laughter were stimulating to the performers. These large studios were the easiest to convert to television. Remodeled radio space and theaters were used everywhere. New studios were built, but much of the space in New York was really a conversion. Studios providing unlimited space were constructed in Hollywood. The initial television production staffs were hired primarily from the fields of radio engineering and production, in part because the personnel was already there. Many artists—key producer/directors and performers—came from the theater. After the experimental period, a few large television studios were built outside Manhattan, for instance in Brooklyn, but the principal activity in drama has remained in converted space in Manhattan or new studios in Los Angeles. The drawbacks of converted space usually include limited floor areas, low ceilings, inadequate air conditioning, and little surrounding storage as well as ancillary rooms. Consequently, early television dramas tended to rely on one interior set.

Radio engineers were forced to grapple with television's visual demands: scenery, makeup, and lighting techniques. These techniques were integrated from theater, tested in radio studios, and emerged, after much

trial and error, suitable for video. Virtually every television drama during the 1930s was in fact an engineering experiment that was considered to be unsuitable for public demonstration. Camera improvements that sharpened picture quality were the basis for the experiments. Achievements in resolution can best be tabulated by the number of lines scanned; the greater the number, the better the picture. The number increased from about 60 lines in the mid-1920s to 525 lines, the commercial standard, twenty years later; simultaneously, the iconoscope camera of the early 1930s was replaced by the orthicon camera of the late 1930s, and it was improved by the image orthicon of the mid-1940s. The electronic scanning capabilities of video cameras were central to quality acceptance for television dramas because the picture was always compared with film resolution.

Origins of Television Drama

At the end of World War I, the United States entered a period of dizzy prosperity. Nowhere was this more pronounced than in the several blocks around Times Square, New York, known as the "theater district." The artistic community consolidated its productions in these ten blocks. The best in theater, film, publishing, and art was discussed and reviewed in the hotels, clubs, and restaurants. It was a rather insular community— 3,500 miles from London by ship and 3,000 miles from Los Angeles by train. Taxis, subways, cars, and buses were prevalent, but everything that mattered was within walking distance.

Vaudeville was alive and well at the Palace; Eugene O'Neill, Elmer Rice, Robert E. Sherwood, and Sidney Howard had plays around the corner; *The New York Times* was just west of Broadway and the *Variety* offices were just east of it; Roxy built the "Cathedral of the Motion Picture"; Texas Guinan managed her tinseled speakeasy; David Belasco was still producing Victorian revivals; George Gershwin and Gertrude Lawrence were appearing at Aeolian Hall; German operas, omitted from the repertoire at the Metropolitan Opera House, built in 1883, gained new favor with the public as they were heard once again; boxing was big business at Madison Square Garden; and Florenz Ziegfeld was charging an outrageous $7 to see *The Midnight Frolic* on the roof of the New Amsterdam Theatre. The theatrical and literary elite met at the Astor, the Algonquin, the Taft, 21, and Sardi's.

A few blocks from the sparkling lights of the legitimate theaters along Forty-second Street and Broadway, a newer entertainment complex was being established at Rockefeller Center, housing the world's largest the-

ater for stage shows and movies and, across the street at NBC, broadcasting the first radio dramas. Nearby CBS was headquartered in the heart of the advertising world on Madison Avenue.

MECHANICAL TELEVISION

Television is a composite invention, combining a number of discoveries in several related fields of electricity, electromagnetism, and electrochemistry. Therefore, no one person stands out as its inventor. During previous decades, the major experimental efforts had been directed toward a mechanical scanning system. A rapidly revolving wheel, referred to as a scanning disk, was developed by Paul Nipkow, a Russo-German scientist, in 1884; and a complete television system using this principal was demonstrated by the Scottish inventor John L. Baird in England by the mid-1920s.

The basic elements in mechanical television were the subject, a pickup camera, a transmission system, and a receiver. Human subjects were required to sit almost motionless under banks of high intensity lights, while the studio itself remained dark. They looked straight ahead into a tiny rectangular opening at the front of the camera. Inside the camera, aided by lenses and a shutter device, an intense beam of light generated within, called a "flying spot," was directed over the subject's image by means of a metal disk that was carefully punched with rectangular holes arranged in a spiral pattern.[12] As the flying spot scanned the subject a dozen or more times per second, the information it gathered, mechanically, was transformed into electrical impulses. It was then sent via wire to nearby locations, where the process was reversed, and the information was displayed on the screen of the receiver, which contained an inside synchronized scanning disk. By the late 1920s "the picture was composed of 60-line images at a frame frequency of 20 per second. The 'camera,' so called, was cumbersome and immobile, limiting action, for all practical purposes, to an area of approximately eight square feet."[13]

The mechanical system presented many problems. The process was slow, the focus was soft, the picture was unstable. The images were limited to facial movements that required abnormal definition through makeup, and lights near the subjects in the studio were so close and hot that actors were sometimes burned. Mechanical television received special attention during the twenties; during the next decade, interest in it was revived from time to time and a color dimension was added.

A major inventor and promoter of mechanical television was Charles Francis Jenkins, who for the benefit of a few guests transmitted the first motion picture on 13 June 1925 in his Washington, D.C., laboratory (for

various "firsts," see Appendix E). The film showed a small Dutch wind-mill. On 17 April 1927 the first artist to appear on television was included in a demonstration shown in the Bell Telephone Laboratories in New York City on two receiving apparatuses, one measuring 2 by 2½ feet, the other 2 by 2½ inches. The demonstration consisted of two parts: the first featured dignitaries viewed by wire from Washington, D.C., and the second part was transmitted from AT&T's experimental radio station 3XN, in Whippany, New Jersey. According to *The New York Times*, "the broadcast consisted of three 'acts': an address by Edward L. Nelson, an engineer at Bell Laboratories, a 'vaudeville act' featuring 'a stage Irishman, with side whiskers and a broken pipe . . . [who] did a mono-logue in brogue,' and then did a quick change and returned in black face 'with a new line of quips in negro dialect'; and, finally, the third act, 'a short humorous dialect talk.' "[14]

At the same time, Jenkins was continuing his experiments in a Wash-ington laboratory at 1519 Connecticut Avenue. Especially noteworthy were his telecasts over W3XK on 6420 and 1605 kilohertz (kHz). The Federal Radio Commission (FRC) noted that "transmission over this station had actually been inaugurated . . . on 5 May 1928, with an elabo-rate invitation announcing the 'birth of a new industry—Radio Movies—i.e., Pantomime Pictures by Radio for Home Entertainment.' "[15] Other movie stories followed, all of them in silhouette. During that same year of 1928, television drama took, what seemed to be, a giant step forward.

The First Television Drama

On 11 May 1928 Martin P. Rice, manager of broadcasting for the General Electric Company in Schenectady, announced that a regular schedule of television programs would be broadcast from 1:30 to 2:00 P.M., EST, that afternoon for the benefit of experimenters and amateurs who had constructed television sets.[16] On a three-by-three-inch television screen that blurred, flickered, and stabilized its 41 lines with uncertainty, viewers could see images of men talking, laughing, and smoking. These transmissions were the results of experiments by Dr. Ernst F. W. Alexan-derson, working in the General Electric laboratories.

Included in the schedule four months later on 11 September 1928 was the first television drama. According to *The New York Times*, "For the first time in history, a dramatic performance was broadcast simul-taneously by radio and television. Voice and action came together through space in perfect synchronization, in a forty-minute broadcasting of J. Hartley Manners's one-act play, 'The Queen's Messenger,' an old spy melodrama, for years a favorite with amateur thespians, which was

chosen for the experiment because its cast contains only two actors, who would alternate before the television cameras."[17] Manners, who had begun his stage career in 1898 as an actor, also wrote short plays. *A Queen's Messenger* had been performed "for the first time on any stage" as part of a matinee vaudeville bill given for charity at the Theatre Royal, Haymarket, in London, on 26 June 1899. Manners wrote several plays. The most successful ones—*Peg o' My Heart* in 1912 and *Happiness* in 1914—starred his wife, Laurette Taylor. The couple made numerous trips between the United States and his native England. He died on 10 December 1928 without realizing that his play, *A Queen's Messenger*, would become a historical benchmark.

A Queen's Messenger takes place in a lonely house on the outskirts of Berlin where, after a masked ball, a mysterious lady entices an English officer into what appears to be a romantic intrigue. The officer is a messenger for the queen and carries a locked valise that the woman finds he will die to retain. While drugged cigarettes take their effect, the Russian reveals that she has saved the officer from spies who are waiting for him at his hotel. The officer makes a romantic gesture toward her, which she rejects because she has learned that his true love lives in England. Rallying from his stupor, a captive and without his valise, the officer decides to kill himself, but the Russian lady undergoes a change of heart, returns the documents, and thus prevents the suicide.

Observers saw front and profile close-ups of the officer and the lady and occasionally male and female hands holding cigarettes, the valise, masks, a fan, glasses, and a key ring. Maurice Randall, a member of the WGY Studio Players, and Izetta Jewell, a former stage actress who was living in Schenectady with her husband, a Union College professor, played the lead roles. William J. Toneski and Joyce Evans Rector provided the hands. The story was substantially rewritten and directed by Mortimer Stewart, an experienced producer/director for WGY radio.

In a locked studio, Stewart began his rehearsals at four in the morning, checking the synchronization of voice and picture on a special monitor placed in front of him, cutting from camera to camera, and fading the picture in and out. The three static cameras were focused on Jewell, Randall, and the hands. The play was presented at 1:30 in the afternoon and repeated at 11:30 that night. Pacific Coast amateurs receiving the signal on short wave reported they were lucky to hold the picture more than thirty seconds. As if a pattern were immediately established, dramas that followed in New York and abroad were presented in the afternoon and the evening, usually being repeated several times.

Although the first television drama stimulated a flow of rhetoric from

Rehearsal for "The Queen's Messenger," WGY, Schenectady, 11 September 1928. (*General Electric Broadcasting Company*)

television enthusiasts, no upsurge in dramatic fare occurred. "The Queen's Messenger" foreshadowed the principal tenants of television drama's future: theatrical adaptations modified by radio formats, performances by stage and radio actors, live broadcasts from radio facilities, and directors who were experienced in stage or radio production. The domination of theater and radio over television drama would last for three decades, at which time television drama would relocate in Los Angeles and merge with the film/videotape industries.

In a prophetic moment, playwright Robert E. Sherwood predicted the prerecorded era despite motion picture resistance:

> Most of television broadcasting will be made from films. It will be an efficient and effective method of sending images and sound through the ether. Some of these films will be full-length photoplays, with the usual attendant short subjects—comedies, scenic pictures, news reels, etc. . . . Broadcasting studios will cease to be scenes of worried confusion. Performers will still be brought in occasionally, to make direct appearances, and there will be announcers on hand to issue the weather reports, stock market quotations, correct time and baseball scores; but the bulk of the activity will be in the control room from which the programmes recorded on celluloid, will be projected into space.[18]

Later experiments at General Electric proved that it was desirable to center actors on the screen because of the limited flexibility of the cameras. For this reason, actors were confined to predetermined boundaries in which they could perform. To increase image definition, each actor worked in front of a white background and applied exaggerated makeup, especially around the eyes and mouth.

Even though "The Queen's Messenger" was principally used to solve engineering problems and the image produced was crude, what it suggested in terms of future development was phenomenal. Demonstrations simpler than this one, together with the imaginings of writers who were stimulated by television's huge potential, ignited public enthusiasm. One radio station owner, after successfully demonstrating an image one and a half inches square, announced: "In six months we may have television for the public."

An occasional exhibit was staged outside the laboratory for the public. Notably, the Bamberger department store and radio station WOR, Newark, New Jersey, combined facilities that summer (1928) to present a two-minute puppet drama. Viewers saw the demonstration in a room in the store where the television signal was generated and heard the sound on a separate signal provided by the radio station.[19] Typically, image and sound were distributed over two separate systems. However, a demonstration of 50-line mechanically scanned pictures with sound had been sent on the same frequency by a single transmitter the previous year (7 April 1927). Such attempts, frail as they were, soon gave theatrical entrepreneurs a new vaudeville-like novelty to include in their stage pro-

grams, just as motion pictures had previously been introduced to the public as a stage novelty.

BIG-SCREEN DRAMAS IN THEATERS

Television was not only demonstrated for home use on tiny screens, but was also projected in theaters on large screens. General Electric was the first company to install rear screen television projection in a theater. The image was televised on a six-foot screen from an improvised studio in Dr. Ernst Alexanderson's GE laboratory, and the voices were transmitted over a loudspeaker system in the RKO Theatre, Schenectady, on 24 May 1930. That same year, the RCA experimental station, W2XBS, broadcast a television signal that was projected in Proctor's Theatre, on 58th Street, New York.[20]

Amidst these activities, B. S. Moss showed the first television drama projected for a theater audience, consisting of 1,500 persons, at the Broadway Theatre on 24 October 1931. Franchot Tone and Margaret Barker "wavered and quavered" on a ten-foot screen while presenting a few minutes of their current play, *The House of Connelly,* by Paul Green. The plot concerns a decadent aristocratic Southern family that must make way for the new democracy. The picture flickered and nearly faded out, but the novelty lingered. Within months, General Electric and the Jenkins Corporation planned to televise scenes from Channing Pollack's Broadway play *House Beautiful.*[21] The play was awful, but, together with other Pollack shows, it made his backer, Crosby Gage, a small fortune. Pollack had appeared briefly at the 1 May 1931 telecast. The public perceived a miraculous invention that would bring Broadway plays, radio personalities, and feature films right into homes; and television, like radio, would be "free."

Technicians experimenting with television tried to minimize the fuss created about the new medium, but for the most part, they were unsuccessful. As Arthur Lynch and C. F. Jenkins commented in *Radio News,* "Folks had all sorts of notions about television. Chief among these notions were the ideas that the machine, when it was introduced, would be small and very cheap and easy to operate; that it could be hooked right into the regular receiver and the National Convention or the World Series or the Grand Prix Race would be thrown on a screen on the living room wall with all the clarity one now finds in the movies. Well—that's just a dream, for some time to come."[22] Eagerly the public attended a few demonstrations, and patiently it awaited the fulfillment of the television prophesy. Yet, as late as 1932, the picture was frequently viewed by a

single person through a peephole receiver instead of on a screen. The image was blurred, coarse, and limited in area. "Under favorable conditions the features of a known person can be recognized," declared *Radio News*. "The movement of the lips, eyes and other features are easily discernible."[23]

STATIONS EXPERIMENTING WITH TELEVISION DRAMA

As public enthusiasm increased, experimental stations in large cities attempted serious kinds of programming soon after the broadcast of "The Queen's Messenger." The stations in the New York City area were W2XAB (CBS), W2XBS (NBC), and W2XCR (Jenkins Corporation); in upstate New York, General Electric's W2XD and W2XH; in Philadelphia, Philco's W3XE and W3XP; in Chicago, Zenith's W9XZY, Western Television's W9XAO and WIBO, and the stations of the *Chicago Daily News*, W9XAP and WMAQ; and in Los Angeles, Don Lee Broadcasting's W6XAO.

Experiments by the Jenkins Corporation in early 1931 included a puppet play telecast from its Wheaton, Maryland, studio and a public demonstration from Aeolian Hall, New York, featuring Gertrude Lawrence and Lionel Atwill (27 April 1931). The principal dramatic presentations, however, were staged in Chicago. Western Television's W9XAO presented its first television drama, "The Maker of Dreams," starring Irene Walker; the company's WIBO, a musical comedy, "Their Television Honeymoon" (7 January 1931).[24] In April, Louis Parker's "The Minuet" was presented by W9XAP (video) and WMAQ (audio).[25] The Midwest's contributions included dramas offered by the State University of Iowa, where at W9XK (video) and WSUI (audio) the Speech Department performed skits on its 45-line system.

In New York, while NBC's W2XBS showed no interest in entertainment programming, the CBS station, W2XAB, took quite another view, as later chapters will reveal.

COMPETITION FROM EUROPE

The only significant competition CBS and NBC would encounter during the thirties and late forties would be provided by the British Broadcasting Corporation (BBC) Television Service, and so a brief summary of the British contribution will be useful at this point.

About the same time that General Electric started its regular program service in the late 1920s, the British television pioneer, John L. Baird, had inaugurated an experimental one-hour schedule on a 24-line mechanical

system that could be seen within a five-mile radius of central London. The programs originated from the Baird television studio—the world's first facility of its kind—located at 133 Long Acre. On 15 December 1928 the Baird station telecast "Box and Cox," produced by Gordon Sherry. The cast included Lawrence Bascomb as Box, Vivienne Chatterton as Mrs. Bouncer, and Stanley Vivien as Cox. The fourth performer was a cat, the first animal performer on television.[26]

When daily television service began on 30 September 1929, the Baird company used a BBC transmitter for the first time. Transmission could be received all over Britain and in some parts of Europe. The program was introduced by Sir John Ambrose Fleming, the inventor, and included a typical vaudeville lineup. Lulu Stanley sang "He's Tall, Dark and Handsome" and "Grandma's Proverbs"; Baird's secretary rendered "Mighty Like a Rose"; and Sydney Howard performed a comedy monologue.[27] By March 1930, when both sight and sound were broadcast simultaneously, numerous television receivers were available to the public.

While engineers in the United States were saying television was at least half a dozen years away, the Baird Television Corporation of Great Britain was asking the Federal Radio Commission for permission to broadcast in the United States. Baird claimed that "teletalkies . . . have been accepted for regular daily transmission over English stations."[28] His London transmissions however, were only 30 lines, while definition in other countries was much higher: Germany 90 and Italy 60 lines. *Radio News* complained:

> The point is that England, Germany, Russia, France and other countries are bringing their television systems out into the open, while the U.S.A. thus far is keeping its sight broadcasting achievements behind closed doors. Much of the American delay is caused by individual manufacturers and broadcasters who hold that television must be perfected before it is launched. We suspect that the delay may be incidental to efforts to grab control of the television industry before it is born.[29]

Transmitted by the Baird company on 14 July 1930, Luigi Pirandello's "The Man with the Flower in His Mouth" became the first television play presented by the BBC. The thirty-minute drama was produced by Lance Sieveking; featured Gladys Young, Earle Gray, and Lionel Millard; and used sets designed by C. R. W. Nevinson. Just as in the GE drama, one cast member appeared before the scanner at a time. Bizarre makeup consisted of heavy blue lines to accentuate features and yellow to fill in facial areas of the forehead and cheeks. The BBC tried to avoid actor recognition for these early productions by refusing to publish names in

Radio Times or by announcing them on the air. Public demand soon changed this, and actors received minimum recognition along with low pay. The next year, Baird developed a system called "zone television." It employed three 30-line scanners in conjunction with a single 90-line picture. According to *The Book of Firsts*, "On 24 April 1931 he transmitted a play called *Another Pair of Spectacles* by this means, and for the first time the whole cast of three—John Rorke, Dennis Lawes and Dorothy Leave—could be seen on a special wide-screen receiver at the same time."[30]

Although Baird's technology lagged behind RCA's, British television programming was significant in drama. The BBC, as a government-authorized monopoly, was obligated to telecast dramas of regional as well as national interest. To this day, it produces significant dramas that express historical, social, artistic, and cultural values of the United Kingdom regardless of audience appeal. The BBC began regular telecasts on 22 August 1932, scheduling four programs a week from 11:00 to 11:30 P.M.:

> The opening programme, transmitted from Studio BB in the basement of Broadcasting House, included Louise Freear singing "I Want to be a Lady" from "The Chinese Honeymoon," a musical comedy in which she had starred in 1901. The service was inaugurated in cooperation with the Baird Co and superseded their transmissions from the Long Acre Studios. The BBC maintained its 30-line low-definition programme schedule until 10 September 1935 [when a high definition standard was recommended].[31]

The first high-definition television programs were broadcast from the BBC television station at Alexandra Palace. Initial program reception was at Radiolympia Wireless Exhibition from 26 August to 5 September 1936. The program schedule was produced and directed by the BBC staff (see Appendix B). Visual transmission was handled by Baird and Marconi-EMI engineers, but the BBC engineers controlled sound transmission. The first program included a Duke Ellington recording; a Paul Rotha documentary film; an excerpt from "As You Like It," also on film; and a live performance by vocalist Helen McKay. The BBC immediately offered excerpts from current plays, the first being "The Two Bouquets," by Eleanor and Herbert Farjson, telecast on 5 October 1936. Most programs were presented in the afternoon. They included sports, interviews, songs, fashion, news, films, variety, and frequent dramas. The last category included T. S. Eliot's "Murder in the Cathedral," Clemence Dane's "Will Shakespeare," Eugene O'Neill's "Ah, Wilderness!", a mime production of Geoffrey Chaucer's "The Pardoner's Tale" in which the words were

spoken off-camera by W. H. Auden, and Christopher Isherwood's verse play, "The Ascent of F6." Within two or three years, the British had experimented with two-hour versions of about sixty plays, even though the television screen was still too small to be viewed more than six feet away.[32]

Productions were telecast from two small studios, each of which could accommodate a maximum of four scenes. The high cost of programs and engineering problems similar to those being solved behind closed doors at RCA were plaguing Europeans. In April 1937 David Sarnoff announced to RCA stockholders: "Recently, the authorities responsible for television in England adopted the Marconi-EMI system of television in preference to the other system they tested. The system thus adopted as the English standard is based on RCA inventions."[33]

As technical quality improved, directors used four cameras and emphasized the artistic potential of the medium, even though they wrestled, as did Americans, with decisions of taste and judgment. Even after the war, the producer of "The Dover Road" was asked to omit "damned" and references to the Devil for the Sunday telecast. Ashley Dukes, a British dramatist and critic of the late thirties, wrote:

> For a reason perhaps unexplainable by logic, the reproduction of this [television] performance differs from reproduction on the motion picture screen. The transference of the picture is as alive and direct as its making is instantaneous—and this with the nearest viewer out of sight of the players and the farthest perhaps a hundred miles away. Authors contrive to speak and express themselves as they desire; and direction is most effective not when it plays tricks of its own but when it allows them full expression, Here then is television drama as it stands today.[34]

From BBC's initiation into the electronic period on 26 August 1936 to its termination of programming on 1 September 1939 because of the war, it produced approximately 400 different television dramas. From late August 1936 to the end of 1937, 102 plays were telecast. These ranged from ten-minute versions of Shakespeare to twenty-minute productions of "The Happy Journey to Trenton and Camden" and "Red Peppers," forty minutes of "Jane Eyre," fifty minutes of "The Importance of Being Earnest" and "Hänsel and Gretel," and one-and-a-half-hour productions of "Journey's End" and "Alice in Wonderland."

During 1938 the drama schedule at the BBC was staggering. Some 172 different plays were produced, many of which were repeated. Among the titles seen in the United States, besides those mentioned above, were a twenty-minute adaptation of "The Maker of Dreams," a thirty-minute

version of "The Monkey's Paw," hour productions of "Tristan und Isolde," Act II, "I Pagliacci," and "Androcles and the Lion," a ninety-minute presentation of J. B. Priestley's "When We Are Married," and hundred-minute telecasts of "Julius Caesar" in modern dress as well as Noel Coward's "Hay Fever." These productions were all presented in England before they appeared on American television. That same year, the BBC piloted a series of short plays entitled *Telecrime,* which preceded the CBS series *Photocrime,* seen after the war.

In 1939, before the abrupt termination of all telecasts that September, the BBC had produced 133 different plays, not including repeated dramas. Of the new titles only one— "The Tell-Tale Heart"—appeared in the United States before 1947. The 1939 BBC program schedule lists, among others, eighty-minute versions of Edna Ferber and George S. Kaufman's "The Royal Family of Broadway" and Karel and Joseph Capek's "The Insect Play," ninety-minute adaptations of Cyril Campion's "Ladies in Waiting," George Bernard Shaw's "Candida," and George Kelly's "The Torch-Bearers," and hundred-minute productions of Shakespeare's "The Tempest" and Goldsmith's "She Stoops To Conquer."

In all, from August 1936 to September 1939 BBC-TV presented a total of just under 400 television dramas, many of outstanding length and quality. During this same period, NBC-TV produced 17 in 1936–37, the most impressive being "The Three Garridebs"; 17 in 1938, when "The Mysterious Mummy Case" topped the list; and 29 by 1 September 1939, when the BBC went off the air. The NBC list was extended to another 90 dramas by 1942, when it too terminated its television programming just after Pearl Harbor. Thus, by comparison, NBC-TV produced a total of 153 different dramas from 1936 to 1942, many of them of high quality, as succeeding chapters will disclose.

The number of receivers in England grew from a few sets in 1936 to about 5,000 in 1938. In September 1939, when the war forced the BBC to cease operation, the television receivers in the land numbered 23,000. When it resumed operation on 10 June 1946, it estimated the television audience at 300,000 people, who viewed programs on about 15,000 receivers.[35]

2
CBS Television Dramas

Soon after the giant corporations managed to arrange an uneasy truce among the estranged branches of the entertainment world, the depression set in. During the 1929–30 season on Broadway, 87 percent of the dramatic shows and 69 percent of the musicals were failures.[1] "Legit. Reports the Worst Holiday Season on Record," read a headline in *The Billboard* in January 1930.[2]

As a result of the slump, talent agencies booked fewer and fewer vaudeville acts until they were eliminated altogether. By the middle of 1929, Publix Theatres had dropped vaudeville from its chain. Even the RKO Palace, the ultimate in this field, presented its last complete vaudeville bill on 16 November 1932. According to Joe Laurie, Jr., "It was Martin Beck's blood that built the Palace, E. F. Albee's sweat that kept it going as the world's greatest vaudeville theatre—and Hiram Brown's tears (when the stock market stopped laughing at vaude) that washed it all away."[3] By 1933 the number of vaudeville theaters had declined from approximately 2,000 to fewer than 600.

Many vaudeville entertainers were forced to find work elsewhere. In 1928–29 Broadway employed 17,000 musicians, but in 1933 only 3,600 union musicians were working. The talkies and the depression were blamed for the 70 percent decline in the vaudeville circuit. Some of the better known performers who found work in film and radio were Ed Wynn, Eddie Cantor, Jack Benny, Fanny Brice, Burns and Allen, Amos 'n' Andy (Amos Jones played by Freeman Gosden and Andrew H. Brown by Charles Correll), Walter Huston, Fred Astaire, and Milton Berle. Eventually all of them would act in or become the subject of a television drama or comedy.

Sketches were the backbone of vaudeville, and many of them became the backbone of early television drama. Among the good dramatic writers whose work in vaudeville was subsequently used on television were W. S. Gilbert, Arthur Hopkins, Arthur Conan Doyle, George Ade,

George M. Cohan, George Kelly, Edwin Burke, Aaron Hoffman, and J. C. Nugent. Supplementing the work of these vaudeville writers and performers were various journalists who also made a success of writing for vaudeville and whose work later appeared on television: Ben Hecht, Charles MacArthur, Bayard Veiller, Edna Ferber, George S. Kaufman, Channing Pollock, Maxwell Anderson, Marc Connelly, Porter Emerson Browne, and Augustus Thomas.

CBS Heyday, 1931–1933

The main thrust of activity at CBS was developing radio. William S. Paley had become president of a small patchwork of money-losing radio stations called United Independent Broadcasters on 26 September 1928. The range of problems he faced was substantial, and so he hired two key figures in 1930. One was Edward Klauber, who handled the administrative details, and the other was Paul W. Kesten, who in later years would not only assume a multitude of general responsibilities for CBS but would take on the guidance of television as well. While Paley was finding new stars—Paul Whiteman, Ted Husing, Kate Smith, Will Rogers, Bing Crosby, Fred Allen, George Burns, Jack Benny—for his fledgling network and Kesten was creating a new image for the company, William A. Schudt, Jr., was director of television programs for the CBS experimental station, W2XAB. Prospects for television looked so promising that CBS, using a mechanical flying spot scanner developed by the Jenkins Corporation, was granted a permit by the Federal Radio Commission on 15 December 1930 and began broadcasting tests over its experimental station on 20 June 1931.[4]

About six weeks later, on 21 July 1931, CBS started a regular program schedule with an elaborate ceremony (see Appendix C). Programs originated from W2XAB, 485 Madison Avenue, and sound was provided by W2XE and WABC, the headquarters radio station in New York. Their broadcasting frequencies, between 2750 and 2850 kilocycles, permitted transmission over vast distances. Some fan mail indicated that sound and/or video signals extended to a 2,000-mile radius from New York. Some response came from the Pacific Coast and overseas. In these frequencies, only very narrow channels could be assigned to television. This narrowness limited the definition to about 60 lines from the top to the bottom of the picture, as compared with today's 525 lines.

For its first anniversary program, on 21 July 1932, Edwin K. Cohan, technical director of the Columbia network, announced the simultaneous sight and sound transmission on one wavelength to an estimated 9,000

television receivers in the metropolitan New York area. Schudt summarized the significance:

> When the history of television is written we will be credited with having presented boxing bouts on a large scale, as well as wrestling, and a play-board vision of football games. . . . We likewise projected by television an authentic art exhibition: classic dancing; miniature musical comedies; sketching before the scanner; especially adapted plays; dancing and piano lessons; palmistry; and programs in connection with news events of the day. W2XAB was the first television station to be synchronized in sound with a coast to coast radio network.[5]

A typical daily program schedule follows:[6]

8:00–8:01	Opening Announcement
8:01–8:30	Muriel Asche and Kiddies
8:30–8:45	Charlotte Wernick—Characters
8:45–9:00	Jack Peterson—Old Sailor
9:00–9:15	Harriet Downs—Songs
9:15–9:30	Henrietta Dunlap—Cartoons
9:30–9:45	Hilliard—Characters
9:45–10:00	Sylvia Sherry—Songs

THE FIRST CBS TELEVISION PROGRAM

The "Television Inaugural Broadcast," which began at 10:15 P.M. on Tuesday, 21 July 1931, featured Ted Husing, an inept CBS office manager who was establishing a substantial reputation as a sportscaster. He suggested that one day perhaps the audience could see, hear, and talk back to those on television. Mayor Jimmy Walker came over from his unofficial nighttime headquarters and the swankiest restaurant in New York, the Central Park Casino, near Sixty-fifth Street, to formally open the new television station; and Natalie Towers, who was chosen as Miss Television, said she was going to act in some upcoming sketches (though her name never appears later on the CBS log as a featured player). Edwin Cohan spoke about the nature of television, and then Kate Smith, who was tired of playing "fat girl" parts in vaudeville, was introduced as "The Songbird of the South." She sang "When the Moon Comes over the Mountain" and "Making Faces at the Man in the Moon."

Dr. Walter Schaffer, the chief engineer of the Reichs-Rundfunk-Gesellschaft, the German broadcasting system, spoke briefly about technical progress; and comedian Henry Burbig gave his own version of

"Little Red Riding Hood." A romantic twosome, contralto Helen Nugent and tenor Ben Alley, sometimes referred to as the "Sweethearts of the Air," sang "Under Your Window Tonight." Nugent would later appear in several feature programs. The singing stylists, the Boswell sisters, rendered the "Heebie-Jeebie Blues." Composer George Gershwin played "Liza," and musical comedy stars Helen Gilligan and Milton Watson, who had begun appearing in radio, were the last act. They sang "Dream a Little Dream of Me" and "Now You're in My Arms." Husing closed the program with station identification and the first television commercial: "This is the COLUMBIA . . . BROADCASTING SYSTEM. 11:00 p.m. B-U-L-O-V-A watch time. WABC New York, W2XE New York."[7]

CBS DRAMATIC PROGRAMS

Dramatic programming was limited to no more than two or three persons on the screen at any one time and did not include any full-length shots. Productions consisted of simple actions that required few hand props. Pantomimes, comedy routines, and dramatic readings were frequent. In the few sketches, actors read their lines from scripts. W2XAB logged its first "Tele Musical" and first "Drama" on 22 July 1931. A number of other CBS "firsts" occurred in 1931: the first puppet show, "Punch & Judy," on 18 August; first "Musical Miniature Comedy," on 27 August; first narrative dramatic anthology, *The Television Ghost*, on 3 September; and the first pantomime on 8 September 1931. Other historical "firsts" that CBS might also claim are the first musical variety series, *Half Hour on Broadway*, which was first telecast on 1 (?) August 1931; and the first musical comedy series, *Ned Wayburn's Musical Comedy*, which began on 27 August 1931 but undoubtedly lacked a "book" each week.

The principal pantomimists were Grace Voss, who appeared nineteen times; Pat Garnell, twelve times; Bob Davis, in his *Character Slants*, eleven times; Charlotte Wernick, occasionally seen in *This and That*, ten times; Bert Hilliard's *Dramatic Moments* and the pantomimes of Estelle Sydney, nine times apiece; and Lilyan Crossman, eight times. Comics Senator Numb, Spaghett and Ravioli, and most notably George Kelting appeared frequently. Kelting appeared at least ten times in *The Television Ghost* series. Information on these early presentations is minimal, especially because no one took them seriously. The first television review in *The Billboard* was published just as W2XAB closed its operation. It mentions Bert Hilliard: "Bert Hilliard doing 'Dramatic Moments' next. In costume. Boy goes in for heavy dramatic stuff, works hard, but his obvious and annoying reading of script kills act. Only when televiz per-

formers realize television differs from radio and lines should not be read should they attempt material of this sort."[8] Bob Davis's *Character Slants,* a similar act, featured novelty characterizations and makeup changes.

The few plays on television were not favorably received. As Benn Hall wrote: "I listen to a rather puzzling dialogue. I am bored. . . . I try to follow the visual action. A mop of hair, downcast eyes or a hairless dome may be the enchanting vision. The players may be reading what we, by courtesy, call their lines."[9] Frustrated with actors reading lines, in a later column he commented:

> The John O. Hewitt players are the chief offenders in this respect, but they are not the only ones. Mr. Hewitt is undoubtedly sincere, either stupidly sincere or sincerely stupid in his efforts to entertain over telev. . . . His epics will, I suppose and hope, be buried. . . . Undoubtedly telev will develop a peculiar playwriting technic, but it will be far different, I hope, from the present-day trash."[10]

The Hewitt Players appeared twenty-five times on W2XAB in *The Silent Drama* and *CBS Tele Talkie* from June 1932 until February 1933.

The most popular television series was *The Television Ghost,* a series of dramatic narratives.[11]

Realizing that printed material, the theater, and the lyrics of songs might be freewheeling, television followed the lead of CBS radio by restricting lyrics:

> No words commonly used in a derogatory or scornful sense of any race, creed, or nationality may be used in lyrics of songs; words such as NIGGER, DAGO, WOP, CHINK and others of that type. Any other words about which there can be the slightest doubt should be referred for special ruling.
>
> No lyrics are allowed that refer to REEFERS, MUGGLES, MARIHUANA or the smoking of same. Such songs as THE REEFER MAN are absolutely banned and any references in lyrics or titles to reefers or synonomous terms.[12]

CBS Engineering Influence on Drama

During the afternoons, engineers and production personnel conducted demonstrations relevant to lighting, scenery, and makeup. All images required high-contrast colors, and so nearly every thing was outlined in black. Under hot, bright, white light images tended to wash away. As a result, the makeup for blonds consisted of a white powder base topped with a medium suntan powder, heavily painted eyebrows, a touch of light

green eye shadow, heavy mascara on upper lashes, and black or blue lipstick. The lights were so intense that some performers were burned. Gradually, a list of recommendations evolved that were summarized in the following 1931 memo:

Hints for Television Broadcasters

1. A make-up room has been provided for your convenience on the 23rd floor. Correct powders, rouges, and lip sticks have been provided for all types.
2. ACTION is a very important factor in visual broadcasting. It has been found that an active image comes through more clearly than any others. Act as much as possible in your program. Use your hands, head, and shoulders—also, where songs indicate, roll your eyes, and shake your finger at the televisor.
3. Any form of light other than that provided under normal operating conditions will partly destroy the projected image.
4. Place yourself at arm's length from the nearest part of the square niche in the bank of photo electric cells (eight globes which look like large unlit electric bulbs). The engineer will take care of the rest.
5. While broadcasting you may move around in a TWO FOOT SQUARE SPACE without getting out of focus. Look into the light or to either side of it. DO NOT LOOK up at the microphone.
6. DO NOT stick your head into the square scanning niche—if you do, lookers-in will see only parts of your face.
7. If you move out of the frame of the picture, the production man will give you a slight tap or push in the right direction. When such corrections are made, try not to look around in an amazed manner. Lookers-in will be quick to notice the unpremeditated move.
8. We regret that, because of Fire Regulations, it will be impossible to allow your friends or relatives in the studios during broadcasting. Before or after the 8:00 to 11:00 PM schedule, they are welcome to visit the studios on an inspection tour. Passes, however, must be secured from The Television Department.
9. Our present studio facilities are limited, therefore, please consider your fellow artist. Do not enter the studio, unless necessary, until the preceding broadcast is three-quarters, or more over. When you enter, be quiet. Avoid talking or whispering.
10. If, while you are being televised, the scanning light suddenly goes out, keep on with your program. The light is put out at intervals, so that the engineers can change the carbons.

11. Remember the sound microphone is *on the air continually* during the evening period.

12. "Who will hear and see you?" A prominent New York radio editor estimates that in New York City alone, 9,000 television receivers are in operation. Columbia's television sound station has been heard regularly as far away as Australia, South America, Europe and all over the North American continent.

13. Since our television broadcasting is experimental, certain research tests will be made during the course of each evening. These tests will not disturb your program, although, changing of screens, and back drop curtain, or the occasional moving of the piano will create a slight, though momentary disturbance.

14. Whenever possible, use costumes or a change of hats. Use of any small "props" is encouraged.

Thank you for your co-operation.

William A. Schudt, Jr.
Acting Director of Television Programs
COLUMBIA BROADCASTING SYSTEM, INC.

[COURTESY OF CBS, INC.]

By early 1933, it was evident that the picture quality of 60-line images was not adequate, that space in which the artists were required to perform was insufficient, and that out-of-doors operations and remotes were not feasible with the equipment owned by CBS: "At moments, a fairly good image would suddenly spread like melted tallow and resemble the grotesque images usually attached to thick mirrors at amusement parks. Black hollows would appear instead of eyes and some clean-shaven persons would suddenly grow mustaches and whiskers. But these distortions were quickly eliminated by men at the control knobs."[13] So, after more than 2,500 hours of television broadcasting since inaugural day on 21 July 1931, CBS stated that it would temporarily suspend its operation at W2XAB:

We now feel that further operation with the present facilities offers little possibility of contribution to the art of television, and we have, accordingly, decided to suspend temporarily our program schedule. . . . it is our intention to resume our experimental transmission as soon as we are sufficiently satisfied that advanced equipment of broader scope can be installed. Until then our activities will be confined to the laboratory and the maintenance of our close contacts with the other organizations in the field.[14]

CBS did not resume operation until after the New York World's Fair in 1939, when it installed an RCA electronic system.

THE CBS FINANCIAL INVESTMENT

During those early days, CBS television had little, if any, observable policy of its own. Its operation depended on personnel who were drafted from regular CBS departments to work on special assignments. The policy that eventually evolved was a reaffirmation of that which had been formulated for CBS radio. Its basis was an ongoing struggle to adjust artistic and scientific aspirations to unyielding budgetary restrictions.[15]

Between 1930 and 1933 available figures cover only the original cost of equipment and the direct cost of programs, Worthington C. Miner observed. The overall investment for equipment was listed at $7,700. In addition, in 1931 the company spent $6,100 for programming; in 1932, $9,600; and in 1933, up to the cessation of program activities in February, $600. The total programming figure is $16,300. The two items taken together show a $24,000 cost for two and a half years of television operations. This is not a complete picture, however, because salaries for the operating staff were not included inasmuch as personnel conducting television operations were drawn from the regular CBS engineering and program departments. Assuming for those two years that eight engineers at an average salary of $2,500 per year were used, the total would be $40,000. Assuming that six program people were employed at an average salary of $3,000, the two-year total would be $36,000. This means that operations during the period of mechanical television cost CBS in the neighborhood of $100,000.[16]

CBS IN HOLLYWOOD

CBS was not totally inactive in television from 1933 to 1939. In Hollywood, in May 1937, it presented a local crime series called *Take the Witness* from the Columbia Music Box Theatre. The shows were experimental and sustaining. The intention was "to prepare players for television."[17] Using scripts written by Ashmead Scott, actors ranged over much of the stage, wore costumes, and memorized lines. Although preparation resembled that of the theater, television cameras were installed in the first few rows of the orchestra. This was not the first indication of television interests in Hollywood. Previously, in May 1933, RKO Radio Pictures had announced plans to construct the "world's largest radio broadcasting studio," which would include television experimentation. NBC radio headquarters remained in New York. The Don Lee Station W6XAO,

referred to later in this volume, was the outlet for CBS programming in Hollywood until 1936.

CBS TELEVISION PRIORITIES, 1933–1941

Television drama made little progress from 1933 to 1941, principally because of the lack of personnel and changes in facilities. CBS policy toward television drama was nonexistent until key administrators were appointed, and they first turned their attention to leasing suitable space and purchasing new equipment before considering types of programming. Once these decisions were made, drama received a somewhat higher priority.

During the two-year shutdown, 1933–35, CBS studied the best television systems available in the United States and Europe. In the summer of 1935, the decision was made that an electronic system was the wave of the future. Paul Kesten, who had left advertising five years before to join CBS as director of sales promotion, was now a vice-president and put in full charge of the CBS television operation. He was close to William Paley's age and was dynamic and intellectually vigorous. He entertained many ideas and strategies for promoting CBS as the equal of NBC. "Kesten and I were so compatible," Paley wrote in his memoirs, "that we understood each other in a kind of mental shorthand. We could cover a lot of ground in a few minutes of conversation. We saw eye to eye from the start on the importance of design and good taste. . . . We proved to be able to work together as a unique and effective team."[18]

Applying his outstanding organizational skills, Kesten decided to focus on three areas: executive, engineering, and programming. He then began an analytical estimate of television's potential from the engineering and profit perspectives, as well as a means of gaining prestige in Washington. But he also found himself overburdened with work, and so later that year he hired a recent psychology graduate from Ohio State University, Dr. Frank Stanton. Stanton became head of research, and, eventually, president of CBS.

About this time, RCA was asked to submit estimates for studio equipment and a transmitter that would be capable of producing 343-line images; and in 1936 Dr. Peter Goldmark, a young, brilliant, Hungarian physicist whose background was in color television, came to CBS as chief television engineer to head the fourteen-member Engineering Department—in a day when television progress meant progress in engineering. Throughout early 1937, research was conducted to determine where the television transmitter and studio should be located. In May a lease was signed for the transmitter to be installed on the 73d and 74th floors of the

Chrysler Building, and in July studio space was leased in the Grand Central Building, 15 Vanderbilt Avenue. Two years later, the transmitter site was completed, and the studio equipment was installed.

CBS PROGRAM ORGANIZATION

Meanwhile, Kesten had continued to improve his organization by hiring key personnel. He had already employed (7 July 1936) Adrian Murphy as his assistant. Within three years, Murphy would become executive director of television. The principal person he sought for the program area was Gilbert Seldes, a former war correspondent, drama critic, and author of a dozen books, including his best-seller, *The Seven Lively Arts*. Prior to becoming director of television programs on 16 August 1937, he had been sent to London and Paris during the spring to observe European facilities. He returned with D. H. Munro, of the BBC, as a television consultant on studio operations. Seldes himself was particularly concerned with program content, and, consequently, demonstrated less interest in technical matters. British television had provided a steady stream of experiments in drama and thereby competitively stimulated those in the United States. As Worthington C. Miner remarked, "The British themselves tended to brush aside the popular reaction to their informal programs pointing with particular pride to their more complex productions of dramatic pieces."[19]

The fact was, however, that dramas cost much money and, even if it were appropriated, the television picture quality left much to be desired. It was as yet unstable, small, caused eye strain, and faded under normal lighting conditions in a viewing room. Of course, NBC's inroads in dramatic production when its regular program schedule was inaugurated on 30 April 1939 bolstered an element of pride at CBS because a major element in its rise to prominence in radio was the development of the dramatic form for the sound medium; inasmuch as television was regarded as an extension of radio, drama would also play an important role at CBS television.

Although Kesten appointed Leonard Hole, who was already on the staff, as manager of television operations on 19 April 1939 to administer the swift-moving technical activities at CBS, someone was needed within the program department who could actually produce programs and train a technical staff in what were perceived as primarily theatrical responsibilities.

Coincidentally, Worthington Miner, who was a director and actor respected for his 1932 production of *Reunion in Vienna* for the Theatre Guild, among many others, was seeking greater financial stability. Not

only was war coming, but also much uncertainty prevailed about how it would affect employment in the theater. Television was a possibility. Miner was undecided as to what his future should be, but fate stepped in. While he and his wife, returning from a weekend with Ilka Chase, were riding with Bill Murray, an executive for the Music Corporation of America (MCA), the car swerved out of control and nearly caused an accident. After recovering control of the automobile, Murray calmly asked Miner whether or not he had ever considered going into television. Miner took this incident as a cue. Within days, he began meeting with Seldes, closed his office at the Theatre Guild, and started his two-decade sojourn into television.

Because of Miner's background in the theater and moving pictures, he provided much of the technical and operational experience CBS needed. He joined CBS on 28 August 1939 as general director of television. Seldes, drawing on his background in print and journalism, dealt with news and the literary content of programs; Miner, experienced in stage and film, supervised all other kinds of programs and trained the technical staff. Eventually, this arrangement resulted in a nebulous and confusing distribution of authority,[20] but it was a starting point in a new industry that was frequently confusing and frustrating.

By the end of 1939, a staff of fifty-four had been allocated: four in administration, twenty-seven in engineering and twenty-three in programming. According to Miner, "In the program area, there was Gilbert Seldes with a salary of $288.46. Worthington Miner with a salary of $150. Edward Anhalt, Philip Booth, Rudolf Bretz, Alice Coss, Virginia DeGaudenzi, Marshal Diskin, Richard Hubbell, Lillian Jacobs, James Lehmann, Charles Marvin, Paul Mowrey, Rose Norman, Reginald Rawls, each of these persons, made between $32 and $45" per week.[21] Others were gradually hired. The program staff included one program head, one studio assistant, one secretary, one office boy, one writer, two announcers, two directors, one special-events man; on the floor, the staff consisted of three camera operators, three assistants, one boom mike operator, one scenic designer, one floor director, one makeup artist, one properties head, one lighting person, and one sound operator.

Once the production staff was in place, CBS managed to produce only two dramas, and they were confined to in-house experimentation. The two one-act plays were "The Happy Journey," by Thornton Wilder, already presented on NBC, on 1 November 1939, and "The Monkey's Paw," by W. W. Jacobs. "The Monkey's Paw" involves a magic monkey's paw that grants its owner three wishes. The owner's first wish is for money. The money he obtains results from the death of his son, and so the owner's second wish is for the son to live again; the third, is for his

return to the grave. The creation of mood through special effects furnished a unique challenge to the production staff.

Development of the CBS Studio

The television studio in the Grand Central Terminal Building consisted of approximately 5,000 square feet and provided space for as many as eighteen different settings. It was 260 feet long, air-conditioned, and soundproof. About a third of it was covered by a rock-wool ceiling at a height of twenty-five feet. At the west end, an additional section of rock-wool ceiling was mounted on towers so that it would be used whenever more playing area was required. Two RCA iconoscope cameras on dollies were installed in the summer of 1939. One camera could boom to a height of nine feet, but the other was kept in a fixed position; within the year, however, four orthicon cameras were on order. CBS engineers had become enthusiastic about this type because it was slightly more sensitive to low foot-candles and permitted a smaller diaphragm opening, which in turn produced a larger depth of field. It was bulkier, however, and created a black outline, or "bloom," around high-contrast areas. At the east end, behind a long glass window was the largest control room in the country, measuring fifty-three by twenty feet. A small announcer's booth was nearby as well as support facilities. By July 1941 three film channels, a 35-millimeter dissector channel, a 35-millimeter RCA iconoscope film scanner, and a 16-millimeter RCA iconoscope film scanner had been installed.

The sound facilities—microphone channels, audio console, and acoustical conditions—were in bad shape. The few microphones were barely adequate for limited productions. The audio equipment was made serviceable with the understanding that the quality of television audio was not up to CBS radio standards. The location of the studio (on the second, third, and fourth floors over the railroad tracks of the New York, New Haven, and Hartford as well as New York Central lines) was subject to periodic violent vibrations and to a heavy demand on the voltage of power lines feeding traffic control for the incoming and outgoing trains during rush hours. The concrete studio floor added to the undesirable acoustics; and the scenery, which was constructed primarily of plywood flats, created highly reflective surfaces.

CBS involvement in color television caused another problem. A third camera that its engineers had built for production was cannibalized by engineers who were working on the color experiments; and a small color studio, built within the Grand Central space, diverted facilities and labor from the main program activity.

Delays in Operation

As soon as the staff was organized and the facilities were installed, CBS planned to telecast three hours per week during the fall of 1939. In reality, November programming was quite suddenly suspended. Miner wrote: "The personnel was not disbanded, no outstanding contracts were cancelled, but lights were removed from the studio, camera rehearsals ended, everywhere planning replaced operations. How long this suspension would last could not be foreseen at the time."[22]

The principal reasons were, first, inconsistency in the second report of the Television Committee that was released by the FCC on 15 November 1939. The report, on the one hand, refused to set definite standards for television; and, on the other, it encouraged the stimulation of public interest through the telecast of programs of high public appeal. Second, a dispute was brewing among various craft unions regarding jurisdiction over television activities. Third, if a second world war should come, and that seemed likely, it would absorb television personnel and matériel. A fourth reason lurked in the shadows: the CBS quest for a color television system.

The potential dispute among unions over jurisdiction is particularly pertinent to drama. When NBC opened its small, in-house television studio, no dispute occurred. CBS was opening a much larger studio, located some distance from its home office building, and it was buying theaters along Broadway for additional studio space. For many years, the International Association of Theatrical Stage Employees (IATSE) had represented technicians who worked on stage productions. The International Brotherhood of Electrical Workers (IBEW) exercised authority over such technicians in radio. Because television production required a mixture of technical services drawn from radio, theater, and motion pictures, the unions were forced to adjust their respective areas of jurisdiction and reach some mutually satisfactory agreement. The reexamination included union technicians on the production staff such as camera operators and artists such as musicians and actors. Actors' unions were the American Federation of Radio Artists (AFRA), Actors Equity, and the Screen Actors Guild (SAG). What actors' union was to make decisions on behalf of actors?

Another case involved lighting technicians:

At this time [1939] in order to carry forward some initial training for the newly assembled staff, CBS television rented from the Century Lighting Company certain units of incandescent light equipment and brought them onto the floor of the studio. Some of these

units were mounted by members of the staff on heavy metal towers that were movable from one part of the studio to another. Even these few units (and they were far from adequate to the demand of television lighting) came closer to the total wattage and power consumption of a motion picture studio than to either a theatrical stage or a radio studio. The presence of cameras mounted on dollies, of microphones mounted on portable booms tends to emphasize the superficial similarity between a television and motion picture studio. Shortly thereafter, the Century Lighting Company was forced by its New York local to pay a sizable fine for delivering equipment to Columbia at its television studios.[23]

A reasonable wage scale needed to be established so that employees who did comparable work to that in the high-paying motion picture industry would receive a wage appropriate to what the fledgling television industry could afford.

In-House Experiments

In view of the decision to telecast only a test pattern throughout 1940, the production staff attempted to prepare itself for the day it would go on the air. Much of its activity was a careful scrutiny of the dramas presented on NBC—now in its peak during these experimental years—and staging mock dramas of its own, even though CBS maintained rigid restrictions against the use of equipment on the studio floor.

Mock Dramas. The mock dramas were staged in a device called a "shadow box." It was located in a small room off from the studio. A series of live objects and still pictures were mounted in the shadow box. Lighting setups, staging, and limited camera operations that included cuts, dissolves, and fades were practiced. One camera, mounted in a fixed position, focused on the shadow box. Inasmuch as the camera operator could only change the focus, the exercise was largely in cueing. The productions began with two dramas, "The Pedestrian" and "The Commuter," and months later, "Next Week in New York." The static nature of the fixed camera position and the increased amount of light necessary for making the shadow box function properly soon rendered it unworthy of further development.

Marking Scripts. Likewise, an attempt to design a shooting script in a horizontal format proved to be futile. Jascha Frank devised a script that was typed on telegraph tape and mounted on cardboard that was 2 feet

by 2½ feet wide, stacked about 8 inches high. Multicolored Scotch tape applied to the script indicated different dimmer settings. Although highly accurate, this script required the expenditure of three or four hours of staff time to prepare one ten-minute program, and so the idea was scrapped.

Director Dominance.   From the director's viewpoint, if the script could meticulously record all cues, those cues could be called on-air by rote, and therefore, needed no artistic judgments while the program was in progress. An engineer or technical director could do that. The struggle for dominance in the control room had been recognized three years earlier, when the engineers controlled studio technicians. The time had come for authority over all technical operations on the floor, except lights, scenery, and props, to be delegated to the program staff. This conflict gave rise to the philosophy at CBS that the director must be the primary decision-maker in the control room during the telecast.

This precedent-setting principle created a major difference in directing programs at CBS and NBC. Both approaches have their supporters. The strain of live programming was substantial in itself, but the tension was worse during the thirty-second station breaks because the director needed to handle everything. He called the shots for three cameras and the film chain, if used. He prepared other camera positions for upcoming shots. Most of these instructions had to be articulated during the thirty-second break. NBC divided the strain by sharing the responsibility between the directors and technical directors. In Miner's view:

> This was but another confirmation of General Sarnoff's short-sightedness as a showman, of his ability to appreciate the vast lone-liness an artist must be granted at such moments of decision. Bill Paley seldom erred in this area. He was a superb businessman, but he was also a supreme showman. He recognized the impossibility of creativity by committee. The technician was there to give technical and electronic life to the Director's dreams. To evade the danger of having a Director ask too often for the impossible, General Sarnoff gave the Technical Director the right to veto the Director's commands; Bill Paley's blunt response was: "Get another Director."[24]

So fundamental was this principle to CBS that, long before television was ready to move into high gear, the bitter jurisdictional battles had been fought and won. As a result, CBS and IATSE experienced little difficulty in hammering out a television agreement.

Comparisons with NBC.   According to Miner, late in 1939 someone at CBS suggested that once an NBC drama was announced, the CBS pro-

gram staff would plan, theoretically, how it would stage the same production so that a direct comparison could be made between the effectiveness of the NBC program and the imagination and ingenuity of the CBS program staff. Typical of the selections was "Burlesque," telecast by NBC on 19 April 1940. Miner recalled:

> . . . after a lot of study and thought, I'd reached the conclusion that no form of play structure was better suited to television than the Elizabethan framework. The Three Act form was surely the worst, the least suited to the new medium. The wide outdoors was a luxury only pictures could afford; and it scarcely seemed feasible to return to the chorus and masks of the Athenian stage, much less the stylized traditions of the Oriental theatre. What else? And believe it or not, it worked rather well. Miraculously well, in fact, aside from one small miscalculation. The first draft of "Burlesque" would have taken three hours of playing time. While structurally effective, it would not have appealed to the money-boys.[25]

By the time an adaptation of "Burlesque" was made, this exercise had become elaborate.[26] A complete model of the studio was built, model sets were constructed, and miniature cameras and sound booths were moved about to simulate the production pattern. The purpose was to show how unimaginative NBC was and how the CBS crew could duplicate the preferred fluid movement of moving pictures.

The mock production assumed the use of four cameras. On the basis of existing studio-floor dimensions, the staff planned seven sets for "Burlesque," one main set and three smaller ones running down the north and south walls toward the west end. The script was fundamentally the stage version, but dialogue at the conclusion of each scene was sufficiently rewritten to allow enough time for a camera operator to break to the next set. This illustrated how smooth transitions could be, if carefully planned. The production made it clear that, if such a high degree of fluid movement were to be attained, for every hour a drama was on the air some ninety-four hours of rehearsal time would be needed. Despite cost-cutting and a generous attitude on the part of actors to work for low salaries, the live production would still cost $1,000, probably an unrealistic sum even in 1939. Motion picture film was considered briefly, but, if major studios released feature films to television, their rental cost per hour was estimated at $5,000 or more, an even less acceptable figure. Consequently, the budgetary analysis pronounced a death sentence on live drama as a feasible source of television material as well as on major motion pictures.

Instead, a review of television's unique characteristics was undertaken.

It indicated that "television is the supreme observer reacting with instantaneous precision to a spontaneous and unpredictable event."[27] Television, it was decided, could report an event better than any other medium, and so the emphasis on CBS programming, at least temporarily, shifted to reporting. Perhaps someday, executives speculated, the vast finances, wide publicity, and huge supply of stars would be available to television for dramatic production.

Nevertheless, a formula was tentatively devised for dramatic production. Schedules were established alloting forty hours of rehearsal time per single hour of on-air dramatic programming. This formula allowed less than half the time the "Burlesque" experiment had projected. Sixteen of the forty hours were to be spent in the studio, involving full equipment (cameras, lights, and switching facilities) and personnel. Once CBS on-air programming exceeded five hours per week, an extra studio completely staffed and equipped, was contemplated. In addition, outside consultants in wardrobe and makeup were to be hired, and from $25,000 to $50,000 was deemed to be reasonable for the acquisition of rights to material.

THE FINANCIAL OUTLOOK

The investment in television prior to 1 January 1940 by the Columbia Broadcasting System was more than $1.6 million. Some estimates follow:[28]

Expenditures for the period of mechanical television, 1930 through 1933 — $100,000

Expenditures for 1934 to 1936 — 4,000

Expenditures for the period 1 January 1936 through 30 December 1939 — 1,312,200

> Transmitter, studio and technical equipment improvements: $764,000.
>
> Materials, test equipment for research and development: $43,100.
>
> Salaries of fulltime television employees: $213,100.
>
> Rent for Chrysler Building and Grand Central Terminal Building: $70,500.
>
> Direct television expenses (utilities, supplies, repairs, insurance, taxes, travel, outside attorneys): $101,500.

General administration, overhead, expenses of other
departments applicable to television: $120,000.

Total expenditures, 1 January 1930 to 30 December 1939 $1,416,200
*(This total excludes $209,500 authorized in 1939 but not spent
within the budget period; $78,000 for a new mobile unit,
$51,000 for four orthicon cameras, and $80,500 for other
technical equipment.)*

In the program department, eighteen persons were hired to initiate
three hours of programming per week during the fall of 1939. The budget
set aside for direct program costs reflected the number of hours planned
for three hours of programming:

52 hours per week in the formal studio at $1,000 per hour	$52,000
52 hours per week in the informal studio at $250 per hour	13,000
26 hours, one every other week of formal remote work at $500 per hour	13,000
25 hours, one every other week of informal remote work at $200 per hour	5,200
Total annual expenditure for three hours of programming per week	$83,200

If the schedule were lengthened to five hours per week, four of them
originating in the studio, it was estimated that the direct program costs
would increase to $148,200 per week and would require a staff of nine-
teen persons in the program department.[29]

The 1939 budget was scrutinized and the projected figures evoked a
semblance of policy along with financial reality. The premise stated that
CBS, as a nonmanufacturing company, derived its role in broadcasting
from programming; and that, if CBS intended to produce television programs, they would need to be equal in quality to programs on radio and
feature films of the motion picture industry when they started.[30] Based
on the television program budget in 1939, an analysis projected that
annual costs would run from $1.5 million to $2 million within a year or
two. The direct cost per program was thought to be somewhere in the
neighborhood of $225,000 a year for studio programs.[31]

Through 1941 policy and economic realities collided to postpone
drama at least temporarily. Accordingly, acceptable programming was
news, animation, art as an educational medium, *Men at Work, The Television People's Platform, Vox Pop, Just Music,* dancing, quizzes,

sports, domestic science, defense programs, variety, and some vaudeville acts.

Comparison of Production Expenses. Miner stated that "during 1939 the cost of NBC programs for a monthly period reached a peak of $9,000 for direct program costs. This meant that they were spending on the average of $140 per hour. At this time they were budgeting between $650 and $750 for their Sunday evening dramatic shows. The CBS budget, for considerably fewer hours, ran to an average of $535 per hour."[32] Likewise, comparative figures at the BBC showed that some dramatic productions were costing as much as $3,000 per program, for longer preparation, overtime for actors, and a larger production staff.

Overall corporate investment in television up until 1940 was made public in various statements by several leading companies:[33]

RCA	$10,000,000
Philco	3,500,000
CBS	2,000,000
DuMont	2,000,000
Don Lee	2,000,000
Western Television	2,000,000
Farnsworth	1,500,000
Hughes Tool	1,000,000
Subtotal	$24,000,000
Several companies:	
General Electric	
Westinghouse	
Zenith	
Other companies	
Several colleges and universities	
Subtotal	$6,000,000
Estimated total:	$30,000,000

Experiments in Color. As though FCC regulations and indecision, union strife, a war in Europe, and high cost were not enough deterrents to television drama, another factor diverted CBS attention from programming: color. Its officials believed that Dr. Peter Goldmark, a highly experienced engineer and innovative thinker, could provide the company with some basic patent that would provide a bargaining chip in the manufacturing field. Because Goldmark was a European, he endured many sleepless nights contemplating the war and what it would mean. In January 1940 he married Frances Trainer, and two months later they

took a skiing trip to Lake Placid. While on that vacation, insomnia plagued him, and, during those wakeful hours, he pondered the illusive problem of color television.[34] Upon his return, he asked for the purchase of equipment, including an orthicon camera, for an experimental color television laboratory. From the first estimate on 10 June 1940 to the end of the year, the cost of materials alone approached $40,000.[35]

The laboratory was operating only two months before the first CBS color transmission took place. It was a private demonstration for Chairman James L. Fry of the FCC, who was tremendously interested in the system because of its simplicity and practical possibilities. A few days later, on 4 September 1940, the first public demonstration of color television took place inside the television laboratories at 485 Madison Avenue. Press reaction was almost universally favorable.[36] Henceforth, CBS would spend enormous energy and resources to promote the Goldmark color system. It contained one flaw, however, in that it was fundamentally a mechanical color system that was incompatible with the black and white electronic systems that were gaining popularity in the marketplace. The ensuing corporate struggle, between CBS and RCA principally, further suppressed a priority for television drama.

Summary of CBS Experimental Dramas. Certain assumptions were formed after more than a decade of programming experience at CBS. If the public was to see dramatic programming, it would need to be sponsored by private capital, and that capital was likely to come from advertising. Advertising agencies and sponsors interested in television were looking for low-cost programs and high exposure for their products and services. Such exposure did not seem probable in the immediate future. Drama, believed to be the most expensive programming, would need to appeal to large audiences if sponsors were to be interested. Broadcasters assumed drama would interest a small, sophisticated audience. This view, which had been widely held since 1936, seemed to be untrue during the decade that followed because of the proliferation of receivers among an eager public. CBS executives also felt that the same conditions fundamental to radio drama would prevail in television. Plagued by weighty corporate decisions, fluctuating industry standards, an untested marketplace, and rumblings of war, live drama at CBS would not see the light of day until the mid-1940s.

CBS Dramas during and after the War, 1941–1947

W2XAB became WCBW, the CBS commercial station in New York, on 1 July 1941. It began regular telecasts for an audience, realistically speak-

ing, of perhaps 150. The programming consisted of dance lessons, news, music, children's stories, and other spontaneous shows. Worthington Miner produced and directed the entire fifteen hours (three hours were on film) of the first ten weeks CBS was on the air. The same two iconoscope cameras that had been purchased in the summer of 1939 were used, but no mobile units, outside rehearsals, or extra studio space were involved. None of the improved equipment listed in the 1939 budget had, in fact, been purchased and installed. As late as fall 1942, the iconoscope cameras being used required such intense incandescent light (1,250 foot candles) that a person whose skin was sensitive could receive a severe burn. Then, once again—this time because of the war—WCBW terminated its television program schedule. That was Thanksgiving Day 1942.

The Resumption of CBS Live Drama

CBS resumed live operation from the Grand Central Terminal Building on 4 May 1944. By this time, the image orthicon camera had already been demonstrated, using only one foot candle for minimum illumination, in Madison Square Garden. The impressive I-O camera was the industry breakthrough needed for adequate black and white picture quality, even though it would take a while for CBS to install new equipment.

The program schedule during the latter part of World War II consisted of two hours of film on Thursdays and two hours live on Fridays. Some celebrities made appearances, and variety formats such as *Backstage,* which featured a puppet presentation, were offered, but no live drama. Typical WCBW programs were:

News and news analysis
Opinions on Trial
They Were There (war experiences)
Documentary film
The Missus Goes A-Shopping (audience participation)
Will You Remember? (music and song)
At Home (musical variety)

According to the *CBS Program Book,* "This pattern is supplemented each week with experiments in adapting various types of radio programs to television, with special events dictated by the news of the day, and with dramatic and educational films."[37]

The first live drama at WCBW was "The Favor," originally written as a war-bond play by Lawrence M. Klee, that was adapted, directed, and produced for television by Worthington Miner. It was selected from several sketches furnished by the Victory Players, a branch of the American

Scene from "The Favor," WCBW, New York, 30 June 1944. (*New York Public Library*)

Theatre Wing, because "it is an exceptionally sensitive piece of writing, with strong simple characterizations—as well as a powerful dramatic appeal to the emotions."[38] The cast included two radio actors: Joseph Julian as The Soldier and Lesley Woods as The Girl.

The first showing, on 30 June 1944, which consisted of a simple succession of a long shot, a close-up, a long shot, and back again, was described by Marty Schrader as "definitely in the worst video tradition."[39] The CBS television staff recognized many limitations created by the lack of equipment, poor picture clarity, and inflexibility in camera movement. Two weeks later, however, WCBW repeated the program because, according to Gilbert Seldes, "we have had from our audience an immediate and remarkably warm response. The audience not only caught the special mood Mr. Miner created, but seemed to sense the extraordinary technical resources on which he called for his results. There were, actually, in this small piece a remarkable variety of new angles, new perspectives, and new effects of movement, space and light."[40]

Schrader's *Billboard* review indicated that Miner's second attempt improved substantially:

The outstanding improvements as of the second scanning were more spirited direction, a trimmed script, intelligent camera work and a

greater air of intensity on the performers' part. The lighting seemed to be more evenly distributed, with the background easily seen and the foreground glare reduced. Very sensitive dolly handling produced a camera that was in motion without blurring. Actors seemed to be able to move freely, without walking out of the screen.[41]

Miner once said the basic difference between television and motion pictures was that, in pictures, actors for the most part moved in and out of a fixed frame; in television, they often remained still, while the frame around them moved.[42] Richard W. Hubbell wrote in *Television:* "Standout was its professional quality, its polish, the feeling of assurance that everything was proceeding on schedule. This was particularly true of the camera handling, the cutting, or editing, all of which were done with finesse equal to any motion picture."[43]

In the fall, Gilbert Seldes adapted one of William Faulkner's short stories—"Two Soldiers"—for presentation on 13 October. It was described as "the best of the few dramas CBS has attempted since its resumption of active broadcasting some months ago."[44] Seldes himself said it was "a moderate success."[45] The opening shot was a still picture of a mountain home where the first scenes took place. The play used eight sets, one of which was an excellent interior of a cabin complete with a kitchen stove. Lighting was spotty. The director was required to give 225 cues; the assistant director gave the music and sound cues. One technical error showed a shot by an unfocused camera. Complex scene changes occasionally required the addition of ten or fifteen seconds to transitions, which were accomplished by displaying symbolic images such as a picture of the exterior of the cabin, a bus sign, or a recruiting poster.

In the spring of 1945, WCBW increased its airtime to three nights a week: Tuesdays, when it competed with WABD; Thursdays, which it held alone; and Fridays, when it opposed WNBT. The general character of the Tuesday night edition, lasting from 8:00 to 9:30 P.M., EST, was news reports, a fifteen-minute vocal or dramatic program, U.S. government and other selected films, and *The Missus Goes A-Shopping*. On 11 April 1945, WCBW offered "Soldiers without Uniforms." A CBS news release speculated that it was "probably the first Franco-American program in the history of television."[46] The play was a dramatization of episodes involving the Resistance movement in Paris that were based on material brought to this country by Pierre Schaeffer and Pierre Garrgues, representatives of the French Broadcasting Service. The events were narrated by Emlen Etting, a correspondent from the Office of War Information. The writer/director of the program was Ben Feiner, who was receiving about $7,000 a year as general program assistant.[47]

On 24 May WCBW presented Norman Corwin's documentary/drama "Untitled."[48] The play, "about the late Hank Peters, Pfc. USA," was the first of Corwin's works viewed on television. Although producer/director Feiner used fourteen sets and every trick known to television—film, slides, stills, and live segments—the effort outweighed the results according to reviewer Lou Frankel:

> There is, as everyone knows, a sweep, a scope, a movement to Corwin's writing which, when the author does the producing on the air, at least stirs the listener, slowly at first, then faster and stronger until the audience gulps, cries or goes thru the emotional wringer in some other fashion. In this television presentation, the words had the same effect to which the visual presentation neither added nor detracted.[49]

On 11 June 1945 CBS, on the occasion of adding 3,000 square feet to its space in the Grand Central Terminal Building, announced that it operated the largest television studio in the country. The new space encouraged the growth of all formats. To make utilization of the enlarged studio economical, CBS said in July that it intended to be more commercial, for to date it had sold only four spots: four twenty-second time signals to Bulova Watch, the same sponsor that appeared on the first CBS telecast in 1931. Speculation arose that CBS would ax some of its sustaining programs to make way for commercial packages the company planned to produce itself or purchase from outside sources.

To show the contribution women were making to the war effort and to experiment with advertising techniques, CBS initiated a series in December 1944 called *Women in Wartime,* which was presented in cooperation with *Mademoiselle* magazine. The series was produced by Seldes and directed by women on the staff, notably Frances Buss. On one program, presented the following April, a bridal fashion show captured attention. This was followed by a drama about a secret courier working for Polish partisan headquarters (Ann Shepherd). She falls in love with a Polish underground worker (William Hollenbeck) whose name she does not even know. In the end, they are married, but, instead of enjoying the usual honeymoon, the woman volunteers for a dangerous assignment. Another skit on the same program, involving two Nazis (Theodore Goetz and Michael Ingram) stressed that, if liberated Europeans were allowed to starve, they would be raw material for a Nazi resurgence. The show provided "a half-hour of intense, effective, princely drama worth anybody's attention."[50]

Women in Wartime, which ran for several months, included the majority of CBS dramatic sequences. One show, on 12 July 1945, "A GI

Dreams of Home," was based on an article in *Mademoiselle* by Irwin Shaw. Produced by Seldes and directed by Buss, the adaptation involved a soldier dreaming of home while stationed in India and enjoying a two-day pass. Fred Hickey complained in *Televiser:* "Outside of the construction of a set which showed an apartment situated in the middle of clouds, the 'dreamlike' quality of the sketch had to depend almost entirely upon dramatic content and background music for its effectiveness."[51] Rear screen projection, smoke, and cloud effects were used, however.

Improvisation began to receive attention as a way of providing low-cost programming. Acting groups received story outlines from which they would work up dialogue and movement in a minimum of time. The sketches were then telecast as a portion of an existing series such as *Tales to Remember,* which offered dramatic monologues, including narration, sketching, and cartoons. Directed by Rudy Bretz, the series originated on 25 September 1945.[52] The Improvisation Group had its own program briefly in the fall of 1946. In one fifteen-minute sketch, a banker tells a Kentucky colonel he is overdrawn by $17,000. The two decide to draw a draft on a distant and unsuspecting maharajah. Unexpectedly, the maharajah honors the check, but he is repaid and made a Kentucky colonel. According to *Television,* "The story unfolds a bit slowly to sustain interest."[53]

In June 1945 "Letter from the Teens," by Lela Swift and Edward Stasheff, was the first drama used as a springboard for discussion of juvenile problems. The direction was one of Worthington Miner's "most perfect technical efforts."[54] On 23 August, WCBW presented its first documentary drama on the atomic bomb, "Experiment in the Desert," by Paul Belanger and Edward Stasheff. *The Billboard* commented: "First such drama outside radio was Columbia television's 'Experiment in the Desert,' a re-enactment of the events leading up to the first atomic explosion in New Mexico two months ago. . . . [It] could have had the tension of *The Petrifield [sic] Forest* and the appeal to the imagination of the atomic bomb. Unfortunately bad acting and spotty writing made it a run-of-the-mill production, interesting but hardly gripping."[55]

Japan accepted the allied terms of surrender on 14 August 1945, though the official surrender did not occur until 2 September. World War II was over. WCBW and other stations ran documentaries heralding its conclusion. Particularly noteworthy was a television version of Norman Corwin's "On a Note of Triumph," which had already been heard over radio on V-E Day, 5 May 1945. Adapted, produced, and directed by Ben Feiner, it was "the right note on which to conclude a day of victory." Feiner was praised for conservative use of camera movement, a prudent adaptation and a "swell" cast.[56]

The end of the war signaled major changes in television's future. Because of the emphasis on commercial advertising, announced months earlier, new challenges and increased competition were beginning along with increased programming, growth of the network, and the struggle over color. The leadership of CBS television programming changed upon the resignation of Gilbert Seldes on 28 September 1946. Because his combined activities represented "too much work," he gave up his responsibilities at CBS to continue writing books and articles, work in the theater, and, eventually, become professor and dean of the Annenberg School of Communications, at the University of Pennsylvania.

Columbia turned to its radio sponsors and successful radio programs to stage two of its commercial television programs during the following months. Since 1936 *Big Sister,* a radio serial created by Lillian Lauferty, had thrived on CBS radio, and so it was a reasonable choice for the first commercial venture. Lever Bros. was willing to sponsor the program upon the recommendation of Ruthrauff & Ryan, the advertising agency that had hired T. H. Hutchinson after he left NBC (1942). Expectations for the telecast on 9 October 1945 ran high despite WCBW's modest experience in drama. Technically, the production, directed by Worthington Miner, was below par because three microphones popped into view, cameras were out of focus at times, and lighting was far from good. Then, too, James McNaughton's set was below standard. Mercedes McCambridge did a fine job as Big Sister, and Julian Funt managed to hold audience attention through a talky script, according to *The Billboard*'s Marty Schrader.[57]

The next effort brought the same team back on 20 November 1945. Lever Bros., Ruthrauff & Ryan, and the WCBW production staff decided to try an adaptation of one of the radio net's other favorites, *Aunt Jenny's Real Life Stories.* "Aunt Jenny" had been on CBS radio for nine years. Whereas "Big Sister" had benefited from a well-written and well-produced script but encountered technical problems, Aunt Jenny's story "to put it mildly, was dull, torpid, never went anywhere and, in fact, never got started."[58] The script, by Joseph Armel Cross, concerned three civilians who are sitting in a lunch wagon complaining about their Thanksgiving dinner. A soldier who overhears them says he is spending his holiday on a bus, grateful to be going home. Such sentiment, popular during the war, was already passé. Neither radio series made it on television past these preliminary outings.

Among the fall experiments was the CBS attempt at a cliff-hanger soap opera, *Three Houses,* originating on 23 October 1945. Reviewer Marty Schrader commented, "Writers Peggy Mayer and Marian Spitzer came up with a script which was far too talky and far too static. And being the

Scene from "Aunt Jenny's Real Life Stories," WCBW, 20 November 1945. (*New York Public Library*)

first act of a dramatic series, it should have done a better job of catching audience interest."[59] The series lasted only three programs.

On 30 January 1946 the CBS *Suspense* classic "Sorry, Wrong Number," by Lucille Fletcher, was telecast. Producer/director John Houseman was scheduled to direct the mystery about a neurotic woman (Mildred Natwick), who, alone in her house, imagines she is about to be killed after overhearing a murder plot on the telephone. After the preliminary work had already been done, Houseman was forced to divert his attention to the Broadway opening of *Lute Song*, and so Frances Buss, of the CBS television staff, directed. Judy Dupuy was critical in the *Televiser:* "Where production fell apart in this three-scene drama (bedroom, telephone central office, precinct police desk) was in its inadequate visual nuances in support of the woman's growing fears, in its routine camera coverage, and in its unimaginative visual denouement."[60]

Fletcher wrote "Sorry, Wrong Number" because "I wanted to write a show that was 'pure medium' [radio], something that could be performed only on the air. It took me about two months to think out this piece and about three days to write it. The character of Mrs. Stevenson is based on an actual person I once ran into in a grocery. My husband

[Bernard Herrmann, the composer/conductor] and I once lived in a small house exactly tallying with the house in the story."[61]

To honor Abraham Lincoln, Raymond Massey appeared in an original sketch by Sam Taylor that takes place at the Wills residence, Gettysburg, Pennsylvania, on 18 November 1863, the night before Lincoln's famous address. John Cromwell played John Hay, the president's personal secretary. Both actors were currently appearing in *Pygmalion* at the Barrymore Theatre. Cledge Roberts directed the telecast on 12 February 1946.

Demonstrating little enthusiasm for wartime themes or adaptation of radio soap operas, CBS television turned to inexpensive crime dramas. *Casey, Press Photographer* (also called *Photocrime* or *Crime Photographer*) was based on characters from *Look* magazine and on a 1946 CBS radio series entitled *Casey, Crime Photographer*. This was the first crime series on CBS television since the resumption of live programming. In the initial story, Casey's woman reporter friend is accused of murdering the daughter of a mind reader. Casey solves the crime. Four sets were used along with a cast of two actors from the radio series and others from stage and screen. Neil Hamilton was "smooth, competent in the detective role." *Photocrime* was "about the best commercial possibility, [CBS] has come up with since John Reed King's *The Missus Goes A-Shopping* hit television a year ago."[62]

Opinions on Trial was a novel forty-five-minute reenactment of a courtroom proceeding, after which viewers were asked to mail in their verdict. *You Be the Judge* was staged in yet another "courtroom." Originating on 4 January 1946, it restaged the trials of famous outlaws of the past. Three judges, selected from the studio audience, attempted to match their opinions with the actual verdict. Professional talent presented the case; Edward Stasheff, as clerk of the court, explained the circumstances. The studio-audience judge whose decision came closest to that of the actual trial judge received $25. The first case concerned ownership of a pearl found in an oyster in a restaurant. The problem was a good choice because "it was so far removed from the more obvious legal cases, and sustained viewer interest until the decision was made."[63]

Another drama, "Delivery Guaranteed," adapted by Gordon Minter and based on a radio play from *The Whistler,* follows the psychological events that force a murderer to confess.[64] The cast, starring Anne Burr, a stage actress, and Robert Bolger, a cousin of dancer Ray Bolger, was supported by Maxine Stewart, Tom McMorrow, and John James. Steve Martin, of the CBS-TV staff, directed the half-hour teleplay on 16 January 1947.

On 5 October 1947, NBC initiated a Sunday night radio series called

Ford Theater. It was moved to CBS the next year and played on Friday nights. Fletcher Markle became the producer, and, instead of using radio actors, guest stars dominant in stage and film were featured. That same fall, CBS began a monthly telecast of *Ford Television Theater.* Three weeks later, it would alternate with another dramatic anthology, *Studio One.* Together, they would contribute to a new era in television drama.

3

NBC Television Dramas

Initially, NBC engineers experimented with mechanical television. "Our original equipment consisted of a 48-line mechanical scanning system, a 250-watt transmitter and several mechanical scanning type receivers," O. B. Hanson, vice-president and chief engineer of NBC, said.[1] One of the major difficulties was a need to increase the number of lines scanned per second. The larger the number, the better the quality of the picture.

Without much fanfare, by March 1930 NBC had converted the old roof garden of the New Amsterdam Theatre, on 42d Street—where Florenz Ziegfeld presented *The Midnight Frolic*—into W2XBS, an experimental television studio.[2] There, engineers discreetly carried on many projects. The mechanical system was advanced to 60 lines, and a 500-watt television transmitter, later boosted to 1 kilowatt, was installed. Even at this early date, NBC received letters from more than two hundred viewers.

Two years later, a 2.5-kilowatt television station was installed atop the Empire State Building. The mechanical scanning was raised to 120 lines, which improved both live pickup and the reproduction of motion picture film.

The Emergence of Electronic Television

Realizing that mechanical television was not a long-term solution, David Sarnoff kept his eye on the experiments of another Russian who had emigrated to the United States by 1 January 1919 and found work as a research assistant at the Westinghouse laboratories in Pittsburgh: Dr. Vladimir K. Zworykin. By the end of 1923 Zworykin had taken out a patent on his iconoscope. Impressed with this achievement, Sarnoff made a major decision to support an all-electronic approach to television equipment. Zworykin estimated $100,000 would be required to develop

the idea, and Sarnoff agreed it was worth it. In fact, according to Sarnoff's biographer, it would cost RCA $10 million; "then it would absorb $40 million more before there was a dollar of profit on the investment."[3]

By 1933 the noisy mechanical scanning system had been replaced by Zworykin's iconoscope, an electronic system that provided flickerless pictures, more detail, and an image of 240 lines. Yet, despite ten years of development, the quality of the picture produced by the iconoscope was not really competitive with motion pictures. Consequently, RCA-NBC experiments continued behind closed doors. In May 1935 RCA released television from its research laboratories for studio and field tests.

Live Talent Studios

NBC had been developed largely as an inducement for the purchase of radio receivers manufactured by RCA. NBC housed radio studios, and some of this space was taken over for experimental television programming. Television facilities consisted of three studios, a technical laboratory, machine and carpentry shops, and a scenic paint shop. The antenna for both sight and sound was installed 1,300 feet above street level on the Empire State Building, the video and sound being transmitted either by coaxial cable or a special radio link transmitter. Of the three studios, one was exclusively for televising film, another for special effects, and a third for live talent.

The live-talent studio was thirty feet wide, fifty feet long, and eighteen feet high. This was small by motion picture studio standards, and the staff found it to be less than ideal. It was a former radio studio simply converted for experimentation. Single sets built in one end of the room were the rule, though multisets were added on occasion. Three cameras on pedestals were relatively easy to move, but focusing and smooth panning were still difficult. The viewfinder lens and the iconoscope scanning lens were not the same, and this displacement caused vertical parallax. The camera operator had to use his judgment to make a correction. Two large green bull's-eye signal lamps mounted below the lens assembly, later referred to as "tally lights," showed when a camera was on the air. A direct beam of high-intensity light could temporarily paralyze a camera tube, causing a resounding reprimand over the control-room PA system if the camera lens was pointed into the lights.

The sets were painted in black and white because the system televised only in those colors. Albert W. Protzman, NBC technical director, made the following summary of the engineering experiments: The average set illumination was in the neighborhood of 1,200 foot-candles of incident

light. The lowest foundation lighting level was 800 foot-candles, a play in which high contrast throughout the set was carried to the upper limit of the iconoscope. The highest foot-candle reading recorded with slightly less than 2,500 foot-candles, a continuity where, obviously, little modeling was attempted.[4] Motion picture techniques were employed to create realistic detail in scenery because the iconoscope camera revealed more to a viewer than a member of the audience could see on the stage. Protzman continued, "This may be a time to correct some erroneous impressions concerning the type of make-up used in television. It never has been necessary to use gruesome make-up for the modern all-electronic-RCA television system."[5] Panchromatic base used for panchromatic film and dark red lipstick were satisfactory.

The control-room personnel included a video director, who was part engineer and switcher, and a "production director," who called the shots and made the artistic judgments. An audio control engineer handled the sound track, much of which was picked up by a microphone on a long boom in the studio. An assistant production man, later called a floor manager or director, wore a headset so that he could convey messages from the director to the performers.

The production of a short play resembled the procedure in practice today: many dry-run rehearsals were held outside the studio, where the production director and the head camera operator worked out visual details. Protzman noted, "All action, including camera shots, cues, and timing, is noted on a master script which thereafter becomes the 'bible' of the production. Timing is very important because of the necessity of having a particular act time in with the other acts or film subject."[6] After several hours of rehearsal on the set, cameras were positioned, technically adjusted, and the action was refined in the play so that the cameras could follow the movement smoothly. Finally, a dress rehearsal was scheduled. Film inserts frequently opened a program and were used for difficult transitions specified in the script. Outdoor scenes were also often filmed. Once the drama was in progress, it was live and had to continue without a flaw.

NBC's Shift to Programming

By 1936 a definite change had taken place in television. Emphasis was shifting from engineering to programming. In June RCA began its first organized experimental field tests, and the following month, 7 July 1936, RCA president Sarnoff announced NBC's first regular television demonstrations (see Appendix D). Technically, the picture was expanded to 7½ by 12 inches, electronically scanned by 343 lines, and the signal was

broadcast within a fifty-mile radius of the mid-Manhattan transmitter, primarily to members of RCA's official family by means of "ultra modern" television receivers. "Private exhibition of progress made to date in television tests was held yesterday Tuesday [7 July 1936] afternoon in RCA building for licensees of company. Seance barred to public," *Variety* reported.[7]

In the lineup of brief presentations was a three-and-a-half-minute monologue from the 1933 Broadway play *Tobacco Road,* by Jack Kirkland and Erskine Caldwell. The monologue was delivered by the original star, Henry Hull, portraying Jeeter Lester, an old tobacco farmer who after seven years of trying to raise cotton on depleted soil, is financially destitute. A neighbor upbraids him for his poverty, and old Jeeter responds.[8] On 9 September 1936 the NBC *Television Master Book* logged the first dramatic scenes, "Romeo and Juliet" and "Park Scene."[9] During the three years thereafter—fall 1936 through April 1939—most of the nearly fifty different productions were romantic comedies or crime dramas.

The exhibition of the first few playlets in the latter half of 1936 made it clear that professional talent needed to be added to the production staff. Bearing overall responsibility for television was NBC vice-president John Royal, who enlisted the services of Thomas H. Hutchinson. Hutchinson, experienced in theater, had originally joined NBC as an announcer in 1928, quickly moving into managerial posts and temporarily leaving NBC to represent a commercial account. Rejoining NBC in New York as a radio producer in 1934, he was already on hand to move into television by 1937 as NBC television program manager. A perfectionist, he directed the principal early television dramas himself.

Assisting him were some of the best television engineering experts available. Albert W. Protzman had been employed in radio since 1922 and afterward in the Fox Film Corporation as assistant sound director. He came to NBC television as technical director in 1936. Likewise, William C. Eddy, a naval officer who had retired because of deafness, was hired as an engineer for the Farnsworth company in 1934 and joined NBC as chief of visual effects in 1937. A radar genius, he convinced the navy to reactivate him in 1941, but he later became the head of WBKB, Chicago.

NBC's Experimental Dramas, 1936–1939

At the outset, television executives scheduled experiments nearly every week showing potential advertisers products and services that could be sold on the new medium. Because young married couples were a key part

of the potential marketplace, NBC hired Grace Bradt and Eddie Albert to write a sketch that would demonstrate the possibilities. Albert, who had begun singing and managing local theaters while attending the University of Minneapolis, moved to New York where he formed a club act and later a radio show with Bradt. By 1935 they were appearing professionally as "The Honeymooners—Grace and Eddie."

Their first original television skit was "Love Nest" on 21 September 1936, but the second, "A Balanced Meal," drew more attention because it was a demonstration for General Foods. The twosome came up with a light meal indeed. The brief play showed Grace serving her hungry husband, Eddie, a vitamin dinner consisting of vegetable soup, nuts, and carrot fluff for dessert. He objects and they go out to eat. "A Balanced Meal" was presented on 16 October 1936. Grace and Eddie were paid $20 for the production rights and $25 for each performance, the fees being about par at the time for rights and acting. The next month, he and Grace performed a third skit, "Just Married." In this one, the couple get away from his milk route for a day to enjoy a honeymoon. After some wrestling on a bed, they order a $15 French dinner they cannot pay for, only to learn later that it is complimentary to newlyweds. At the time of the November telecast, Albert was only a month away from his Broadway debut as Bing Edwards in *Brother Rat* (16 December 1936).

More than 200 spectators watched these demonstrations in clusters of twelve to fifteen persons looking at receivers in a darkened room. *The Billboard* commented: "Altho previous laboratory television has been shown by RCA, yesterday's show ['Just Married'] before some 200 guests represented the first showing of a complete program built for entertainment value as well as a demonstration."[10] Personnel came from radio and the theater. Scripts were in radio format, the dialogue being typed across the entire page in upper and lower case letters and the sound cues being identified by capital letters. Actors frequently read from scripts that they held as though speaking into a microphone. Heavy makeup application was carried over from the days of mechanical scanning because image definition was still not at optimum. Staging and lighting was theatrical, allowing one interior set and limited movement. Studios were still very hot from the use of numerous intense lamps. To improve these conditions, the program department began learning entirely new techniques in continuity writing, makeup, staging, and other details.

COMEDIES PREFERRED

Within the first three years of operation, W2XBS produced more than twenty romantic comedies. Most of them were sketches from revues or

one-act plays that had small casts and involved low royalty ($10–$15) though they offered some prestige to potential sponsors. Collaborations by the brilliant playwright and journalist George S. Kaufman epitomized the kind of plays that were desirable for television. They were light, contemporary (about ten years old), funny, romantic male-female relationships that required only a simple setting and delineated a theme or plot that was easy to understand. By the mid-thirties, Kaufman was at his peak as a highly respected director and master playwright. However patronizing the plaudits from his newspaper colleagues may have been, more than once two of his highly successful plays were playing on Broadway at the same time, such as *Stage Door* and *You Can't Take It with You* (1936).

Two of Kaufman's plays appeared on television during this early period: "If Men Played Cards as Women Do" and "The Still Alarm." The first of these was originally presented on 12 November 1936 and many times over the next year; its last performance was 7 October 1945. The original television cast included Mark Smith, Arthur Maitland, Alan Bunce, Max Waizman, and Alvin Simons. Besides this satire on women who play cards and gossip, Kaufman's "The Still Alarm" (1930) is a fifteen-minute satire involving two men who are trapped in their hotel room during a fire. They carry on their best drawing-room conversation while two firemen enter, one with a violin. He experiences difficulty finding time to practice "Keep the Home Fires Burning."

Two of Roland Jeans's revue sketches were repeated frequently. "The Matchmaker," a blackout written in 1928, concerns a young man named Charles (John Moore) who wants to marry a young lady, Stella (Helen Walpole), who is playing hard to get. Charles receives little encouragement from his friend, John (James Meighan) because he is so henpecked that he finds it difficult to remember the virtues of marriage. Another sketch, sometimes appearing on the same evening and reappearing six times, was Jeans's farce from *Charlot Revue* (1925), "Not Lost." The original cast included Robert Strauss, Ralph Locke, Jack MacBryde, and Helen Walpole.

In "Little Old Lady" (or "Romantic Interlude") an elderly couple reminisces about how they met at a ball. In the flashback sequence, Helen Walpole appeared as Grandma when she was a girl, and Lawrence Gray played the role of The Boy. Several extras were in the ballroom scene. The sketch ran about ten minutes. A large cast that included a five-piece orchestra was assembled for an adaptation of Robert Wallsten's original short story "When They Play a Waltz." The plot concerns a flirtation Diana has with an unknown man. She enlists the aid of her friend, Archie. Come to find out, Diana is flirting with Archie's friend.

Some months later, "The Noble Lord" and "Sauce for the Gander"

continued the series of light romantic comedies. "The Noble Lord" is about a young lady (Helen Lewis) who pretends to be drowning so that she can attract the attention of a nobleman (Harold DeBecker). He saves her and learns of her deception. Pretending to be his own valet, he tests her motives. She is not interested in a mere valet and proceeds to try the deception again. This time, the nobleman sends his real valet to her rescue. In Margaret Freshley's "Sauce for the Gander," Terry (Ned Wever) is paying attention to another woman, Luella (Kay Strozzi). His wife, Linda (Marjorie Clarke), pretends to be interested in his friend Tom (William David). The women get together to discuss Terry's wandering eye, and as a result, Terry and Linda are reunited. The action takes place on the terrace of a Palm Beach Hotel.

CRIME PAYS

The first crime drama presented by NBC was "Midnight Murder," a one-act play by Arthur Ashdown. When it was originally telecast on 15 July 1937, the actors included Irving Lewis, Arthur Maitland, and Neil O'Malley. The library of the Towers, Yorkshire, England, was the setting. In October 1939 Thomas H. Hutchinson adapted a story by Harry Stephen Keller, "The Services of an Expert." The setting for the fifteen-minute comedy is a New York apartment where a husband (Arthur Maitland) entices another man (Ned Wever), whom he believes to be an intruder but is really the apartment owner, into opening a safe belonging to the tenant's wife so that the husband can procure some letters. When repeated on 6 July 1939, *The Billboard* said it was "choice entertainment beautifully adapted."[11]

The first crime drama that captured the attention of the press in a substantial way was "The Three Garridebs," a Sherlock Holmes adventure by Arthur Conan Doyle. While in search of a lost member of the Garrideb family, Holmes discovers a wanted killer and $5 million in counterfeit money. The script, adapted by T. H. Hutchinson, ran thirty-three pages. Actors Louis Hector as Sherlock Holmes and William Podmore as Dr. Watson received $125 each; Arthur Maitland and Harold DeBecker, as John and Nathan Garrideb, $115. Other cast members—Violet Bosson as Mrs. Hudson, Selma Hall as Mrs. Saunders, and Eustice Wyatt as Inspector Lestrade—received $95 each. The production required twenty-two hours of rehearsal over four days.

Louis Hector experienced some difficulty with his lines, a trait somewhat characteristic of many radio actors. He was a veteran actor who had appeared as Moriarty in a radio version of *Sherlock Holmes* as early as 1930. He was remembered by audiences for parts in *Pretty Kitty Kelly*

Scene from "The Three Garridebs," W2XBS, New York, 23 November 1937. (*National Broadcasting Company*)

(CBS, 1937) and *Lorenzo Jones,* which originated at NBC that same year. "I was floor manager," Arthur Hungerford once said. "So we had to work out a scheme—because if you throw a line to an actor when he doesn't really want it, you may throw him off. He'd [Hector] like to work himself out of it. So we had a deal. . . . If he really couldn't do it, he'd make a vast gesture with his right hand like he was saluting the Pope or something and that would be my cue to throw the line."[12] William Podmore was also a radio veteran. His credits included *Second Husband* on CBS and *Terry and the Pirates* on NBC at the same time he was acting in "The Three Garridebs."

Three performances were given on the evening of 23 November 1937. This first full-length mystery enabled NBC to invite ham radio operators, members of the American Radio Relay League, to look into the future. Such groups were frequent guests. Sherlock Holmes, a favorite character from the novel, was one of radio's early dramatic successes. This was the first teleplay to integrate film and live studio production. The opening

and transitional London scenes were filmed at London Towers in Queens using a hansom cab from the Plaza Hotel. These filmed sequences allowed actors time to change costumes. The two major studio sets were Holmes's apartment and the home of John Garrideb. *The New York Times* said, "At times, due to limitations of lighting, distortion or some other cause, the figures and objects in the room became somewhat vague and shadowy, but by and large the pictures were well-defined, the action smooth and it was always possible to recognize objects such as microphones and museum pieces littered about the quarters occupied by Holmes and the eccentric Garrideb."[13]

By spring 1938 crime-related one-act plays were rivaling the number of romantic comedies. "Confessional," by Percival Wilde, sometimes called "Hour of Truth," appeared on 12 May. He was the most prolific writer of one-act plays of the time. His subjects varied as did his occupations of banker, navy veteran, and inventor. In "Confessional," a well-known play of social comment, John Gresham (Earle Larrimore) is held for the misappropriation of bank funds. For a large bribe, he asks Robert Baldwin (Wilmer Walter), a witness for the prosecution, to say that he does not remember vital information. Baldwin, despite pressure to accept the money, remains honest. ("Confessional" was being repeated more than a year later.)

Within two weeks, "The Valiant," a very popular play by Holworthy Hall and Robert Middlemass, was produced. The story tells of a convicted killer on death row, Warren Holt (William Daniel), who is confronted by a girl, Josephine Paris (Flora Campbell), looking for her lost brother. The killer will not admit he is her brother. Scenes for the half-hour drama take place in the offices of the warden and the governor. From this start, Flora Campbell became one of the most frequently used actresses in television.

Kenneth Sawyer Goodman's 1913 one-act play, "A Game of Chess," was dusted off for a later presentation. The scene is a room in a nobleman's palace, where a "Red" peasant, Boris (Eugene Sigaloff), attempts to assassinate the nobleman, Alexis (Anthony Kemble Cooper). Alexis is weary of life anyway; he prefers chess with his rival, Constantine (Calvin Thomas). Nonetheless, Alexis manages to trick Boris into drinking poison. Such cleverness revitalizes Alexis to the extent that he plays his opponent with renewed vigor.

A crime story gave television prognosticators something to talk about for a second time when "The Mysterious Mummy Case" was produced on 11 May 1938. The tale, adapted by Thomas H. Hutchinson from a story by Tom Terriss, involves an evil-spreading mummy case whose macabre influence kills several men and finally is sent to the bottom of the

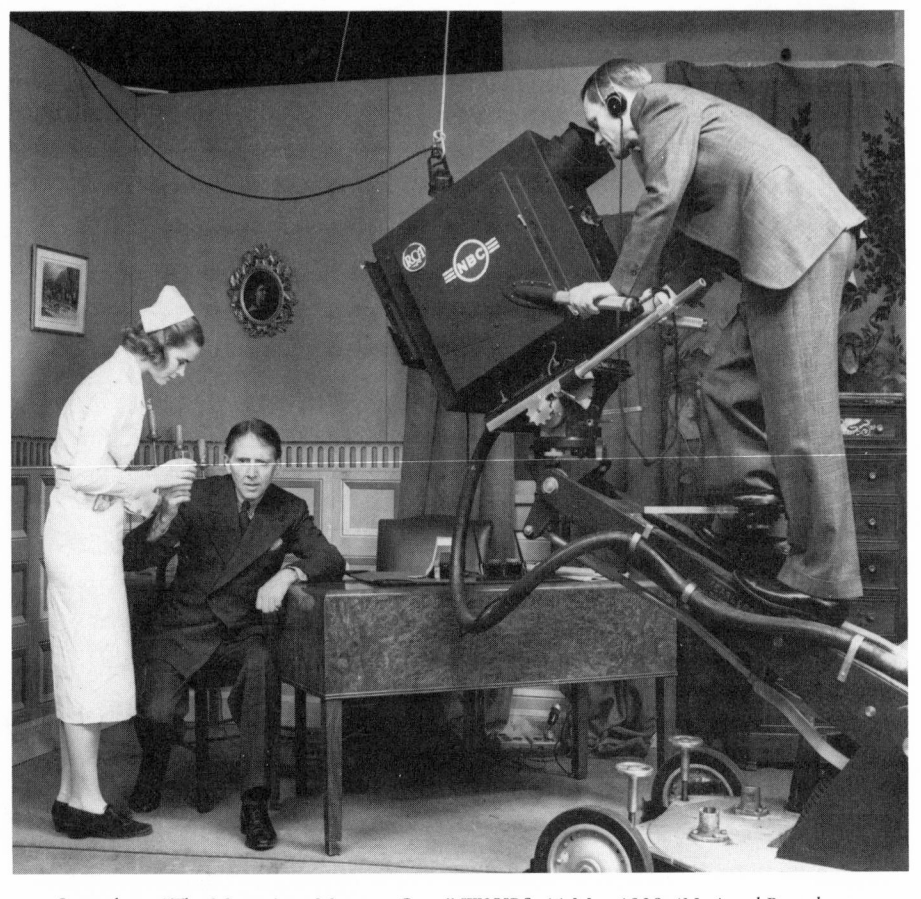

Scene from "The Mysterious Mummy Case," W2XBS, 11 May 1938. (*National Broadcasting Company*)

Atlantic on the SS *Titanic*. A cast of well-known radio actors supported Tom Terriss, who played himself. It included Arthur Maitland as The Doctor, Anthony Kemble Cooper as A Friend, Ned Wever as Piquard, and Harold DeBecker as Gregory. Dorothy McGuire played Miss Clark. McGuire, at age twenty, had just been selected to understudy Martha Scott in *Our Town*, a title simply borrowed by the radio network from the Wilder Broadway stage hit (1938). Quick changes by the actors, moving picture film, slides, and accurate timing enabled the drama to move swiftly.

Variety's first review of a television drama appeared on page one. Bob Landry hailed "The Mysterious Mummy Case" as the television equiv-

alent of the movies' benchmark narrative "The Great Train Robbery." He wrote: "Television is still crude. Very crude. . . . But compared with the rain streaked flickers of the nickelodeon days the entertainment offered by 'The Mysterious Mummy Case' is relatively advanced."[14] *The New York Times* agreed:

> "The Mysterious Mummy Case," presented by the National Broadcasting Company, as a twenty-five-minute television drama during the past week at Radio City, was generally applauded by veteran teleobservers as the most professionally staged show seen so far in the air over New York. Sixteen hours of rehearsal were required to "polish" the program.
>
> The [five] sets, art of make-up, costumes, the camera work and acting all dovetailed into real showmanship that held the eye far more entrancingly than have many of the loosely fitted productions of the past "experimental" days. The spectator forgot that he was viewing television; it was more like sitting in a movie theater.[15]

Little wonder that reviewers like Landry sounded a note of hesitancy. The costly cathode-ray tube, the eye of the iconoscope camera, was causing various problems. Within an hour's use, for instance, the edge of the picture began to blur substantially. Picture quality and expense were considerations when the Baird company of England decided to return to a 120-line mechanical system, now scanning in color.

"SUSAN AND GOD"

Television dramas enlisted the services of prominent radio actors, stars in their own right. For example, James Meighan was a familiar voice on *Just Plain Bill* (CBS, 1932); as Flash Gordon for Mutual in 1935; as Valentine in *Alias Jimmy Valentine* (NBC Blue, 1937); as Larry Noble in *Backstage Wife* (NBC, 1935); and as Reid Wilson in *Against the Storm* (NBC, 1939). Another leading man was Ned Wever. He participated in the first full-hour radio dramatic series, *The True Hour Story with Mary and Bob,* for CBS in January 1928. He early worked for both networks: *Pages of Romance,* NBC, 1932; *Little Italy,* CBS, 1933; *Big Sister,* CBS, 1936; *Valiant Lady,* NBC; and as Dr. Anthony Loring in *Young Widder Brown,* NBC, 1938. A later role as Captain Hugh ("Bulldog") Drummond made him well known on Mutual.

Helen Lewis was a frequent ingenue. During the early thirties, she played Gladys Pendleton in *Ma Perkins* (NBC, 1933) as well as Tess Trueheart in *Dick Tracy* (Mutual, 1935) and appeared in *The Road of*

Life, which originated in 1937. Helen Walpole was a writer for *Our Gal Sunday* and *Second Husband* (1937) an well as an actress. Among her acting assignments were *Just Plain Bill* in the early thirties and *Lorenzo Jones* on NBC about 1937.

Jack (or John) MacBryde enjoyed a substantial career. He was Peewee in *Peewee and Windy,* a radio show about two young sailors in the early thirties, but his vocal qualities brought him roles as the Old Ranger in *Death Valley Days,* originating on the NBC Blue Network in 1930, and as Dan Cassidy in *Eno Crime Club* later on CBS. By 1938 he was appearing in *Young Widder Brown* when it premiered in September. Ralph Locke was perhaps best known as "Papa David" Solomon on *Life Can Be Beautiful,* CBS, 1938. Robert Strauss was Pa Wiggs in *Mrs. Wiggs and the Cabbage Patch* for NBC in 1936 and appeared on *Our Gal Sunday* the following year. John Moore played Captain Goodhue in *Terry and the Pirates* on NBC in 1937 before he was on *Life Can Be Beautiful* for CBS. Arthur Maitland, another character actor often on television, came from radio's *David Harum,* originating at NBC in 1936, and *Your Family and Mine,* NBC, 1938. Wilmer Walter held the title role as Andy Gump on CBS in 1934 and as David Harum in that series for NBC radio in 1936.

Although the voices of these people were familiar to millions because of their roles on continuing radio serials, none of them became television stars nor possessed the charisma of the first star to appear on television: the British actress, comedienne, and musical comedy favorite Gertrude Lawrence. Enticed by the opportunity to present "an epoch-making event," John Golden, noted for producing "clean" sex plays, agreed to the telecast of a scene from his current hit, Rachel Crothers's three-act comedy *Susan and God* on 7 June 1938. The play had opened the previous year and was still at the Plymouth Theatre. *The New York Times* reported, "The experiment marked 'the first time in television history that a current Broadway hit with its original cast' went on the air in New York." [Earlier televising of Broadway shows was in theaters.][16]

"Susan and God" is the story of a flighty and selfish woman, Susan Trepel (Lawrence), who has just returned from abroad with new religious values. Her alcoholic husband, Barrie (Paul McGrath), is eager for reconciliation so that they can provide a home for their lonely, neglected, fifteen-year-old daughter, Blossom (Nancy Coleman). The husband and daughter respond to the improved home life, and so Susan decides to keep the family together. The television production used only the bedroom scene: Susan has just returned home and Barrie pleads for another chance.[17]

Scene from "Susan and God," W2XBS, 7 June 1938. (*National Broadcasting Company*)

Gertrude Lawrence was no stranger to television for she had appeared at Aeolian Hall in 1930, and now she was "the first big star to try television" in a dramatic scene.[18] Ten years later, she would make television history again by being in the first George Bernard Shaw teleplay, "Great Catherine." An amusing incident was involved with this Theatre Guild production. Lawrence went to meet Owen Davis, Jr., an NBC executive, at the Guild's brownstone headquarters on 53d Street. Several children saw her arrive and then attempt to enter the building by knocking loudly on the front door. Exhausted, she returned to the street to hail another cab. As she did so, the children, who were used to disappointed actresses, chided, "You didn't get the job, did you?" It seems someone had inadvertently locked the outside door so that Davis could not hear her knocking.

Everyone at NBC was flustered over the arrival of the charming and talented star. Arthur Hungerford recalled:

We made the scenery ourselves. Got the stencils and put the wall-paper on that way, instead of getting real wallpaper because that cost too much. We got the whole studio set and on comes John Royal, who was the vice president in charge of programs at NBC. He said, "The place stinks." Of course it did from casein. So he sent me out with $50—we hadn't spent that on the whole set—to buy Gertie's perfume. We came in and sprayed it all over the place, and when she came in it was fine. Sarnoff was so delighted to see Miss Lawrence that we had to really take Sarnoff off the stage in order to start the show.[19]

Actors depended on stage makeup and did not attempt to adapt their acting technique, especially their voices, to the more intimate medium. It was a sizzling afternoon and the studio, heated by equally intense light-ing, was extremely warm. Lawrence looked "quite tired" afterward. The half-hour production began at four o'clock in the afternoon. An audience of thirty-five watched the show on a seven-by-ten-inch screen at Radio City while others observed it at various places within the viewing area. A printed synopsis of the play provided the continuity for the scenes. John Golden, who was an actor, writer, and producer (*Seventh Heaven, The Bishop Misbehaves*), paraphrased Shakespeare to enthusiastically predict: "Soon television will make a stage of the world."

Gertrude Lawrence's appearance may have accelerated recognition for actors. Those in major roles received $25 apiece through the summer of 1938, but, when the fall season began, actors' compensation doubled and they benefited from the security of a contract. Improved payments for talent and for royalties at a time when unions were weak in television and copyright enforcement was not yet well defined largely foreshadowed the industry's efforts in preparing for public demonstrations during the com-ing spring.

During the next several months, the list of familiar one-act plays length-ened. In "Good Medicine," by Harold P. Godwin and Edwin Burke, produced on 23 August 1938, Dr. James Graves (Pat Lawrence) learns, after tests, that a millionairess patient (Lily Cahill) referred to him by his wife (Barbara Weeks) is a hypochondriac. John Kirkpatrick's "The Nine Lives of Emily" takes place at the engagement party of Emily (Mona Moray) and Douglas (Burford Hampden). During the party, Emily nearly drowns. "Speaking to Father," by George Ade, is a romantic comedy in which Edward Worthington Swinger (Ronald Bennett) asks Septimus Pickering (James Spottswood), of the Pickering Pickle Company, to marry his eighteen-year-old daughter, Caroline. In a second Ade comedy that month, "The Mayor and the Manicure," an older manicurist (Paula Mac-

Lean) takes advantage of a vulnerable mayor (George Taylor) who wants to run for governor by threatening a breach-of-promise suit involving his young son.

In "Emergency Call," by Ted Byron, a husband (Robert Light) discovers his love-starved wife (Doris Light) making a suspicious phone call to a stranger. In "The Trimmed Lamp," an O. Henry adaptation by Edward Padula, Nancy Danforth (Dana Dale) searches for a rich husband. Previous scripts followed radio format, but the script for "Emergency Call" was divided into three columns: for dialogue, actor movements, and camera shots. On 9 September 1938 "The Ace Is Trumped," by H. H. Stinson, gave television viewers the first glimpse of gangland characters, when Big Ace Jacobs (Clarence Rock) struggles over territorial jurisdiction with Eddie Reilly (Neil O'Malley).

Susan Glaspell's popular 1916 one-act play, "Trifles," presented on 28 March 1939, takes place in the kitchen of a New England farmhouse. Mrs. Wright (Edmonia Nolley) is under suspicion for the strangulation of her husband. While authorities search the premises for clues, two neighbor ladies find a strangled canary in a broken cage and other evidence of the husband's abuse and cruelty. The women do not reveal her motive and probable guilt.

When Llewellyn Hughes's "Dark Eyes Mean Danger" was telecast on 30 March 1939, public programming was only a month away. This play takes place in a London hotel, where Audrey Stair (Mary MacCormack) and Dwight Gray (Robert Light) are clashing over an alleged infidelity before their trip on the *Queen Mary*. Gray is a young diplomat who had seemingly been involved with a female counterspy (Lili Valenti). This production cost $237.60, about twice that of most previous shows. It was the first time a credit was given to a contributing store: Russek's Fifth Avenue, for the use of an evening wrap and furs.

Summary of NBC Experimental Dramas

Of the ninety-two comedies and dramas that NBC produced from 7 July 1936 to 30 April 1939, eight were repeated as many as six times and several others were repeated at least twice. Frequently, they ran under ten minutes; a few consumed an hour. Half-hour one-act play adaptations were common. Initially, the sketches were demonstrations promoting the sale of products and services, but they quickly became entertainment vehicles without commercial references. Although regarded as the most complex and expensive of television productions, dramas have consistently held the attention of the public and critics. The fledgling productions during this period were primarily technical experiments in performing, staging, lighting and makeup.

NBC Public Demonstrations, 1939–1941

After more than two and a half years of experimental field tests and closed-circuit viewing by invitation only, RCA head David Sarnoff told the Radio Manufacturers Association that, despite many technical, artistic, and financial problems, NBC would begin a regular public television program service from its transmitter on the Empire State Building when the New York World's Fair opened on 30 April 1939.

So long as experiments were conducted behind closed doors, the television staff was kept to a minimum. Thomas H. Hutchinson took most of the major producer/director assignments, and Thomas Lyne Riley and Edward Padula shared the others in drama. Riley was primarily a radio producer, but he also knew a good deal about theater. He was married to Marjorie Clarke, a highly competent actress, who appeared in several of his telecasts. Padula was a bright young man just out of Yale Drama School, and many of his dramas showed quite a bit of imagination.

To carry out a more complex schedule of regular programming, NBC vice-president John Royal decided in March to place Max Gordon in charge of television production. Gordon knew almost everybody in show business. He had been a writer in vaudeville and at one time booked acts for the Palace. He ran an agency with Al Lewis and produced many plays with Sam Harris, such as *The Family Upstairs, The Farmer Takes a Wife* (1934), *Ethan Frome* (1936), and *Missouri Legend* (with Guthrie McClintic, 1938). They would all be telecast by NBC within two years.

Gordon immediately hired Edward Sobol to serve in the vague capacity of liaison under Hutchinson, the senior man in longevity and television experience. Sobol had begun his directing career working for Gordon on vaudeville sketches for silent film stars in 1929 and during the intervening ten years directed productions on Broadway, in London, and in Hollywood. He was a fortunate choice; by 1947 he was to receive more industry honors than anyone else. The press expected Gordon and Sobol to put on two-a-day vaudeville, and in a way, they did by turning to the short plays of Aaron Hoffman, Arthur Hopkins, George Ade, Harry Delf, George S. Kaufman, and others who were writers for newspapers, vaudeville sketches, and the Broadway stage.[20] From the two rather small studios in Rockefeller Center, two program schedules lasting at least an hour each were telecast on Wednesdays and Fridays, for a total of ten hours per month.

Clearly, a lot of promotion and selling was required so that the public could view this limited schedule. The cost of television receivers ranged from $199.50 for a 3⅜-by-4⅜-inch screen to $600 for the larger 7⅛-by-9¾-inch picture. Although the New York World's Fair was an auspicious occasion to announce television's arrival, twenty-four comedies

and dramas telecast through August were routine reminders of the recent past. During the year that followed, however, NBC presented an impressive array of sixty long dramas and comedies, nearly one a week, through July 1940. Then, the next month, it shifted to election coverage that included the Republican and Democratic conventions, sports events, and feature films. Dramatic productions were not resumed until January 1941. The growing audience for these programs was estimated at more than 20,000 viewers.[21]

THE FIRST PUBLIC DRAMAS

For the initiation of regular public service, NBC revived the twenty-minute Aaron Hoffman play "The Unexpected," originally televised a year earlier. He was judged by many to be vaudeville's greatest comedy writer, but this sketch about a fellow who plans to rob a woman of a ruby was below expectations in *Variety*'s view:

> For the dramatic interlude the program builders singled out a mossy piece by the late Aaron Hoffman, "The Unexpected." George Nash did the playlet in vaudeville back in 1916. . . . Technically the results showed a considerable advance over the demonstrations of an excerpt from "Susan and God" televised by NBC last summer. The definition in both the long-shots and close-ups was consistently okay but the sketch itself offered but a minimum of interest.[22]

The production required 12½ hours of rehearsal and cost $115.

SHORT COMEDIES AND DRAMAS

For the most part, in the late spring a continuation of one-act plays occurred. Telecast on 10 May 1939, "The Faker," by Edwin Burke, showed "a definite superiority to radio in the field of drama," which was credited in part to the superb performance of stage actor Walter Greaza, and the debut of Edward Sobol as producer and of Edward Padula as director.[23] The story concerns a man (Greaza) who wants to establish a colony where he can raise his children without the influence of women. He espouses his view by selling a book, *The Protection of Man against the Blandishments of Matrimonially Maddened Women*.

Elaine Sterne Carrington's "The Red Hat" told of a marital problem between Ted (Boyd Crawford) and Jean (Jean Muir) over another woman (Blanche Gladstone). Carrington was an expert in writing about romance through her radio serials *Pepper Young's Family*, originating on the Blue Network in 1936, and *When a Girl Marries*, carried by CBS radio in

1939. The camera work in the television show, one reviewer thought, was unflattering to women.[24] On 17 May another triangle found Jean (Martha Sleeper) and George (Burford Hampden) planning to run off while husband Mark (Ned Wever) seems to give her up too easily. One complaint was that Sleeper emoted too much; short and pudgy Burford Hampden did not seem to be the gigolo type; and tall, villainous Ned Wever was also miscast.[25] The play was "The Smart Thing," by Frank Conlan.

On 16 June 1939 "Family Honor" was at stake when Joshua, played by the author, William E. Shea, and Enoch (Paul Ballantine) tried to win the same girl. In another Aaron Hoffman sketch, "The Honeymooner," a couple is tired of being teased about being newlyweds. A few plays dealing with serious themes appeared in May and June. Harry Delf's "Any Family" concerns a father (Grant Irvin) and mother (Anne Athey) who are tired of working without help from ungrateful children. In "Likes and Dislikes," by Edwin Burke, Mildred (Margaret Callahan) invites a man (Alan Bunce) her husband, George (John Baruff), dislikes to dinner. Frequently performed by schools and civic groups, "Afterwards," by Geraldine McGaughan, is a fantasy about a boy (Robert Baren) and a girl (Doris Young) who meet after being killed in an automobile accident. On this occasion, the actors were students from Bogota High School, in New Jersey.

Noel Coward's 1925 three-act farce *Hay Fever* was not outstanding when seen on the stage, and it lost much of its satirical bite on television. The plot takes place at the weekend home of eccentric, retired actress Judith Bliss (Isobel Elson); Judith and members of her family invite friends for a visit and then are impolite to them. Elson performed "very well" and received good support from Dennis Hoey as the author, Virginia Campbell as the daughter, and Montgomery Clift—in his first television appearance—as the son.[26]

CRIME STORIES

Crime stories continued to hold their own. "The Unexpected," "A Game of Chess," "The Valiant," "Confessional," and "The Services of an Expert" were alternated with some longer dramas and musicals. "Moonshine," a backwoods yarn by Arthur Hopkins, appeared as part of an evening devoted to hillbilly life. Hopkins, sometimes referred to as the "Sphinx of Show Business," was a well-known producer and writer, who worked out of a tiny office in the Plymouth Theatre.

In late June "The Donovan Affair," by Owen Davis, was one of the more impressive programs. The play takes place in the home of Professor

Donovan, where Inspector John Killigan is proceeding to solve the murder of Donovan's son. The prolific Davis, who won the Pulitzer prize in 1923 for *Icebound,* wrote more than three hundred plays between the ages of twenty-seven and forty. It was said that he seemed to do nothing else, yet somehow he married and raised a family, including sons Owen, Jr., a film and stage actor and later NBC executive, and Donald, who produced *The Donovan Affair* on Broadway. In the fall of 1939, Donald would join NBC as a television writer/adapter and eventually director. Frequently seen in several telecasts was his actress wife, Dorothy Mathews.

The schedule had become more complex by July, when "Missouri Legend," by E. B. Ginty, and "Hay Fever," by Noel Coward, were telecast. The Ginty work, produced by Max Gordon on Broadway, is a melodrama about Jesse James that takes place in the Ozark mountains in 1882 and starred Dean Jagger and Mildred Natwick.

MUSICALS

Over the summer, four different kinds of musicals were staged. The first, on 2 June 1939, was an hour-long presentation with music called "Jenny Lind" that dealt with P. T. Barnum's promotion of the "Swedish nightingale." Within two weeks, an entirely different change of pace featured a scene from the Negro tragedy "Mamba's Daughters." *The Billboard* commented: "The first scene of the third act from *Mamba's Daughters,* starring Ethel Waters and members of the original cast, was well adapted for television. . . . The scene, marking the return of Lissa, after she achieved fame as a radio singer, offered Miss Waters a chance to sing, *Lonely Walls.*"[27] The third kind of musical was a delightful version of "The Pirates of Penzance," by Gilbert and Sullivan. To assist director Thomas L. Riley, two light-opera experts were called in: Harold Sanford, who supervised the music; and Ivy Scott, who worked with dialogue, movement, and detailed stage action.

Director Riley remarked: "Among the techniques learned were the fact that in television a much smaller cast and orchestra could be used than is required on the stage. The script and score were cut closely making the plot completely coherent but with very little repetition thereby maintaining the rapid pace essential to good television."[28] After a few days of dry rehearsals, the cast was on camera for two days. A commentator was used to describe the scene as well as the cast and provide other program information during the intermission. Two scenes were required, one showing the exterior of a castle.

The fourth attempt at musical dramatization used a showboat setting

for the staging of brief melodramatic moments that were based on *Uncle Tom's Cabin*. Harriet Beecher Stowe's antislavery novel portraying the life of a devoted slave, Uncle Tom, had been produced as a play the year after publication (1852). An abbreviated version was filmed by Edwin Porter and shown during the nickelodeon era (1903). The showboat sequences at NBC—"The Marriage of Little Eva" and "Topsy and Eva"—bore little relation to the principal theme of the book. Both sequences were televised in July 1939. These musical forms would be revived in later years.

NBC's Major Productions

When the fall season opened in 1939, NBC telecast a series of ambitious productions in rapid succession. Several of the plays ran an hour and a half. Although romantic comedy and crime were still the dominant categories, samples of historical and period dramas, classics that included the first major production of Shakespeare ("Julius Caesar"), and fantasy were presented. A few original dramas, light dramas, or comedies incorporating music as well as musicals such as Gilbert and Sullivan's "H.M.S. Pinafore" (5 September 1939) were occasionally attempted. The programs for the most part were reviewed erratically but enthusiastically by the trade press. The sixty productions telecast from 29 August 1939 through 31 July 1940 mark the high point in NBC's output during the experimental era. Frequency, range of content, length, complexity of production, and critical acclaim indicate that this was NBC's best period, and indeed, the most outstanding year in television drama anywhere in the United States during that era.

NBC DRAMA's "BEST YEAR"

Drawing upon substantial knowledge that had been obtained from experimentation with short productions and utilizing the momentum of public programming at last, NBC launched an all-out effort to show that television was ready for the marketplace by presenting the best television had to offer in drama. Although no precise formula for scheduling emerged, a four- or five-week cycle usually included one serious drama, one classic, and two comedies. Nearly every drama was adapted from a Broadway play, which had probably been adapted from some previous work.

The noteworthy exceptions were "Roosty," a rare original crime drama on 1 December 1939 and Gertrude Berg's anniversary play, "prepared

particularly for television," "The Glass House," telecast on 1 May 1940. *Variety* said: "Gertrude Berg's playlet registered impressively as it had done in the past on airwave programs," when it had helped mark the completion of one year of regularly scheduled programming on NBC. It was part of a variety format entitled "Milestone in Television."[29] Berg was known to radio audiences as Molly Goldberg in *The Goldbergs,* a series she created and wrote, since it had made its debut on the Blue Network on 20 November 1929. She would receive the Academy of Television Arts and Sciences' first Emmy award as the best dramatic actress of 1950.[30]

Comedies. As might be expected, NBC initiated its fall season with its most popular genre—romantic comedy—by its most frequently used playwright, George S. Kaufman. In 1939 two of his plays were on Broadway: *The American Way* and *The Man Who Came To Dinner.* The 1921 three-act comedy "Dulcy," written by Kaufman and Marc Connelly, was telecast on 29 August 1939. It is the story of a loquacious wife, Dulcy (Helen Claire), whose endless blunders almost cost her husband (Tom Powers) a chance for an important merger. By some miracle, however, she blunders onto success and saves his business. *The New York Times* reviewer, O. E. Dunlap, Jr., wrote that this show "proved beyond all doubt that drama is one of television's aces, and that this new department of radio acting belongs to the theatre folk, who live their lines and go on the air without scripts."[31] NBC had improved its equipment. New lenses made the images remarkably clear. Four major television adaptations would emerge from Kaufman plays within the twelve months: "Dulcy," "The Butter and Egg Man," "Stage Door," and "June Moon."

"The Butter and Egg Man," a 1925 comedy authored solely by Kaufman, was adapted to a seventy-minute version and produced by Reginald Hammerstein, making his first appearance at NBC. The play is about show business. Theatrical producer Joe Lehman (Anthony Blair) needs money to rehearse his new show. Among those in the cast were Helen Twelvetrees as Mary Marlin, Zella Russell as Fanny Lehman, and Theodore Leavitt as Peter Jones.

"Stage Door," a 1936 drama written by Edna Ferber and Kaufman, tells the story of Terry Randall (Margaret Curtis), who endures many hardships to learn her craft in the theater. She finally obtains a role that establishes her as an actress. The play takes place at Mrs. Orcutt's boardinghouse, where sixteen young women hope for theatrical careers. "Stage Door" was a mid-December offering. Later that winter, on 2 February 1940, "June Moon" was telecast. Based on the 1929 three-act comedy by Ring Lardner and Kaufman, it also involves show business. Freddy (Rich-

ard Quine), a young songwriter from Schenectady, has made a good deal of money from his first song hit and has spent it on a blond. Eventually, realizing the error of his ways, he returns to the girl back home.

Aside from the Kaufman plays, two others dealt with show business: "Burlesque," on 19 April, and "The Barker," on 25 May 1940. The first of these is a 1927 three-act play by George Manker Watters and Arthur Hopkins. Variety acts are woven into the storyline, which concerns a husband and wife team, Skip and Bonny, who are on the burlesque circuit. Skip receives an offer to join a big Broadway show. As a result, his interest in Bonny wanes, and she divorces him. After Skip's career declines, he meets Bonny in burlesque once more, and they are reunited. Audrey Christie, Edwin Muchael, Bette Harmon, and Robert Allen were in the principal roles. As was pointed out in an earlier chapter, "Burlesque" had been used as a prototype by the program department at CBS for intensive study during a period in which the company was unable to produce dramas of its own.

"The Barker" is a 1927 three-act drama about carnival life. Written by J. Kenyon Nicholson, it is the story of barker Nifty Miller (Len Doyle), who wants his son, Chris (John Craven), to become a lawyer. Chris falls in love with Lou (Judy Parrish), the snake charmer, and marries her. Discouraged, Nifty plans to leave the carnival, until he realizes it needs him and that Chris has obtained a job in a law office.

Other comedies during the fall included "Brother Rat," on 7 September, "Art and Mrs. Bottle," on 14 September, "The Dover Road," on 18 October, "The Milky Way," on 20 October, and "Three Men on a Horse," on 24 November 1939.

"Brother Rat," originally a 1936 stage play by John Monks, Jr., and Fred F. Finklehoffe, was, after a forty-second opening, presented in three acts averaging somewhat over twenty minutes each. The comedy concerns Bing Edwards (Lyle Bettger), a star pitcher on a baseball team in a military school who hopes to win a $200 prize as best athlete. On the day before the big game, Edwards, who is secretly married, learns he is to be a father. Marriage is against the regulations, and so he fears exposure. His friends help him out of his trouble. The cast included Tom Ewell as Dan Crawford. The cost of artist fees amounted to $595. Despite a strong appeal to the youth audience, the play was not a big money-maker for producer George Abbott. In fact, he and Warner Bros. not only waived all television rights for the production but also even loaned props. It was directed by Edward Sobol and dubbed "a worthwhile presentation."[32]

"Art and Mrs. Bottle" was the first time that NBC brought in an outside group, intact, to televise its own production since the company had initiated a policy of public programming. The 1939 comedy, by Benn

W. Levy, was staged by a professional summer theater company from the Surray Playhouse, in Maine. The romance centers on a middle-class English family, in which the mother, a wayward soul, becomes concerned about the behavior of her daughter. The daughter has fallen in love with a young artist who was the mother's previous lover. Meanwhile the son is swooning over a cockney model, and the father cannot seem to understand his offspring at all. Donald Davis directed the seventy-minute program. He had been handling daytime shows; this was his first nighttime venture. He received good marks for using close-up shots and for restricting the number of actors on the screen at any one moment, but his critics said he needed a lot of practice in the use of cameras to produce a fluid style resembling motion picture technique.[33]

When it opened at the Cort Theatre in 1934, *The Milky Way*, by Lynn Root and Harry Clarke, was a fairly successful play. The plot involves a milkman who reluctantly turns to prizefighting. As usual, in the television version, the action was staged primarily in one interior set: a dressing room. However, to show the milkman's struggle to qualify even remotely for a championship fight, "for the first time" a filmed sequence was projected. Scenes in "The Cheese Champ," the show's original title, showed him honing his physical condition by working out on a road tour. Sobol generated many laughs through his adept directing of the teleplay, but, lasting ninety-five minutes, it caused too much eyestrain.[34]

A. A. Milne's "The Dover Road" lasted more than an hour and a half. Director Thomas Lyne Riley and the cast rehearsed for nearly fifty hours. In this delicately ironic comedy, Mr. Lattimer has an unusual hobby. He allows couples who are contemplating a change in their marital status a place to stay for a week so that they can become better acquainted and think about the potential breakup of their marriages. Charles Webster, an erstwhile stage and radio actor, was Lattimer; and Marjorie Clarke, a frequent television actress, played Anne.

The 1935 three-act comedy, "Three Men on a Horse," by John Cecil Holm and George Abbott, concerns Erwin Trowbridge (Jack Sheehan), a man who has always lived a sedate life in the suburbs. He goes to a New York bar, where he meets two men and a woman whose livelihood is betting on horses. Trowbridge figures winners as a pastime while riding home on the bus. Relying on his advice, the bookies make a lot of money. Eventually, he returns home to his wife. This was another of Reginald Hammerstein's productions.

A dozen more comedies appeared over the first six months of 1940. Lynn Sterling's "Meet the Wife," "The Impossible Mr. Clancy," and "Tickets Please," a 1937 play by Felix Fair, were among the early entries.

J. B. Priestley came in for attention when two of his plays were presented within a week: "When We Are Married," on 3 March and "Dangerous

Corner," on 8 March 1940. The 1932 three-act play "Dangerous Corner" shows how the truth about a murdered man gradually disrupts family and friends, who turn out to be unpleasant characters. Both comedies required one interior set. "When We Are Married" was "the first production of the legitimate stage to be telecast in its entirety during its run on Broadway."[35] Although it was playing at the Lyceum Theatre in New York, the television production, with permission from Actor's Equity, originated from NBC studios in Radio City, where duplicate scenery and properties were constructed using shades suitable to television. Previously, the play had been telecast in November 1938 by the BBC directly from the stage of the St. Martin's Theatre during its London run.[36] Except for somewhat more limited playing space, the video play was almost exactly like the theater version. One reviewer said there seemed to be no reason to go to the theater.

"When We Are Married" was televised at 8:30 P.M. and ran slightly over an hour and a half. The uncut story told of three Yorkshire couples who learn they are not legally wed. The actors—Estelle Winwood, Alison Skipworth, J. C. Nugent, Tom Powers, Ann Andrews, Sally O'Neil, and A. P. Kaye—were introduced by announcer Ray Forrest. They appeared two at a time on the screen. The cast rehearsed for two days. Numerous long shots of six to eight persons were taken on three cameras, but close-ups of two persons aided the viewer considerably. The makeup was heavier than necessary on the stage.[37]

"Ode to Liberty," a comedy by Marcel Duran that was adapted for the stage in 1934 by Sidney Howard, was televised on 5 April 1940. The multilingual Howard had won a Pulitzer prize (*They Knew What They Wanted*, 1925) and became a major force in contemporary American theater. He adapted several foreign works and some novels of Sinclair Lewis (*Dodsworth* and *Arrowsmith*) for the stage and the movies, in addition to writing his own plays (*The Silver Cord* and *Christopher Bean*). In years to come, these plays would appear on television, but Howard would never see any of them. After spending the morning working on a new play, he was accidentally hit and killed by a tractor a few months before the "Ode to Liberty" telecast.

The May schedule included a comedy a week. On the 5th, Austin Strong's "Three Wise Fools," a 1918 three-act comedy, was directed for television by Warren Wade. The adaptation was largely as a musical and featured Percy Kilbride, Stephen Courtleigh, John Craven, and Betty Furness. A judge, a physician, and a financier share a home. Their masculine world is invaded by the daughter of a woman whom they had all loved previously. What at first seems to be total destruction of their male refuge turns out to their delight.

"Miss Moonlight," another play by Benn W. Levy, ran an hour and a

half on 12 May. Leslie W. MacLeod's (or McLeod) "We'll Take the High Road" appeared on the 19th and included Frances Fuller in the cast. An established actress, she was the wife of Worthington Miner. A short sketch entitled "The Old Book Shop," featuring Arthur Allen and Parker Fennelly and based on *The Simpson Boys of Sprucehead Bay*, a radio serial by Henry Fiske Carlton and William Ford Manley, was also presented. It was directed by Warren Wade. The "Simpson Boys" were in various serials for a decade, most of them taking place in rural New England, but the life of the material was short on television. Clare Cummer's only really notable comedy, "The Rescuing Angel," was adapted by Thomas H. Hutchinson and ended the month. It featured Sally O'Neil, Eric Dressler, and Robert Allen.

Serious Dramas.   Continually seeking public favor, NBC presented romantic comedies and crime dramas. Nevertheless, a trend toward diversification was evident as dramatic themes turned to more serious matters. During 1939–40, when NBC put forth its best effort of the experimental era, serious dramas included seventeen domestic dramas and eight classic plays. Often the domestic dramas were short, perhaps two being staged in a single evening. As a rule, they received less press attention than adaptations of classic plays.

The fall season was hardly underway when Thomas Lyne Riley rehearsed "Death Takes a Holiday," Walter Ferris's 1930 three-act adaptation of an Italian play, *La Morte in Vacanze*, by Alberto Casella. "Death," on a holiday, visits an Italian family and falls in love with the young daughter. The drama was frequently produced on radio, but at the last moment television rights for the production could not be cleared, and the show was canceled. A B film was run in its place. This jolted Riley into preparing two short dramas the following week, neither of which would cause rights complications: "When the Nightingale Sang in Berkeley Square," a fantasy based on a Michael Arlen short story, and "Dr. Abernathy," a second brief drama that had already been televised in London. The two dramas ran about an hour.[38]

Dramas of the 1930s often dealt with domestic situations. The depression brought a new emphasis on family life that stressed pulling together for the common good and enjoying the simple pleasures of home life. Among the domestic dramas in 1939–40 were: "The Happy Journey," on 12 November; "Another Language," on 8 December; "Post Road," on 29 December; "The Gorilla," on 19 January; "The Long Christmas Dinner," on 4 February, "The Passing of the Third Floor Back," on 22 March; "A Fine Place To Visit," on 29 March; "My Heart's in the Highlands," on 28 April; "Joe and Mary's Place," on 8 May; "Double Door," on 6 June; and "Jack Rabbit Plays," on 13 June.

For two Thornton Wilder plays, "The Happy Journey" and "The Long Christmas Dinner," Edward Padula directed members of the American Actors Company. In "The Happy Journey," a family discusses a variety of human problems and reactions while on a short automobile trip. The mother's role, typifying the backbone of the nation, is a wonderful characterization. "The Long Christmas Dinner" represents the culmination of nine decades in the Bayard home. Brief sequences showing changes in the countryside, differences in attire, acquisition of property, and the growth of the family provide a vivid portrait of American life. Both dramas consumed about half an hour each, but a major production of the 1934 play *Post Road,* by Wilbur D. Steele and Norma Mitchell, was also offered. In essence, George (Percy Kilbride) is unemployed because of the depression and so he and his wife are staying with her sister, Emily Madison (Edith Shayne), who accommodates tourists at her home on the Boston Post Road. The trio become involved in the complicated lives of their tenants. One of them is a sick girl (Marjorie Clarke) who is believed to have a kidnapped baby. This complex drama required thirty-seven hours of rehearsal for the cast of eleven, directed by Thomas Lyne Riley. Another play, telecast on 6 June 1940, was Elizabeth McFadden's Broadway and movie success "Double Door." Mary Morris, as the neurotic Victoria, who dominated the Van Brett household, headed a large cast directed by Edward Padula. This play is noteworthy because it would be the debut production for the *Kraft Television Theater.*

Although relatively few attempts at classic works had been made during the earlier years by any of the American television stations, in the 1939–40 season eight, or about one a month, were presented: "The Streets of New York," on 31 August; "Jane Eyre," on 12 October; "Treasure Island," on 4 November; "Little Women," on 22 December; "Ethan Frome," on 5 January; "Julius Caesar," on 15 March; "The Marriage Proposal," on 3 April; and "Dr. Jekyll and Mr. Hyde," on 4 June 1940. Many of these plays had been very popular during the Victorian era.

The Dion Boucicault melodrama *The Streets of New York* was originally staged at Wallack's on the lower Bowery in 1857. Boucicault was a well-known writer of nearly forty plays and a major promoter of the first U.S. copyright bill the previous year. During the 1860s the Wallack Company, under the management of Lester Wallack, "the most conspicuous figure on the American stage," was the most brilliant company of actors in the nation.[39] "The Streets of New York," a five-act piece that introduced the work of Anton Bundsmann as producer/director, takes place in the private office of Gideon Bloodgood's banking house. Lucy Fairweather (Joyce Arling) tells Bloodgood (George Coulouris) to keep his "gold"—some $100,000—which he has actually robbed from her father, a ship's captain (Whitford Kane), so that he can trick young Mark

Livingstone (Derek Fairman) into marrying his daughter Alida (Sheila Trent). Mark loves Lucy, however, and in the end rescues vital papers from a burning tenement that proves Bloodgood's misdeed. The caliber of stage actors making up the eighteen-member cast was remarkably good because many of them had just returned from summer-stock engagements. During rehearsal breaks, Bundsmann encouraged the actors to cool themselves from the hot studio lights by standing in the outside corridor.

The 1939–40 television season included a version of "Dr. Jekyll and Mr. Hyde." This was a freely adapted rendition of the Stevenson story by Luella Forepaugh and George F. Fish. Warren Wade tried his luck at producing a showboat sequence, as he had done the previous summer with scenes from *Uncle Tom's Cabin*. Winfield Hoeny, already on hand as Simon Legree, played Jekyll and Hyde in the mawkish, villainous style of nineteenth-century melodrama.

The Theatre Guild decided to stage Helen Jerome's adaptation of *Jane Eyre*, in which Katharine Hepburn played the lead. After two months on the road under the direction of Worthington Miner, Jerome was asked to rewrite part of it because it just was not ready for a New York opening. She stubbornly refused. The Theatre Guild canceled any plans for New York, and Hepburn luckily found herself playing the lead, Tracy Lord, in Philip Barry's *The Philadelphia Story* (1939).

Nevertheless, Jerome's version of Charlotte Brontë's *Jane Eyre* (1847) was soon picked up for television by NBC. It was telecast from Studio 3-H in Radio City beginning at 8:30 P.M. and continued for ninety minutes without interruption. The love story, staged in the library of Thornfield Hall at Millcote in winter, involves Jane Eyre (Flora Campbell) and Edward Rochester (Dennis Hoey), owner of Thornfield Hall, who keeps his first wife, now insane, locked on the third floor of the mansion.

The production required sixteen characters and two sets. It was distinguished in that it emphasized characterizations rather than plot. At times, Campbell spoke too rapidly and did not look directly at the person to whom she was speaking. Hoey occasionally "boomed and bellowed" even though "with proper direction [he] could handle any TV assignment."[40] Effie Shannon appeared as the housekeeper. The supporting players gave "uniformly good" performances, except for Mary Newnham-Davis who as Diana was "probably the best in the entire cast."[41] The production errors, such as facial shadows, made Campbell look gaunt and drawn. She wore the same dress throughout the show, and her coiffure was not particularly flattering. Occasionally, principal characters were left out of the picture.

For the television adaptation of Robert Louis Stevenson's 1883 adven-

ture romance, "Treasure Island," Donald Davis retold the yarn about Jim Hawkins, who falls heir to a map of an island where treasure is believed to be buried. Accompanied by his friends Dr. Livesey and Squire Trelawney, as cabin boy of the *Hispaniola*, he sets sail for perilous adventure along with the ship's cook, Long John Silver. Because neither the limited studio space nor the small television screen could do justice to the scope of the story, the production seemed amateurish.

The first presentation of Louisa May Alcott's "Little Women" occurred at Christmastime 1939. Marion DeForest had adapted the play for the theater in four acts in 1912. As television sought broader commercial and public acceptance, it followed trends in dramatic selections, especially in movies. The motion picture industry was heavily into the revival of nineteenth-century novels during the thirties. George Cukor had made a feature film of *Little Women* in 1934 and *Wuthering Heights* was one of the big hits of 1939. The telecast recounted the main incidents of the novel: the writing and rehearsing of the Christmas play, Jo's courtship and marriage, and the love affair of Meg and John Brooks.

Edith Wharton's 1911 domestic tragedy, *Ethan Frome,* was notably adapted for the stage by Owen and Donald Davis in 1936, and revised for television by son Donald in 1939.[42] In the one hour and twenty-one-minute version for television, Ethan Frome (Robert Allen), a poor farmer, marries Zeena (Ann Revere), a woman he does not love. The sickly Zeena requires the assistance of a cousin, a lovely person, Mattie Silver (Dorothy Mathews). Frome falls in love with Mattie, and they form a death pact. Zeena fires Mattie, and the lovers realize they will be permanently separated. They attempt suicide, but end up in a semiparalyzed condition. Now Zeena must take care of them. The telecast included nine scenes in and about Frome's New England farmhouse in winter.

A modern dress version of "Julius Caesar," little changed from Shakespeare's work, was the first full-length play of his presented on American television. It was adapted by Warren Wade and telecast on the ides of March 1940. Although the production was praised for its staging and the use of a new effect—superimposition—to show the ghost of Caesar, the acting was criticized. The familiar story tells of the assassination of Julius Caesar (Judson Laire) as a result of a conspiracy to gain power in Rome. Two armed camps result: Mark Antony (Douglas Gilmore) leads one and Brutus (Stephen Courtleigh), Caesar's onetime friend, heads the other. A battle ensues that Antony wins. The modern dress concept had already appeared on television in England and would be seen again, 6 March 1949, on *Studio One*.

The last of the classic plays of the 1939–40 season was Anton Chekhov's half-hour, one-act "The Marriage Proposal," which was

adapted in English by Helmar Baukhage and Barrett H. Clark. The farce tells of an excitable, nervous man who proposes to an attractive woman. While he does, however, a quarrel erupts over their common boundary line. The cast for the spring 1940 telecast included J. Gray as Stephan S. Tschubikov, Frieda Allen as Natalia Stephanovna, and Robert Allen as Ivan V. Lamov.

"The Night Cap," a 1921 two-act mystery comedy by Max Marcin and Guy Bolton, tells the story of Robert Andrews (Douglas Gilmore), a bank president who is short $500,000 in his accounts. He plans to have himself murdered so that his life insurance can save the bank and his ward, Anne Maynard (Claudia Morgan). Eventually a way is found to repay the money and to enable the two to marry. The script ran 145 pages and required a cast of twelve.

"A Criminal at Large," by Edgar Wallace and produced by Anton Bundsmann, was very well received. Bundsmann, already recognized as a promising television director, made the most of his material to sustain interest, according to *The Billboard*.[43] A highly competent cast included Dennis Hoey, Nance O'Neil, Charles Jordan, Carl Harbord, and Frances Reid.

"Roosty" was one of the few original plays telecast on NBC. The plot involved some criminals hiding out in the Adirondack Mountains. They are dependent on a fifteen-year-old boy named Roosty for supplies. The drama was written by Martin Berkeley, and Andy Donnelly played Roosty Nelson. Young Donnelly had performed in radio for some time. He played the role of Jimmy in *Tom Mix,* which made its debut in Chicago on NBC (1933); Junior Tracy in *Dick Tracy* on Mutual (1935); and Billy Wiggs in *Mrs. Wiggs and the Cabbage Patch* on NBC (1936). "The Perfect Alibi," by A. A. Milne, had appeared on Broadway in 1932. The telecast was produced and written by Thomas L. Riley.

Historical Dramas.   In addition to the comedy "Ode to Liberty," three historical dramas were presented: "The Farmer Takes a Wife," on 10 November 1939, "Charlotte Corday," a new play by Helen Jerome, on 8 February, and "Prologue to Glory," on 23 February 1940. E. P. Conkle's "Prologue to Glory" is a biography in eight scenes depicting the life of Abraham Lincoln (Stephen Courtleigh) from his early days as a poor, uneducated rail-splitter through his love for Ann Rutledge (Frances Reid) to his departure for Springfield. The production, including a cast of more than twenty persons and running an hour and eighteen minutes, was directed by Anton Bundsmann. By this time, however, he was already involved in casting assignments for David O. Selznick in Hollywood and was well on his way to becoming a screen director, when he changed his name to Anthony Mann.[44]

"The Farmer Takes a Wife," based on a novel by Walter D. Edmonds called *Rome Haul,* was dramatized in 1934 for the stage by Frank B. Elser and Marc Connelly and was purchased for a movie starring Janet Gaynor and Henry Fonda. The television adaptation by director Thomas Lyne Riley emphasized the basic love story and provided a semidocumentary treatment of life along the Erie Canal in upper New York during the 1850s. A young farmer, Dan Harrow (Wylie Adams) comes to the Erie Canal looking for work. He finds various hauling jobs, meets an assortment of amusing characters, and becomes romantically involved with a cook, Molly Larkins (Mary Hutchinson).

Scenes depicting the canal itself were filmed at a similar one in Pennsylvania; and sequences of old trains, which eventually reduced the importance of the canal, were combined in a filmed montage using a voice-over narrator. A miniature replica of a portion of the lock was required to open and close. The scene designer built an interior of an Erie Canal Hotel in 1850, a section of the canal wall with a canal boat tied to it, and the interior of a canal boat cabin. Costumes and sound effects such as boat horns, insect noises, train whistles, bells, and water sounds helped create a realistic atmosphere. Director Thomas Lyne Riley said:

> A final checkup the day before "The Farmer Takes a Wife" went before the cameras revealed the following: a shooting script, a cast which had been rehearsing for almost two weeks, a set of titles, a narrator, four special film sequences, a miniature, sound effects, marked and timed phonograph records, costumes, properties, and three sets which almost overflowed our floor space, in addition to all basic studio equipment. It was now up to the director to blend all those factors into a television production.[45]

Musicals.   Another hour version of Gilbert and Sullivan was telecast on 5 September 1939. This time it was "H.M.S. Pinafore," whose cast included Colin O'Moore, John Cherry, and Ray Heatherton. The big news in musical drama did not come until the spring of 1940, however. NBC's "first" telecast of grand opera was a brief scene from "Tristan and Isolde," conducted by Dr. Walter Damrosch on 10 May 1937. Because of David Sarnoff's love of fine music, in 1927, when Dr. Damrosch was about to retire, Sarnoff convinced him to broadcast *The Music Appreciation Hour* (1928) on NBC radio.

For the first telecast of grand opera that took place during the period of public demonstrations, a much longer presentation was staged at Radio City under the auspices of the Metropolitan Opera Company. The first half of the program consisted of several arias in concert form; the second half, an abbreviated rendition of *Pagliacci.* The singers received much

criticism from the press for not being sufficiently attractive, straining on delivery, and being generally inadequate on the tiny television screen.[46] Soon marked improvements in opera production would satisfy viewer demands.

After a year of public television demonstrations, 30 April 1939 to 7 May 1940, the total production outlay was estimated at $750,000, of which talent, including eighty full-time employees, cost $90,000. Although salaries were very low, this did not discourage the flow of talent. About 620 hours of all types of programming were televised, a third of them originating in the studio, a third from remote pickup, and less than a third on film. The estimated 1,000 program items used approximately 750 dramatic roles, 180 singing acts, 70 dancing sequences, and numerous other novelty acts mainly from the theater and vaudeville.[47]

No dramas were telecast from August 1940 to January 1941. NBC turned its attention to other kinds of programming, such as the Republican and Democratic conventions, elections, sports events, and feature films.

SUMMARY OF NBC PUBLIC DEMONSTRATIONS

By the mid-1930s program activity had shifted to NBC's experimental station in New York City, W2XBS. From 1936 to 1942 NBC experimented with dramatic television programming that laid the foundation for the next two decades (see Appendix D). The six-year period may be divided into two parts: the experimental demonstrations designed for in-house use from 7 July 1936 through April 1939; and the public demonstrations from 30 April 1939 to 1 July 1941 that were intended to capture public attention and acceptance of the new medium.

The six-year period began with weekly (1936), then biweekly (1937) brief, light, commercially oriented sketches and one-act theatrical comedies. Second year programming included mysteries, romantic comedies, crime dramas, a few serious sketches, and fantasies, all running from less than ten minutes to more than half an hour. Nearly all these demonstrations were adaptations from plays or short stories. The programs originated at Rockefeller Center in NBC studios 3-H and 5-A and were sent via coaxial cable to the transmitter atop the Empire State Building. The signal was then transmitted to various locations in the RCA Building, principally the board room on the 62d floor. Potential sponsors, advertising agency representatives, government officials, engineers, reviewers, and numerous persons from diverse fields were guests on these occasions.

On 30 April 1939, in its third year, NBC offered regular television

programming two or three times a week to the general public. After a shaky start, it presented by the fall of that year one-hour, three-act television adaptations of well-known stories involving multisettings and large casts. The 1939–40 season was the high water mark of dramatic demonstrations in NBC's precommercial period. During the remaining months before World War II, the imminent conflict and growing interest in commercial formats influenced the dramatic programming. W2XBS became WNBT, a commercial television station, on 1 July 1941.

NBC Dramas during the Commercial Era, 1941–1947

On 2 May 1941 the FCC issued a press release stating that commercial television, under existing regulations, could make its debut in two months. The FCC also encouraged stations to continue work in color. On 1 July 1941 W2XBS became NBC's WNBT and W2XAB became WCBW, the principal CBS station in New York. Both stations planned to telecast fifteen hours per week in black and white. NBC estimated that in the New York area television receivers were located in 4,500 homes and 900 in public places, serving a total of 90,000 residents.[48] The approach of World War II was slowly affecting the number, length, and content of dramas, though weeks before Pearl Harbor the press reported: "Hollywood has been unable to turn out a single smash hit picture with a serious modern war theme."[49] The recording and nightclub businesses showed that "in terms of box office, let's fight themes are not so hot—at the moment."[50] When the United States entered the war in December, however, the limited dramatizations that survived reflected patriotic themes and requirements of the war effort.

By spring 1942 the television stations had virtually shut down for almost three years, 1942–44, programming minimum schedules geared to wartime needs. Experiments in television engineering were conducted once again behind closed doors. At New York's three television stations—WNBT, WCBW, WABD (DuMont's W2XWV)—typical programming from the middle of 1942 to mid-1944 is illustrated by this schedule for a week in October 1942:

> Sunday: W2XWV (variety show)
> Monday: WNBT (air warden's course)
> Tuesday: No programs
> Wednesday: No programs
> Thursday: WCBW (news, film, quiz)
> Friday: WCBW (news, Red Cross, quiz)
> Saturday: No programs

This schedule was hardly conducive to drama. Yet, in March 1942 NBC announced that it intended to expand its civil-defense program by including a one-hour dramatization explaining defense activities and the war effort to the general public. The series, called *The City Awakes,* was essentially an educational program for civil defense that contained brief skits. One observer described the techniques that were employed: "Camera No. 1 may be kept trained on the Police Lieutenant who is the lecturer, but is standing by while Camera 3 is picking up a diagram illustrating some technical point. Meanwhile Camera 2 may be wheeled into position to pick up a corner of the 'Brown's' living room where husband and wife are listening to Post Warden 'Smith.' "[51] The series, using thirteen volunteer actors, was written and directed by staff producers Warren Wade, Martin Jones, and Thomas Lyne Riley. Its theme stated that it was up to the civilian public to catch and to surpass the enemy. In dramatized sequences, the civil-defense messages explained "Bombs and Fire Protection," "Gas Warfare," and "Allies in Arms."

A NEED FOR FILM

In view of the scarcity of personnel and materiel for live television drama during the war years, this was the perfect time for feature films to take over programming. The motion picture industry, unlike fifteen years earlier, was enjoying huge profits and had established a large film library. Nevertheless, the old obstacles remained. Television was administratively the "child" of a growing and powerful radio industry. As one source indicates, "From 1938 to 1948, the advertising volume of the four networks more than doubled. From 1937 to 1944, broadcasting profits of all networks and stations rose from $23 million to $90 million."[52] Second, the public desire for live talent still prevailed. As *Business Week* reported, "R.K.O. is careful to give live talent programs their due, but like most film companies, R.K.O. looks forward to the time when film transcriptions will be used even more widely than the radio transcriptions of today."[53] Third, the cost of producing a live telecast was less than producing a similar drama on film:

> The expense to be faced is almost terrifying. Translated into terms of running time on the screen a motion-picture play may cost from $1,000 to $35,000 a minute, with $1,000 representing the worst that the public will tolerate. If we are to have every day a new television comedy or tragedy lasting an hour and a half, the studios incur an outlay that dwarfs anything with which producers are familiar. . . . Television promoters talk hopefully of keeping the cost of production down to $500 a minute or even much less.[54]

The most important obstacle was distributor-exhibitor resistance. Current features of A, B, and even C quality were withheld from television, and new contracts for film stars carried special clauses in 1944 that specifically restricted television appearances. Withholding films from television proved to be "an obstacle in the way of television which is more real and immediate than the over-strict government regulations," *The Saturday Review of Literature* reported.[55] The motion picture industry encouraged unions to insist on wage scales at parity for television. As *The Billboard* explained, "The pic boys on the other hand feel that anything that competes with pix should be forced to operate under the same standards that they do—and they're going to do everything to see that television entertainment is going to cost plenty."[56] To avoid such union demands, the television industry concentrated for a time on forming an identity separate from film, originating a vocabulary wherein cameras were, for example, called "iconoscopes." Regardless, because the feature film was judged to be the standard of quality, refinements in live drama produced in radio studios occurred. Such effort might not have been pursued had the motion picture industry furnished its products in the first place.

Thomas H. Hutchinson, in his role as television director of RKO Television Corporation, correctly surveyed future demand: "Actual checks of dramatic programs produced live have proved conclusively that the television audiences will not care in the least whether a *good* program is on film or is produced live in the studio. As a matter of fact, film is going to be the medium that makes economic operation of many television stations possible."[57]

DIVESTITURE IN ENTERTAINMENT

Significantly, during this wartime hiatus, the government, maintaining its pressure against big industry to refrain from monopoly, won two fundamental decisions against the giants of the entertainment industry. One decision was a Justice Department suit against RKO, Paramount, Warner Brothers, 20th Century Fox, and Metro-Goldwyn-Mayer. A consent decree resulted in the Big Five divesting themselves of their exhibition branches, which forced them to sell approximately half of the 3,137 theaters they owned in 1945. The court battle spanned fourteen years and was finally concluded in 1952.

In litigation against NBC and CBS, the FCC adopted a set of "Chain Broadcasting Regulations" that was supported by the U.S. Supreme Court. These rules forced NBC to divest itself of one of its two networks, either the Red or the Blue network. In 1943 the Blue Network was sold; two years later, it became ABC Radio and Television. ABC Television

competed, without facilities of its own, as a producer of dramas over local television stations throughout the forties. Other major stations contributing to drama during that decade were in Schenectady, Philadelphia, Chicago, and Los Angeles.

By the end of 1946, the screen was six by four inches; the 525-line picture was black and white; and a major struggle was looming between CBS and RCA/NBC over standards, compatible versus incompatible color systems.

NBC DRAMAS IN THE FORTIES

Dramatic programming resumed at NBC in January 1941, after the respite for national elections. In anticipation of going commercial and the possibility of war, the choice of dramatic material differed slightly from previous years. Thirty-four dramas were produced in the period immediately preceding the war, 1 January 1941 through April 1942, though by fall 1941 the war had already closed down NBC's live programs. The few shows telecast from 1942 through 1944 were typified by the feature film *Gunga Din; The War as It Happens,* a U.S. Navy film, one of many provided by the War Department; and a live production, "The Freedom Ferry," by Ruth A. Brooks, a vaudeville showboat routine familiar at NBC from previous summers. The last of these was designed to encourage the sale of U.S. Savings Bonds and to fight racial prejudice.

Military requirements and the lack of live programming reduced the NBC production staff to a skeleton crew. Hutchinson and Riley went into advertising, Bundsmann was already in Hollywood, and Sobol rejoined Broadway producer Max Gordon. Colling and Wade fell heir to most of the directing assignments. Colling was more of a producer than a director. His public-relations style at first brought him into conflict with the accounting department because he took actors to posh places for food and entertainment that ran well over budget. Wade was a radio producer, a vaudeville type, a big man "who wore his heart on his sleeve."[58] He was a wonderful person to work with, but one who would break into tears through job pressure or a sense of personal rejection by his peers. By the mid-forties, he had assumed executive functions in television.

Late in December 1944, when the war's end was in sight, NBC resumed dramatic productions Sunday nights for the next two years, through 1946. The public viewed over eighty comedies, serious dramas, crime stories, dramatic reenactments of history, and musicals.

NBC Dramas to Wartime Cessation. An analysis of the thirty-seven dramas telecast before the war and until the wartime cessation, during the

period 1 January 1941 through 10 April 1942, reveals that within several months NBC drama made transitions from an artistic ideal reflected in the 1939–40 season, to potentially successful commercial fare, to serving wartime needs, to cessation of virtually all programming at the height of the war. The noticeable shift in concentration during the early forties was toward series that were already successful commercially on radio.

About midyear 1941, minor productions of serious dramas and the filmed series *The Chronicles of America Photoplay* took the spotlight. In the fall, attention turned to bizarre and crime stores, which once again were adaptations of successful radio series. Most of them were short plays that ran from five to twenty minutes. The longer dramas—"Blind Alley," "The Thirteenth Chair," and "To the Ladies"—appeared at the time the United States became seriously involved in the war.

Comedies. The three comedies telecast during the prewar days began with adaptations of *The Aldrich Family* and *The Parker Family.* Both were supposed to demonstrate the potential of converting successful commercial radio situation comedies to television.

The Aldrich Family, for example, had been a highly popular program on the NBC Blue Network since 1939. It was based on the Broadway play *What a Life,* by Clifford Goldsmith. The plot centered on the difficulties of a young teenager, Henry, whose voice and world were changing simultaneously. Immature and awkward at making social adjustments, he was always in trouble, though not because of mischief on his part. He lived in Centerville with his family, headed by his father, Sam, the district attorney. The television story, adapted by T. H. Hutchinson and directed by Warren Wade, posed the same situation, when it was presented on 24 January 1941.

About four months later, an episode from *The Parker Family* was directed by Wade. It, too, was a situation comedy that had first been heard on the NBC Blue Network in 1939. For the television adaptation, Leon Janney, who frequently played the lead, Richard Parker, on radio appeared in that role for the 9 May telecast.

The third comedy, presented on 15 February 1942, about two months after the declaration of war, was a television version of Kaufman and Connelly's 1922 play *To the Ladies.* The plot concerns John Kincaid, a young, ambitious man of little talent who is aided by his wife in the promotion of the Kincaid Piano Company.

Serious Dramas. Beginning in the middle of 1941, a miscellany of eleven serious dramas were offered over the following months. Most of them were inconsequential. Louis N. Parker's perennial favorite, "The

Minuet," the first drama performed on Chicago's W9XAP-WMAQ in 1931, was shown a decade later on NBC (24 June 1941). The twenty-five-minute verse drama takes place during the French Revolution. A marquis and a marquise, long separated and estranged, meet in prison on the eve of their execution. Reunited, they bravely go to the guillotine.

"A Cup of Tea," a short play by Florence Ryerson, was directed by Thomas Lyne Riley on 6 September 1941. From their California ranch, Ryerson and her husband, Colin Clements, fueled the accolades for their writing with the terse motto: "Keep on keeping on."[59] They turned out volume after volume, including three each of short plays, long plays, and monodramas. Their principal claim to fame was about fifty feature films, among them *The Wizard of Oz* (1939).

"A Constitutional Point," by journalist-turned-playwright Augustus Thomas, was aired in October. The following month, Riley directed James Warwick's "Blind Alley," a semiclassic in its genre. In this study of terror, a psychiatrist (Maurice Wells) and his wife (Katherine Warren) are held hostage when gangsters on the run enter their home. A battle of minds revealing the ghastly background of the principal gangster results in the collapse of his defiance. Riley's direction was "tightly drawn, deftly balanced and incisively paced," but the ninety-minute script needed cutting. The cast was first-rate and potently sustained the roles. *Blind Alley* had opened on Broadway in 1938, and it became a motion picture the next year. Once again, television showed a penchant for recreating successes from other media.

In "Dust of the Road," a religious drama by Kenneth Sawyer Goodman, Peter (Blaine Cordner), an avid reader of the Bible attempts to recall a tramp (Graham Velsey) who had been turned away from their farmhouse door by his wife, Prudence (Dorothy Blackburn). The mysterious tramp wanders from place to place in expiation of a crime he had committed years ago and prevents the farmer from selling his soul for "thirty pieces of silver."

"The Clod," (1914) by Lewis Beach, is a forty-minute, one-act play that involves an 1863 Civil War setting. An uneducated woman refuses to take sides in the conflict. A Yankee soldier is hiding in her house and is being sought by two Confederate soldiers. In a dramatic climax, she admits she does not like either side. Several vignettes lasted only minutes, such as "Shanghai," by W. Stuckes, and "The Heiress," by Emma B. C. Wells. "The Victorian Christmas Tree," by Helen Morley, was a monologue, partly in Negro dialect.

Historical Dramas. On 7 July 1941 NBC announced that it was initiating a filmed series of major potential value because it would dem-

onstrate the worth of television as a medium of entertainment and education. The series dramatized major events and pioneers of American history. *The Chronicles of America Photoplay* or simply *The Chronicles of America,* as it was usually referred to, was based on a fifty-volume series published by Yale University Press and, subsequently, released through the Yale University Film Service. Various script writers and directors participated.

The first telecast was on 31 July 1941 and the series extended over nine weeks; the final episode was in the fall, on 16 October 1941. The programs were presented in the afternoon. *The Chronicles of America* was repeated, beginning on 6 December 1945 and running through February 1946. The initial offering, "The Puritans," was written by J. Raymond Hutchinson, who was chairman of the Committee on Television, Department of Secondary Teachers, National Education Association, as well as chairman of the Education Committee, American Television Society. He was also director of visual instruction for the public schools in Elizabeth, New Jersey. Other programs included "Peter Stuyvesant," "Gateway to the West," "Columbus," "Jamestown," "Wolfe and Montcalm," "Vincennes," "The Pioneer Woman," "Daniel Boone," "Alexander Hamilton," "Dixie," "The Eye of the Revolution," "The Declaration of Independence," and "Yorktown." The filmed series eventually consisted of more than a dozen programs.

Crime and Bizarre Stories.   In the fall, more attention was given to crime and bizarre stories. Of the twelve dramas of this type, three were popular radio programs. *Believe It Or Not* was a newspaper feature by Robert L. Ripley that often consisted of two- or three-line descriptions and drawings of strange factual events and people. This newspaper "sideshow" was converted into a radio series for NBC in 1930. Two *Believe It Or Not* vignettes were presented: "A Hundred Thousand Dollar Kiss" and "Laugh, Clown," both telecast in October 1941. The series was revived a decade later, and again in the 1980s.

The adventures of *The Bishop and the Gargoyle* were typical radio crime formula. Heading this radio series, written by Frank Wilson, was a former Sing Sing parole board member, referred to as "The Bishop," and his ex-convict sidekick, known only as "The Gargoyle." Together they solved crimes, The Bishop providing the brains and The Gargoyle, the brawn. The first of these formula plays was telecast on 29 November 1941. An innovation in the crime category was five episodes in a series called *False Witness.* This involved a mystery quiz by Henry W. Senker and Arnold Lever that was directed and produced by Martin Jones and sponsored by the Bulova Watch Company and Botany 500. The dramas

allowed the audience to identify the culprit. In one program, a man is stabbed when three persons are present, and the audience is asked to figure out who did it. Romeny Brent appeared as The Inspector. The initial program was on 21 October 1941, and the series ended the following 20 February.

Aside from "Prince Gabby," on 1 August 1941, three principal dramas, all produced early in 1942—"Fright," on 12 January, "The Thirteenth Chair," on 25 January, and "Suspect," on 1 February—supported the popular belief that crime drama would play a major role in television programming. In "Fright," by James Beach, John Fairbride thinks someone is trying to kill him. Beach once said that he had never written a play that satisfied him, but then most of his career as a newspaperman and in the theater as an actor and playwright was disappointing.[60] This one-act play, which had been popular for a decade, required only one interior set—the study of the Fairbride home—and five characters.

NBC Dramas after Wartime Cessation.

Within the last six months of the war, NBC began offering the public a wide array of dramas—over eighty of them. Nearly equally represented were the four categories that had emerged through the experiments of almost two decades: comedies, serious dramas, crime stories, and historical dramatizations. The latter category was primarily a rebroadcast of *The Chronicles of America* series. These dramas drew material from all media. For example, four radio series were attempted on television during the war years, and they became part of NBC's 1949–50 television programming: *The Aldrich Family* (1949), *Believe It Or Not* (1950), *Lights Out* (1949), and *Mr. and Mrs. North* (1949).

Appearing as a harbinger of things to come, Edward Sobol returned to NBC in the summer of 1944. Although live telecasts were scarce for the remainder of the year, his production of "Men in White" in January 1945 was outstanding.

Because so many staff members were involved in the war effort, by fall 1945 the NBC production department began hiring new talent, including a lanky, blond theater director—who was 4-F—named Frederick Coe. He had been born in Mississippi to a widowed public health nurse and spent his early years in Nashville, where he gained considerable experience as an actor, playwright, and director through the church and later, the Nashville Community Playhouse. He produced and directed Shakespeare's *Julius Caesar* (1939) in modern dress and *Twelfth Night* (1940) for the summer Playhouse, while on vacation as a student from Yale Drama School. After four years (1940–44) as director of the Town Theatre, Columbia, South Carolina, he went to New York to direct on Broad-

way. The venture was *Bonanza*, a play set in an old mining town, which he would produce for television on 10 December 1950.

Coe's television debut for NBC was, however, "Ring on Her Finger," by Charles P. Hoffman. The plot concerns Shiela Rourke, a woman who thinks she is in love with two men at the same time. "Petticoat Fever," by Mark Reed, is staged in the northernmost wireless station in Labrador and was another of Coe's efforts at comedy two months later. Although neither his debut on 30 September 1945 nor "Petticoat Fever" were distinguished in themselves, Coe would complete his television apprenticeship in less than three years and become one of television drama's most noted producer/directors.

Comedies. The Kaufman comedy "If Men Played Cards as Women Do" was revived again in October 1945; it had originally been telecast nine years earlier. The new production featured a distinguished cast consisting of Sidney Blackmer, Leo G. Carroll, Neil Hamilton, and Ralph Dumke, but *The Billboard* said, "None were more self conscious than this quartet of stars."[61] A month later, another Kaufman play, "You Can't Take It with You," was presented. The 1936 collaboration with Moss Hart won the Pulitzer prize for its story about the Sycamores, a family that believes in emphasizing human affection and self-development rather than money. Contrast with the Sycamores is brought about when young Tony Kirby, the son of a wealthy but unhappy clan, the Kirbys, falls in love with his secretary, Alice Sycamore. Joe Koehler again complained about an "adequate" cast that was not good enough to do the show well and uninspired technical work under Colling's supervision. Tom Seidel, as Harvey, forgot his lines several times, and the cameras were frequently out of focus. Colling "has to take the rap for not bringing the play thru the ike [camera]."[62]

The first comedy in 1946 was a 1920 three-act Broadway hit, "The First Year," by Frank Craven. Grace and Tommy, a young married couple, invite one of her former suitors, Dick, to dinner. The meal-time conversation nearly results in a breakup of-the marriage. Grace goes home to her mother, and domestic tranquillity is not restored until Tommy gives Dick a thrashing. Grace returns home and announces that Tommy is about to become a father. *Television* reported that the "lines were for the most part, very amusing and well acted out."[63] Criticism focused on the use of extreme close-ups, which showed the actors perspiring. On 24 February 1946 the Broadway play *Knockout,* by the father-and-son team J. C. and Elliott Nugent, was presented. J. C., his wife, his son, Elliott, and daughter, Ruth, were a well-known vaudeville team for many years.

The high point in comedy for the two-year postwar period was Noel Coward's farce "Blythe Spirit." The play was in an anthology series, *NBC Television Theatre,* which initiated NBC's return to the air on its new Channel 4, WNBT. It was adapted at home over a two-week period by Edward Sobol. Three settings—a living room, a terrace, and Madame Arcati's home—were used to enhance movement and to underscore the time element. After two weeks of preliminary rehearsals of four hours a day, fifteen hours of on-camera rehearsals followed, including dress rehearsal. In addition, four hours of technical rehearsal for makeup, costumes, lighting, and production trick shots were required.

As the plot develops, Charles Condemine (Philip Tonge) is plagued by the return of the ghost of his first wife, Elvira (Leonora Corbett). Confusion arises when he talks to the ghost, which is unseen by his second wife, Ruth (Carol Goodner). Desperate, he enlists the aid of a spiritualist, Madam Arcati (Estelle Winwood).

According to *Television,* the "program was in line with NBC's policy that the show's what's going to put television over. Equipped with a good script, obtaining a star cast and putting the necessary rehearsal time into producing it, such shows are sure to hold home viewers."[64] And Sobol said, "At NBC the policy is to cast theater people rather than radio people because radio actors rarely know how to use their bodies, to move about the stage, to talk with and play to other performers."[65] *The Billboard* contended that the production "was about the finest type of air-pic entertainment that has been scanned to date."[66]

In the summer of 1946, playwright George Kelly attracted much attention when three of his Broadway plays were produced. His first one for the theater was *The Torchbearers,* and he won the 1925 Pulitzer prize for *Craig's Wife.* His *The Flattering World* was adapted by Sobol and telecast on 2 June 1946. The plot is about a famous actor who would like the wife of a pompous clergyman, the Reverend Loring Ridgeley (Edward Kreisler), to attend his play. Knowing the minister will not take her, the actor flatters him into thinking he too could be an actor. A curtain-call technique introduced cast members, such as Enid Markey as Mrs. Zooker and Joyce Van Patten as Lena.

"The Weak Spot," by Kelly, played on 14 July. While Mr. West and his wife quarrel, she spills some salt, which according to superstition predicts bad news. Later, a messenger arrives from the hospital to tell her he is dead. As it turns out, however, a friend who borrowed his raincoat is dead, and his apparent demise was only a case of mistaken identity. Finally, on 4 August, Kelly's 1924 comedy, "The Show-Off," told about a braggart who builds a world of fabrication. Although in fact Aubrey Piper has a humble job, to satisfy his ego and his self-respect he lies in ways that

bring embarrassment to his relatives and friends. To provide exposition in
the character study, actors gave their impressions of Aubrey as they were
introduced. The production consumed seventy minutes; however, according to producer Sobol, "Further tightening of the script would have quick-
ened the pace and sustained interest easier."[67]

Boston at the turn of the century is the setting for "Enter, Madame," by
Gilda Vavesi and Dolly Byrne. The Broadway adaptation is about a tem-
peramental opera star, Madame Della Rabbis (Carol Goodner), who has
a Latin entourage, and her husband, Gerald Fitzgerald (John Graham).
He wants to divorce her so that he can marry the widow next door and
enjoy a more tranquil domestic life. The situation resolves itself and no
divorce occurs. *Television* questioned the choice of the show, which was
"cleaned up" considerably from the stage version, as well as some of the
dialogue.

John Kirkpatrick's "The Strangest Feeling" (1912) was adapted by
Colling for telecast on 16 June 1946. When Ethel refuses to go on a date
with Johnny, he takes her younger sister, Naomi. On the way, he meets an
old flame, who convinces him to enroll Naomi in her dancing school and
to become her business manager. Colling also adapted "Seven Keys To
Baldpate," a 1913 melodramatic farce by George M. Cohan, for his July
program. The play, based on a novel by Earl Derr Biggers, tells of an
author, William Magee (Vinton Hayworth), who bets a friend $5,000
that he can write an entire play if he can enjoy a weekend of absolute
quiet. He is offered a cabin on Baldpate Mountain, where unknown to the
owner, thieves hang out. The author completes the play despite their
antics. Heavy-handed directing, including 80 percent long shots and few
close-ups, drew criticism of Colling in the press.

"The Homelife of a Buffalo," by Richard Harrity, tells about Eddie, his
wife, and son Joey, a vaudeville team down on its luck. Discouraged,
Eddie prepares an elaborate suicide scene for the trio: death by asphyxia-
tion. The situation inspires a new act, and the vaudeville team starts
anew. Fred Coe had received a number of unfavorable reviews, especially
from *The Billboard,* but "The Homelife of a Buffalo" was a triumph:
"Swell acting, top direction and keen adapting turned this play into a
sock video seg." The review continued, "Here in the tele-flesh was a four-
a-day song-and-dance team, one that would never make the top grade.
Never for a moment did Fred Coe, the director, permit himself the luxury
of making the hams terrific. . . . Check this as perfect proof that Coe has
put on his directorial long pants to stay."[68]

The eighteen comedies were adaptations of famous works of major
playwrights: Kaufman, three; Kelly, three; the Nugents, one; Kirkpatrick,
one; Coward, one; and Cohan, one. Sobol, Colling, and Coe were the

main adapters, producers, and/or directors. The only classic comedy attempted during the two years was Molière's "The Bourgeois Gentleman."

Serious Dramas. The list of serious dramas during the latter war years and the postwar era lengthened to twenty. About a fourth of them dealt with veterans or war. The initial effort was presented in December 1944, when a *Collier*'s short story, "Birthday," by James Hopper, was adapted. Retitled "Christmas in Alsace-Lorraine" and reworked by Hugh Chain, the story tells of a young French girl, Fauvette (Jimmy Somers), who relates how the people suffered at the hands of the Germans. A gift of a chocolate bar by a GI (Lyle Bettger) stimulates her spirit of hope at Christmastime.

A month later, on 24 January 1945, one of the outstanding dramas of these early days, "Men in White," was produced by Edward Sobol and directed by Ronald Oxford. The 1933 three-act, Pulitzer-prize winner by Sidney S. Kingsley recounts a personal challenge in the life of Dr. George Ferguson (Vinton Hayworth), an intern at a large hospital. He must decide whether to marry and have a comfortable practice or study abroad to perhaps become a great surgeon. He chooses the latter course. The telecast was recognized as "the best production of the year" by the American Television Society, and *The Billboard* commented that it provided an "extremely pleasant evening."[69]

Ernest Colling faced a hectic schedule during the early months of 1945. He adapted "The Veteran Comes Back" from a book by Willard Waller on 3 June 1945. The story concerns a veteran's readjustment to life at home. "The Copperhead," a Civil War story by Augustus Thomas, was revised by Colling and Helen Morley. Colling adapted "Portrait in Black" from a story in *Charm* magazine, and produced "Winter Wheat," which was reworked by Maxine Word from a novel by Mildred Walker. The story is about an easterner who settles in Montana with his Russian-born wife after the last war. Their daughter (Mary Patton) falls in love with a man she meets at college, but he is killed while serving in the Army Air Corps. She remains faithful despite attention from a Montana neighbor. Patton was criticized for failing to give a strong performance. As *Variety* said, "Direction may have been responsible for poor performances, but whatever the reason, television, in the presentation of drama, has a long way to go."[70]

Colling also adapted the 1918 Joseph Conrad novel, "Victory." The plot follows the travels of Alex Heyst, who goes to the East Indies searching for meaning to his life and finds love (Uta Hagen). Late in the year, Colling adapted Stephen Vincent Benét's "The Devil and Daniel Web-

ster." In a nineteenth-century New England courthouse, Daniel Webster defends Jabez Stone, who has sold his soul to the Devil. The Devil technically outmaneuvers Webster, who makes his appeal to a ghostly jury and wins a verdict of "not guilty."

WNBT's fall season opened on 2 September 1945, when "Another Language," by Rose Franken, was presented. This adaptation was an encore production, originally offered on 8 December 1939. The plot concerns the lives of the Hallam family. Although well acted, it moved slowly partly because too much time was spent on character delineation—the Hallam family numbers about twelve—and too little on plot development. Nevertheless, in reviewer Marty Schrader's opinion, "Another Language" "came well up to the standard which Producer Edward Sobol set for himself (and, incidentally, for television) in previous successes."[71] Robert Wade's set enhanced the play.

Sobol received added praise for his November selection, "The Front Page," a 1928 comedy-melodrama by Ben Hecht and Charles MacArthur. Ace reporter Hildy Johnson (Vinton Hayworth) uncovers an exclusive story about an escapee and alleged murderer, Earl Williams, for whom he helps obtain justice. *The Billboard* reviewer exclaimed, "Ed Sobol has done it again. As with *Men in White,* he has taken a Broadway play and turned it into a sock air pic, one that moved so evenly that the hour passed as tho it were 15 minutes. Of course, there were a few seconds during which one of the cameras was out of focus and another one or two in which players went up in their lines, but none of this was important."[72]

Louisa May Alcott's "Little Women," adapted from Marion DeForest's four-act play, appeared the second time. The original telecast had been on 22 December 1939. For this Christmas offering, on 30 December 1945, Margaret Hoyle played Jo; Dorothy Emery, Meg; and Gene Blakeley, John Brooks.

Among the noteworthy dramas of 1946 was "The Children of Ol' Man River," on 30 January 1946. One reviewer found that, instead of telling about the human experiences of the Valley Belle showboat family, the production "leaned too heavily on so-called show boat attractions, *Ten Nights in a Barroom,* Bryants' Old-Time Minstrels and 'polite' vaudeville between acts."[73] But, once again, this was part of a persistent effort to make the showboat format attractive.

A rare original drama, "Laughter in Paris," written by the erstwhile writer of war dramas for radio and head of NBC's script department, Richard P. McDonagh, was televised on 17 February. He reveals, mostly in flashback, how Henri, a once carefree Frenchman, and his mercenary, wealthy brother Pierre fall in love with the same girl. Rejected, Pierre

plans to murder the girl and have the blame fall on Henri (Frank Lea Short). Pierre fails and is sentenced to Devil's Island. The play ran more than an hour, during which fifteen scenes were squeezed into NBC's small studios. Producer Fred Coe was criticized for the overuse of close-ups, and Short for failing to build the part.[74] This was an effort to pilot a new script on television that might be suitable for feature films.

By the mid-1940s, some commercial sponsors were supporting variety formats that included a short sketch within the evening program. The *Tender Leaf Tea Hour* was one of these. For instance, on 1 August 1946, Percival Wilde's "The Finger of God" was included in the telecast. Sponsors and advertising agencies were considering different kinds of program material that would be suitable for selling products. Wilde's play, which requires only two men, one woman, and one interior set, involves a company head who plans to steal large sums of money from the firm when he is interrupted by stenographers.

In November an unusual fantasy, Neil Grant's one-act "The Last War," involved a cast cleverly costumed as animals. They discuss man's fate when they find that they have inherited the earth. The year closed with a dramatization of how the poem "The Night Before Christmas" was written. The evening's presentation was the first combination studio and remote show, which included a playlet. The vignette "According to Joseph" originated from the NBC studio and outside Rockefeller Plaza. Part of the Christmas program was produced in cooperation with the Veterans Production Group of the American Theatre Wing's Television Workshop.[75]

Crime Stories.   The year 1945 began with a series of crime dramas that were based on a novel, *The Black Angel,* by Cornell Woolrich. In the story, Mia Mercer has been murdered. Each episode is a different attempt to determine which suspect is guilty. The four parts were: "Black Alibi," "The Black Angel," "Playboy," and "The Last Name." They played in January and February. The first two parts were repeated nearly two years later, in October 1946. The series was "well acted" and well received despite the difficulties created by the use of seven sets in the "bandbox"-sized NBC studio.[76] This series of programs, a forerunner of miniseries that are based on novels, was adapted and directed by Colling.

A highly successful version of "The Perfect Alibi" was telecast in two parts on 4 and 11 March 1945. It was directed by Edward Sobol and performed by a Broadway cast. "The set, by Robert Wade, like everything else associated with the show was solid, real and believable," said *The Billboard.*[77] The second part, however, lacked sufficient action.[78]

"Air-Tight Alibi," by Walter Hackett, telecast on 7 October 1945, "packed a punch that would have kept any viewer chained pretty close to

his video set." A farm wife, Abby Cosgrove (Ann Elster), is abused by her domineering husband (Gayne Sullivan), whom she poisons. *Television* reported, "Probably to escape the accusation that the show justified murder, an anti-climax note was introduced as the director burst onto the set, bawling out the actors for muffing their lines."[79]

"A good college try for NBC" was "Bedelia," directed by Fred Coe. It was an adaptation of a novel by Vera Caspary; she wrote *Laura*. The scene is Christmas in the home of Charles and Bedelia. The adequate cast needed stronger performances to bring off a weak story about a second wife who attempts to poison her husband.[80] The telecast was on 21 October 1945.

A 1935 romantic tragedy by Maxwell Anderson, "Winterset," was produced for WNBT by Colling that same October. The three-act play, based on the Sacco-Vanzetti case, consumed ninety-five minutes in its television debut. Mio's (John McQuade) life is blighted by the belief that his father, who was executed for murder, died an innocent man. Although praised as "excellently done" in *Television*, Joe Koehler complained that the play was dated and that the production and playing were uninspired.[81] He advocated originality: "Television doesn't advance even a shadow, when it transcribes entertainment from another medium. The 'art' of presenting air-pic has something all its own and, during these days, NBC should be in there developing it—or at least someone should."[82]

"Crime plays are now enjoying unprecedented popularity on stage, screen, and on the air," John Reich observed in 1946.[83] Not only in New York but also in other major cities crime dramas were typical experiments. The Victorian thriller "Angel Street," by Patrick Hamilton, was directed by Colling on 20 January 1946. A woman is frightened at the prospect that her husband might be a murderer who is sought by the police. Tension heightened as Colling used long shots to establish the mood of the nineteenth-century setting, and then went to close-ups. The Broadway cast demonstrated an "excellent video translation of the script."[84]

Five months later, for NBC's second western, Colling adapted Porter Emerson Browne's story "The Bandit" under the title of "The Bad Man." And Sobol adapted "The Lady and the Law" as NBC's third western. The action takes place in a lonely cabin, where an outlaw wanted for murder bursts in on a sleeping housewife who is alone. He is being sought for killing her "dearly departed" husband. By the time the sheriff arrives, the couple realize they are in love. The improbable plot was criticized as below NBC's usual quality.[85] "Moonshine," the Arthur Hopkins play that also takes place in a cabin, was repeated with Paul Douglas in the cast.

Although most of the crime stories were the work of Colling and Sobol,

Coe directed a series of short stories from the radio fantasy horror series *Lights Out:* "First Person Singular," on 30 June 1946; "Something in the Wind," on 11 August; and "Dr. Mortius," on 1 September. "First Person Singular" began with the familiar gong that identified the series and depended on a voice-over narration. Reviewers complained about Coe's adaptation as well as direction. The second program was even less effective.

On 22 September 1946 Coe directed a successful version of "Mr. Mergenthwirker's Lobblies," a fantasy adapted by Nelson Bond and David Kent from their short story. This was a joint venture of NBC and the Dramatists' Guild. Henry Mergenthwirker (Vaughn Taylor) is a pure of heart, simple soul who is hit by a truck and believed dead, but, aided by two invisible, little, beer-drinking boys called "lobblies," he survives. Through them, he can foresee the future. He tells a newspaper that a murder is going to occur and he later solves it.[86]

Historical Dramas.   Most of the fifteen dramatizations based on historical events or biographies were part of *The Chronicles of America* series. The programs presented during the period were "Columbus," "Jamestown," "Peter Stuyvesant," "Wolfe and Montcalm," "Vincennes," "The Pioneer Woman," "Daniel Boone," "Alexander Hamilton," and "Dixie."

The two principal dramatizations were biographical. "Conquest of Darkness" related episodes from the life of Tom Davenport, inventor of the first electric motor. The production originally was staged at WRGB, Schenectady, and then it was moved, along with the cast, to Radio City.

"Abe Lincoln in Illinois," the 1938 Robert E. Sherwood historical chronicle, was presented over four nights. The last act was repeated. In the first act, which appeared on 15 April 1945, Lincoln, a backwoodsman, is taught by Mentor Graham, who encourages him to enter politics. Opportunity arrives when Ninian Edwards asks Lincoln to run for the state assembly. Meanwhile, Lincoln has revealed his love for Ann Rutledge, but she dies of fever before he leaves for Springfield.

In the second act, on 20 May 1945, "The Springfield Lawyer," Lincoln is in despair because of the death of Ann. He meets Mary Todd, an ambitious woman he decides to marry, but hesitates because he does not love her. Abe encounters an old friend, whose child is ill. The friend, with whom Abe had once planned to trek westward, feels that, if his child dies, he and his wife will lack sufficient courage for the journey. In a flash of insight, Abe sees the child's sickness as symbolic of the nation's sickness because the Dred Scott decision had made it possible to extend slavery to the West. Lincoln prays for the health of the child, and there-

fore the nation. Now obsessed with national political objectives, he marries Todd, who he thinks can help him achieve them. The third act, "For President—Abraham Lincoln," is staged on a speaker's platform in an Illinois town, where Lincoln tries to tell a crowd about his views of the nation's future. Although nominated for the presidency, Lincoln is haunted by his marital difficulties with the domineering Mary and by his own tendency toward melancholia.

Stephen Courtleigh made a "splendid Lincoln," and "NBC's courage in choosing this vehicle, its initiative in providing the play with an excellent cast and fine production are praiseworthy and creditable," according to *Variety*.[87] Much of the review discussed whether the play could be shown in a single evening instead of presenting one act a month for three months. Such delays reduced the dramatic impact, and some acts, like the second one, were dramatically weak anyway. Edward Sobol was the producer/director.

Musicals. By the summer of 1944, excerpts from grand operas were among NBC's few live productions. A former stage director of the Metropolitan Opera, Dr. Herbert Graf, had been engaged as director of television opera. His first presentation was a scene from *La Bohème*, featuring John Hamill as Rodolfo and Lois Eastman as Mimi. An excerpt from *The Barber of Seville*, in which Hugh Thompson appeared, soon followed. Evidently NBC had learned a good deal since its earlier experiment with opera on 10 March 1940, when it had staged scenes from *Pagliacci*. *Television* lauded the performance: "Adding to Dr. Graf's tasteful staging was the freshness of the singers. They were young, attractive, believable and the soprano did not look like a mantelpiece. The three principals, with voices as pleasant as their looks, sang in English with such good diction that it was possible to understand the meaning of the words."[88]

Another significant experiment was bringing former silent film star Mae Murray before the television cameras in a musical dramatization based on her 1925 hit, *The Merry Widow*, as part of a new series entitled *Memories with Music*. This gave the critics a chance to recall Murray's past musical successes, but *Television* complained, "If there had been a bit less of Miss Murray, if her lines had been less flowery, and her gestures toned down a bit, show would have gained considerably."[89] Colling was the producer.

4

Other Television Dramas

Beyond the activity at WNBT and WCBW, few other individual stations throughout the United States had carried on extensive programming. During the 1930s, little of it was in drama. Lack of equipment, space, and funds to hire talent were among the reasons. By the 1940s, WRGB and WABD, the DuMont station, had joined the other two leaders in originating dramas and in encouraging outside groups to use their studios for dramatic programming. By mid-decade, some professional acting groups, notably the Television Workshop of New York City, were packaging live dramas for television and traveling from station to station. Companies anticipating a future in television—ABC Television and WOR-Mutual Radio—supported acting groups and underwrote the cost of producing dramas at existing studios. These efforts gave everyone expertise in various formats. The medium seemed complicated, expensive, yet promising, if not irresistible. Probably because of the lack of manpower during the war, a few women assumed significant roles as administrators and producer/directors, and several others gained the opportunity to start their television careers.

Significant Dramas

As previously discussed, WNBT was clearly the most prominent station in drama, and WCBW presented little in this field until mid-1944. General Electric's WRGB and DuMont's WABD rivaled each other for the second most active spot, though WRGB enjoyed an edge. Dramatic production at Chicago stations was infrequent but a comfortable fourth place behind CBS, while dramas at WPTZ, Philadelphia, and the Los Angeles stations were minimal. An examination of these key locations suggests the frequency of the experiments, their repetitive nature, and the

limited extent of innovation. Dominance in dramatic television production definitely resided in New York City.

WRGB, SCHENECTADY

General Electric (GE) was primarily interested in manufacturing equipment, not programming. WGY, its Schenectady radio station, served the public well, however, and in 1928 presented the first television drama, "The Queen's Messenger," in its experimental laboratory. Most of GE's attention during the 1930s centered on solving problems in broadcast engineering. Technically, the state of the television art was not ready for drama until the 1940s and that was when the WRGB effort accelerated. More than seventy dramas were telecast between 1940 and 1945. The three-act dramas were adaptations of plays or books; the short dramas were usually one-act plays. WRGB produced seven original television dramas, more than any other company during the experimental era. This was indeed an outstanding accomplishment.

Although WRGB maintained its own in-house radio acting group that presented a television drama now and then, the station encouraged prospective clients, advertising agencies, colleges, and community groups to become familiar with television. As early as 1940, the J. Walter Thompson advertising agency, already deeply involved in radio drama, used WRGB's facilities to present Milton Geiger's "Sentenced to Life" and Agnes Ridgeway's "Courage a la Carte."

The WRGB Players appeared in Glenn Hughes's "Red Carnations" on 10 October 1940. The simple love story requires only a park bench for a set. According to author Judy Dupuy, "Both times it was well-received [also 9 March 1944]. An attention-getting opening helped to sustain interest. Credit slides, backed by music, introducing the play, were dissolved in over a huge carnation, which in turn dissolved into a flower in the buttonhole of the waiting park-bench swain. Similarly, 'The End' was dissolved in over the flower as it was plucked from his lapel and tossed away."[1]

Highlights at WRGB included its first full-length production, "The Betrayal," a passion play, telecast on 3 April 1942. Performed by actors from Siena College and the College of St. Rose, it began with a series of filmed scenes from the Passion Play at Oberammergau. A one-hour version of Harriet Beecher Stowe's *Uncle Tom's Cabin*, presented on 12 May 1942, was the work of writer/producer/director Robert B. Stone and a well-rehearsed cast. Five sets were used and full camera instructions were provided. The Schenectady Civic Players appeared in a successful pro-

duction of "Help Yourself," a three-act farce by Paul Vulpius, on 13 November 1942.

The increase from ten dramatic productions between 1940 and 1943 to sixty between 1943 and 1945 was attributable in part to the installation of new facilities.

In January 1943 Yale University drama students put on "First Came Fire," originally a play by Harry Kleiner. He was invited to observe the conversion to television. The Mountebanks of Union College presented Shakespeare's "Twelfth Night" on 24 March 1943. "But in spite of the professional caliber of the show, the two-hour performance proved tiring," in Dupuy's opinion.[2]

Two original dramas were produced during the summer. "The Tower Room," a psychological mystery, projected the mood of a gloomy, ghost-haunted castle, but lacked story content. "Meet Miss Subways" told of the glamorous new life of a girl after she is selected as Miss Subways. The script was well acted, but lacked reality, perhaps because of its close link to its commercial for Vimms Vitamins.[3]

On 26 August 1943 Tchaikovsky's grand opera *Pique Dame,* sung in the original Russian by a professional troupe, lasted an hour. A full-length opera version of "Hänsel and Gretel" was also performed before the year was over. An experiment on 13 September called *The Martins* consisted of two episodes in a soap opera that would be the equivalent of a daytime radio serial. Dupuy, who also wrote frequent reviews during this period, commented, "The first episode was staged as if for a radio broadcast with actors reading from script. The second episode was written, staged and directed as an incident in the lives of the Martins. The actors memorized their lines and were rehearsed in stage business. This was an improvement over the first camera reporting method but was 'still a soap opera.' "[4] The "commercial announcements" were made on behalf of a mythical sponsor.

On 11 November viewers saw the second full-length Shakespearean play at WRGB, "The Taming of the Shrew." Shakespeare was a natural source of television material. His plays provided many long speeches and soliloquies that could be edited to meet time restraints; they required fewer stage settings than realistic modern plays; they possessed definite educational value; and they offered a challenge to producers. They were also in the public domain.

On 18 February 1944 a detective comedy written especially for performance over WRGB, "The First Time I Saw You," by Charles Wilde, contained a complete fashion show within the framework of the story. An experiment on 28 April 1944 televised a dramatization of "Penny," one of

the comic strips appearing in the Sunday edition of *The New York Her-ald-Tribune*.

THE TELEVISION WORKSHOP

On 11 August 1944 the Television Workshop in New York City made its debut on WRGB with "The Woman Who Was Acquitted," a psychological play that tells the story of an acquitted murderess who confesses her crime while in a cataleptic trance. The cast included Steven Roberts, Mason Andrews, Josephine van Fleet, Jack Bittner, Ronald Alexander, and Donald Keyes, all members of the Television Workshop group. The workshop had formed a touring company that, after two weeks of rehearsals, sent three or four actors to various stations on the East Coast to provide a form of live syndication; that is, the repetition of a single drama on the few local television stations. In an adaptation of "The Return," based on George Lowther's *The Submarine,* a sailor recounts a Nazi attack on his hospital ship. Because the play called for eight characters, each of the four actors in the touring company played two roles. Other plays in the repertoire included "The Clod" and "Dust of the Road."

The first episode of "Conquest over Darkness," entitled "The Golden Ox," was performed on 13 October 1944. This dramatization of the life of Tom Davenport, inventor of the first electric motor, included a model of the first motor, copied from the original in the Smithsonian Institution, and utilized live action, film, and titled mood pictures. The script, written by Larry Algeo, was an institutional commercial for General Electric, but it had entertainment value. A National Book Week presentation on 16 November included a historical sketch that took place in the bookstore of children's writer John Newberry. A video version of "Jack and the Beanstalk" was also presented.

On 7 March 1945 an original drama was based on the writing of O. Henry's short story "The Furnished Room." A period setting, nostalgic vocal music, and the use of film with voice-over narration established the mood. Author Dupuy claimed that "of the seven television originals telecast over WRGB [1943–45], five dramas were rated 'better than good' by televiewers and two as 'acceptable.'" The shows ran the gamut from patriotism to romance, adventure, and dyed-in-the-wool mystery. Dupuy reported, "In analyzing these plays, it is concluded that the top rating of 'excellent' was based on superior performances and production. No unique television techniques were employed for picture effectiveness other than well-planned camera work."[5]

Community Involvement

The policy at WRGB in 1945 was to encourage sponsorship of experimental programs. No charge was required for the use of facilities so long as the program met certain standards of quality. The management believed that such a policy, instead of relying solely on its own staff and talent, not only resulted in better and more varied programming but also permitted a wider scope of productions. Any commercial enterprise desiring to present and sponsor a show on WRGB might do so, the management said, merely by demonstrating a program idea or script that was good television or by applying for sponsorship of one of WRGB's own shows. A sponsor could furnish his own talent or use the station's acting group. WRGB actors were paid $10 to $15 a performance.

Television reported, "WRGB uses ten minute program periods, with shows running ten, twenty, forty, fifty or sixty minutes. While this allows a possible maximum of six different shows an hour, as against radio's four, the average segment is twenty minutes. No stipulation or limitations as to types of commercial programs have been set up and the station is particularly interested in any new, unusual, unorthodox programs with real viewer interest."[6]

In the spring of 1946, WRGB had a staff producer/director sit in on rehearsals of stage productions, make suggestions for camera movements, and plot camera angles. The productions, often originating at schools in the area, were then rehearsed on-camera in the television studio. Examples are "The Tragedian in Spite of Himself," a fifteen-minute drama presented by the Yale Drama School under the direction of Professor Edward Cole; "The Shadow Passes," a twenty-five minute play put on by students from Russell Sage College; and "Joint Owners in Spain," a twenty-minute program offered by personnel from Mount Pleasant High School.

Other WRGB full-length productions were "The Rivals," which ran two hours and eleven minutes, and Eva Le Gallienne in "Alice and Wonderland." Superimposition of the Cheshire Cat and the construction of scenery of abnormal size that contributed to the illusion of Alice shrinking created an atmosphere of fantasy. Shorter dramas included Kenyon Nicholson's "Trifles," John Kirkpatrick's "When You Marry the Navy," Dorothy Parker's intimate character sketches "Here We Are" and "The Waltz," Anton Chekhov's "The Marriage Proposal," Arthur Hopkins's "Moonshine," and Holworthy Hall and Robert Middlemass's "The Valiant."

Aside from plays that had become standard fare at television stations,

WRGB not only initiated original dramas, musicals, and improvisational experiments but also invited others to perform them. In July 1946 WOR's Ad Lib Theatre of the Air, an improvisational acting group, appeared on WRGB. "The Pay-Off," an original fifteen-minute drama by Ted Beebe, was presented with one camera. Director Larry Algeo said that preplanning a one-camera show for his three actors required as much or more time as would have been necessary if he had used two or three cameras.[7] Two of WRGB's musicals, "Pagliacci" and "The Old Maid and the Thief," were produced by Arthur Weld in cooperation with the Colony Opera Guild, a professional opera group.

On 27 September 1946 the Television Workshop in New York City produced "Writer's Cramps," directed by A. Vance Hallack. It involves an author who suddenly finds the characters in his novels stepping into his room and accusing him of stealing plots and lines from Shakespeare. A complaint of *The Billboard* was that this "show should prove once and for all that radio actors are not for television unless they have enough training and consistent stock background to carry themselves."[8]

The interest General Electric showed in television dramas did not lessen in later years. On 1 February 1953 it would inaugurate the *General Electric Theatre,* a half-hour, filmed anthology featuring well-known stars in plays that had been successful. The host and occasional star was Ronald Reagan. *General Electric Theatre* was produced live for a short while during the fall of 1954. The live debut starred Gene Tierney, Luther Adler, and Patric Knowles in "Nora," based on the principal character in Ibsen's *A Doll's House.* The following season, the series returned to film. By 1956 *General Electric Theatre* ranked second in the Nielsen Top Ten rating. Although infrequent, good dramas still appear under this aegis.

WABD, New York

DuMont telecast an experimental schedule as early as 1941, but its W2XWV did not actually begin operating until 28 June 1942, in small studios on the 42d floor of 515 Madison Avenue. The schedule of this station, which at first produced a variety show on Sundays and later on Wednesdays, resembled the typical lineup of variety acts that most stations had offered during the preceding decade. An evening's entertainment frequently featured monologists or a group of actors performing scenes from plays. Glorianne Lehr appeared in an excerpt from "Susan and God" and a melodramatic skit about women whose men were on a bombing mission over enemy territory. Mady Christians acted in condensations of four Shakespearean plays: "A Winter's Tale," "The Merchant

of Venice," "Romeo and Juliet," and "The Taming of the Shrew." Klaus Lollmar and Scott Selmar participated in scenes from R. C. Sheriff's "Journey's End."

During the summer of 1943, W2XWV was off the air for revamping. In the fall, Sunday evening programs occasionally included plays of fifteen to thirty minutes. The schedule for Sunday, 31 October 1943, listed at 8:30 P.M. a play called "Lonely Soldier," at 9:00 a singer, at 9:15 "City Missing Persons," at 9:30 "Chills and Thrills," and at 9:45 "Face the War." In December the two-hour variety schedule featured a presentation of Dickens's *A Christmas Carol*, probably the station's most ambitious undertaking in the dramatic field until then.[9] The familiar story was adapted by William Podmore, who played Scrooge. Although Podmore was said to have carried the show, he received good support from the Mountebanks. The camera opened on a view of the book and panned up to Noah Julian reading. He faded out and Scrooge appeared. Authentic scenery, properties, and costumes were unusual highlights during this period of wartime restrictions and limited studio space. The director was George Lowther.

According to *Television Daily*, "Throughout the war W2XWV telecast from five to 10 hours a week—the only television station in the U.S. to maintain a regular program schedule."[10] By 1944 the Allies were gaining the upper hand, the war had peaked, and Allen B. DuMont's experimental station had changed its call letters to WABD. In an effort to encourage sponsor and agency interest in drama, the station began a series of plays, fashion shows, musicals, and novelty acts on 28 March 1944. George S. Kaufman's "If Men Played Cards as Women Do" was the opening presentation.

THE HARVEY MARLOWE PLAYERS AND OTHER GROUPS

For the most part, DuMont sought outside productions. The Harvey Marlowe Players were frequent performers at WABD. In May it telecast "The Valiant," which, when repeated later, proved to be the only bright spot in a variety lineup. After twelve hours of rehearsal, the cast performed well. Critic Wanda Marvin stated, "Clever camera work helped immensely by variation of shots, and good lighting contributed much."[11] The Marlowe group performed a half-hour adaptation of "Footsteps of Hate," a Rupert Brooke story. Twenty hours of rehearsal resulted in "a high mark in tele entertainment."[12] The play created an atmosphere of hate and ugliness brought on by the fear of starvation that was sustained throughout the drama and built to a powerful climax.

In August the Marlowe group presented "Gander Sauce," a script

written by Betty Smith, author of *A Tree Grows in Brooklyn*. It, too, was offered more than once. *The Billboard* was critical: "The supposed piece-de-resistance of the evening . . . was disappointing in its content, altho technically and scenically the production, directed by Harvey Marlowe, wasn't bad. Aside from technical errors, the acting at times was a bit hammy, a throwback to the old mellerdrama days, tho we have seen other video that was worse."[13]

The Marlowe dramas were frequently part of WOR's series *Video Varieties*. A performance of "The Valiant" by the Marlowe Players helped to celebrate the station's first anniversary. For September the group, after thirty-six hours of rehearsal, presented another thirty-minute drama: "The Ring of General Macias," by Josephina Niggli. The plot concerns the wife of a Mexican general who talks a young girl out of taking her life. The cast featured Gloria Mann and Elaine Barrie. One reviewer was ecstatic: "Marlowe's skillful direction, coupled with a careful, concise interweaving of cameras and lights, made the one-acter a dramatic video tapestry of color and movement."[14] Harvey Marlowe became executive producer for ABC Television, which telecast its dramas over WABD and WRGB.

WABD presented on 28 September 1944 "The Boys from Boise," the first full-length musical comedy written especially for television.[15] The following month, it offered Florence Ryerson's "Angels Don't Marry," a half-hour comedy about a couple of scrapping ex-mates who really love each other and eventually reconcile. One of the scenes resulted in the rare occasion when a critic questions good taste: "And while on the seeing business, it's questionable video taste to have the scene end with the couple in bed and milady's hand seen in close-up hanging over the side of the bed holding a handerchief which falls from her hand as her arm relaxes. One little boy asked, with good reason, 'Why did the lady drop her handkerchief, mama?' "[16]

Like the Marlowe Players, the Television Workshop in New York City tried to produce several low-cost dramas. Because of the high royalties demanded for most Broadway shows, the workshop's directors turned to little-known one-act plays, original material, and discarded radio scripts.[17] Television was unable to compete for top writers to prepare original material. One-act plays by well-known writers brought only $15 to $25 for noncommercial performances and $75 to $100 for sponsored telecasts.

"The Eighth Step" was a radio play originally written for radio's *Columbia Workshop* by John Hugh, of the Donahue & Coe advertising agency. It was adapted by stage director/writer/actor Sanford Meisner for the Television Workshop of New York City. "The Eighth Step" is a

psychological thriller about a demented hillbilly girl (Elizabeth Wilson) who is falsely accused by a parson (Donald Keyes) of killing her uncle (Robert Harris). The telecast was reduced to one interior cabin setting and one exterior scene. The production was first prepared for WABD after eight hours of dry-run rehearsal and three hours on-camera. The actors restaged it for an engagement at WRGB on 7 September 1944.

The Television Workshop began experimenting with live-actor syndication in 1944 by providing weekly, half-hour dramas. These programs usually originated at WABD, then went to WRGB. Two years later, WPTZ, Philadelphia, became a third city (16 August 1946). It was estimated that as many as fifty cities would eventually be tied into a nationwide itinerary network, whose stations would be visited by different groups every week.[18] This did not happen because, as networking expanded, touring companies became unnecessary. The Television Workshop productions were packaged at a cost of $200 to $500 per program.

Meanwhile, DuMont had continued to allow groups to telecast dramas. Students of the New School of Social Research presented "Surrender," a twenty-five-minute play originally written for radio by Arch Oboler and adapted for television by Ruth Forma, and "The Boor" by Anton Chekhov. Critic Wanda Marvin was pleased: "Both *Surrender* and *The Boor* were well chosen, carefully directed and splendidly acted. Tho neither one-acter had much camera rehearsal, technical work on both was first-rate due, undoubtedly, to scripts with specific shooting instructions for the studio crew."[19] The same group presented William Saroyan's "People with the Light Coming through Them" and "Hello, Out There." According to *The Billboard,* "The cast was good, imagination employed and details like having some of the atmosphere characters drawn in cartoon form on the set was Saroyan okay."[20]

As 1944 ended, DuMont offered "Private Johnson's Christmas," an original video script by David Kaplan. It was about two GIs: one receives mail, the other does not. The latter dreams of what it must be like at home. The production was well acted and produced, but a miniature of a war-torn countryside was "badly modeled." WOR Television Producer Bob Emery directed the children's fairy tale "Hänsel and Gretel," described as "a neat well-done job, with almost professional polish."[21] Emery was familiar with children's programming for WOR radio and would become a major producer of drama for WOR using the WABD facilities. Charles Dickens's "A Christmas Carol," featuring Helen Jerome as Mrs. Cratchit, Carl Eastman as Bob Cratchit, and Bobby Hookey as Tim, concluded the year's dramas.

By the mid-1940s, the cry for new, original dramas written especially for television was becoming louder, as expressed by Harvey Marlowe:

One of radio's great contributions was to begin to indicate the value and importance of the half-hour dramatic vehicle. It was left to such writers as Corwin, Oboler, and others to really make the transition from stage to radio in a truly individual style. It was men like Corwin and Oboler who first realized that it wasn't sufficient merely to transpose a play from stage to radio, but that there were both advantages and disadvantages in this new medium. It was only after such men had begun to write specifically for this new art that radio thirty minute plays [emerged].

All this indicates one thing . . . that the sooner we realize this, and begin to write for television as a completely new art medium with a full understanding of its limitations and advantages today, only then will we be materially aiding the pioneering of television programs.[22]

On 15 April 1946 WABD opened the finest television studio in New York: the John Wanamaker studio, located in the Wanamaker department store, 9th Street and Broadway.[23] It was a gala evening, crowded and exciting. Many celebrities, such as Mayor William O'Dwyer, attended. The studio, equipped with four cameras, was completely furnished with DuMont facilities. The printed program, issued to guests, featured two principal productions: "Let's Have Fun," a charades-variety quiz directed by television pioneer Thomas H. Hutchinson; and a thirty-minute dramatic fantasy entitled "Experience," written by George Lowther and directed by Louis Sposa, director of commercial operations. "Experience" concerned the erotic wanderings of a dental patient under the influence of gas. John Graham played The Patient, Lawrence Deacon The Dentist, and Abby Lewis The Nurse.

Despite the glamour of the evening, "those who sat at home or visited the studio were offered an astonishing evening of ineptitude in the theatre, an amateur pot-pourri in concept, production and projection," commented Jack Gould. "What should have served as another step forward for television was only a major disappointment through failure to acknowledge video's current technical and economic limitations."[24] The *Televiser* complained, "There was no continuity. In fact, there wasn't a show—just some sophomoric writing."[25] "It was a really cornball [drama]," Florence Monroe remembered, "but the evening was spectacular." And, indeed, it was, because, as *The New York Times* reported, "the world's first permanent television network, linking New York and Washington by coaxial cable, went into operation last night in the auditorium of the John Wanamaker store here. The Mayflower Hotel was the sending-receiving station at the Washington end of the cable."[26]

Although the performance purportedly featured the latest in television

The DuMont (Wanamaker) Studio, New York, 1946. (*New York Public Library*)

facilities, the lights were still extremely hot for both day and night scenes. Monroe remembered that one director complained about studio noise. No one could find where it was coming from. Finally, the cause was determined to be crew members slushing around in perspiration collecting in their shoes.[27]

On 29 April 1946, "The Headmaster," Jay Strong's first one-act play with the new DuMont facilities, was presented. According to one review, it was "adequate, professional and indicated what can be done at the John Wanamaker studios. Nevertheless it didn't hold much interest."[28] In May the one act "Angels Don't Marry" also suffered from a weak script. On 21 August WABD presented a dramatic monologue version of "The Tell-Tale Heart," by Edgar Allan Poe. The actual murder occurred on camera, which raised the question of how literal television should be. Theater and films tended to have gruesome scenes take place offstage, off-camera, but WABD took the viewer to the murder bed.

THE FIRST SERIAL ON COMMERCIAL TELEVISION

Late in the year, on 9 October 1946, *Faraway Hill,* the first soap opera on commercial television, was presented by the Caples advertising agency. David P. Lewis was the director of the programs, which were budgeted at $300 each. An off-camera voice helped to reveal the thoughts of a woman who, after the death of her husband, tries to escape the memories of their life together. The story was essentially about a rich young woman who becomes romantically involved with a poor fellow. The woman was played by Flora Campbell, and the male lead by Mel Brandt. The drama involved love, heartbreak, noble rejection, death, gossip, and the eternal triangle. After eight episodes, the Caples Company conducted a survey to determine public acceptance. About 80 percent of the viewers rated the series from good to excellent.[29] The more of the series the viewers saw, the more favorably they responded.

On 30 October 1946 WABD presented a comedy skit for Westinghouse. The $4,000 effort turned out to be one long commercial for the Westinghouse electric blanket. Jerry Colonna backed out after the dry-run rehearsal because his part was too small and in pantomime. The director was changed at the last minute, too, and so the production ended up being a "pretty bad job."[30] The American Television Society ran some experiments over WABD, including "Date with Destiny" on 20 December 1946. This experiment was so modest and poorly done that the project was "a complete waste of time."[31]

By the end of 1946, WABD was offering the only two sponsored dramas on television, aside from those that appeared as part of the variety program *Hour Glass,* sponsored by Standard Brands on WNBT. The WABD telecasts were *Famous Jury Trials,* underwritten by the American Broadcasting Company, and *Write Me a Love Story,* sponsored by the Manhattan Soap Company (Sweetheart Soap).[32]

DuMont diligently attempted to form a fourth network along the East Coast, but the reluctance of stations to purchase the company's programs and services, the lack of sufficient financial support, and the limited number of channel allocations in major markets resulted in failure. The DuMont assets eventually became WNEW, New York.

WOR, NEW YORK

Radio station WOR, owned and operated by the Bamberger Broadcasting Service, a subsidiary of R. H. Macy and Company, and the principal station for Mutual broadcasting, began developing television dramas in 1944 under the direction of Harvey Marlowe and then Bob

Scene from "The Tell-Tale Heart," WABD, New York, 1945. (*New York Public Library*)

Emery. Emery, who had produced a children's series, *Rainbow House,* for WOR since 1939, said:

> I got definite instructions from Mr. Norman Livingston, my immediate superior in the matter of programs at WOR. Following the policies laid down by Mr. T. C. Streibert, our President, and Mr. J. R. Poppele, our Vice President in Charge of Engineering, Mr. Livingston assigned me to produce a series of dramatic programs, with the provision that I use two of the WOR regular radio programs as "vehicles" or "frames." They were *The Brownstone Theatre* and *The Sealed Book.* This classified my play material as: (a) old time standard plays for *The Brownstone Theatre,* (b) terror and mystery plays for *The Sealed Book.*[33]

Emery usually staged his productions at WABD and later at WRGB.

With the help of Margaret Webster of the Theatre Guild, several short plays were identified and produced weekly in half-hour telecasts. In the spring of 1945, "The Necklace," "The Bells," "The Heritage of Wimpole Street," and "The Man Who Came to Gettysburg" were chosen for *Brownstone Theatre.* Such thrillers as "The Singapore Spider," "Trifles," and "The Green Skull" were scheduled for *The Sealed Book.*

Scene from *Faraway Hill*, WABD, fall 1946. (*New York Public Library*)

The Brownstone Theatre opened with producer Emery, as the host, inviting the audience to join him at the "theater." The camera took a long shot of the theater facade and dollied in through the door to give the impression of entering. The noise of the theater filling up, the raising and lowering of the curtain, the applause of the studio audience, and the taking of curtain calls by the actors all contributed to the theater atmosphere.

A review in *The Billboard* commented on one play in the *Brownstone* series: "The play, 'David Garrick,' was corn, but it was done in period manner that made it good fun. It was played straight—and that is what all good corn must be. . . . Emery handled the curtains well, and the fade in from sketch to scene was so well cued that few realized that the curtain was in miniature and the cast life-size."[34] "Crime in the Cabin" tells of a playwriting couple who are in a lonely cabin trying to write a murder mystery. At the height of a storm, a gun-toting couple, wanted for murder, arrives. Practicing some of their techniques employed in previous crime dramas, the playwrights capture the criminals. In this experiment, Emery tried to work out technical problems before the play was finally drafted. In "Absinthe for One," a psychological murder mystery in which a three-year-old murder is solved, the dialogue was prerecorded and the actors lip-synchronized the video; this cut rehearsal time in half. Emery claimed that the use of cue cards distracted the actors.

Using his own WOR stock company, Emery enjoyed flexibility. As *Television* explained, "By having a stagewise cast, they are used to the 'business' which makes good theatre—the gestures, the ease of moving, the right spacing, all the little intangibles that can add importance to a scene. Then too it simplifies production and casting problems."[35] Emery determined what each actor should do, for what roles they were best suited, how long it took them to learn lines, and how much rehearsal they would require. Usually, he rehearsed his dramas four times in New York and presented them over WABD. When he later went to WRGB, he prepared complete plans for scenery, audio, and video in advance, and spent five hours in rehearsal there. He believed that, because of such an investment, good plays should be repeated for a week over a station so that a sufficient audience could view them.

As WOR's production supervisor, Emery devoted himself mainly to script adaptation, casting, scene design, property and set supervision, and dramatic direction. The work called for close coordination between the artists and technicians. As WOR anticipated opening its own television station in Washington, D.C., executives speculated that "experimentation on live dramatic and variety programs will probably come far down on the list as station feels it has a good file of data on this programming from the Bob Emory [*sic*] Brownstone Theatre and Sealed Book series."[36]

ABC Television, New York

ABC Television, which, as yet, did not have a television studio of its own, used WABD for dramatic purposes. When the FCC's ruling on chain broadcasting was upheld by the Supreme Court in 1943, NBC sold its second radio network, the Blue Network, to WMCA (New York) owner Edward J. Noble. On 25 February 1945 the Blue Network had launched its series of "radio shows-on-television," which, according to Paul Mowrey, in charge of television for the Blue, used the facilities of WRGB and WABD in an effort to answer the question: "Can radio programs be successfully transferred to television?" Despite the negative view of most of the experts, the radio network attempted to adapt various radio formats to television.[37]

Chosen to head the ABC Television operation as executive producer was Harvey Marlowe. Florence Monroe recalled, "Harvey was more of the modern show biz type. . . . Harvey was a lot more high powered [than Emery]. The Madison Avenue type that you think of now, Marlowe was very charming, good looking, jovial, very imaginative, and responsive to the needs of the crew."[38]

Marlowe directed episodes that were adapted to television from radio's *Famous Jury Trials*. "The State vs. Dolly Steele" was telecast on 18 April

1946. This "whodunit" demonstrated, according to the *Televiser,* the professional quality fine actors—Elissa Landi as Dolly Steele, Sidney Blackmer as the defense attorney, Zachary Charles as Lou Diamond, and Dennis James as the prosecuting attorney—would bring to television, even though too much of the story was read by a voice-over narrator.[39] WABD charged ABC Television $625 per half-hour for each of its twice-weekly telecasts.

After directing his dramatic programs, Marlowe commented, "One of the major cost factors in both movies and the theatre has been the elaborate and pretentious sets. This has been necessary due to the all-encompassing eye of the movie camera and the wide expanse of stage from proscenium to proscenium which must be furnished in detail. However, in television, the small size of the screen has demanded for successful production, the use of at least eighty per cent of close-ups, thus immediately cutting down the need for huge sets that the movies and theatre have employed."[40] In 1947 the director formed Harvey Marlowe Television Associates, Inc., a consulting firm.

Meanwhile, Paul Mowrey, formerly at CBS in 1939 and now ABC Television manager, had announced plans to begin a half-hour dramatic series, *ABC Tele-Theater,* on 20 April 1946 over WRGB. The first drama was "The Devil on Stilts," by Florence Ryerson and Colin Clements. Bobbie Henry directed the program, and Beverly Roberts played the leading role. "Fit for a King," on 11 June 1946, was a half-hour show that featured King Cole and his court. The royal setting was an attempt by Marlowe to imply that General Motors craftsmanship was worthy of the discriminating taste of the affluent, a major theme in early television advertising. This represented a good try at an effective commercial, but it was not entertaining.

The American Broadcasting Company applied for a television channel allocation in New York. While it waited for FCC approval, it utilized WABD, WRGB, and WPTZ facilities not only for experimenting in dramatic productions but also for training its staff in television techniques. On 15 November 1946 Mowrey announced that ABC would increase its airtime on television to nine and a half hours, the heaviest video schedule in the company's history. Yet, ABC Television would wait until 10 August 1948 to go on the air with its own channel and would not become a major competitor in drama until the 1950s.

WPTZ, PHILADELPHIA

As the notion of networking became more prominent, WRGB, WABD, and WPTZ telecast programs by means of coaxial cable or exchanged programs by repeating live dramas produced by touring companies, as

discussed earlier. WPTZ's function was to introduce these dramas to the Philadelphia area. By late 1945, WPTZ did not yet have complete facilities for telecasting commercial programs. It did, however, telecast football games from Franklin Field under the sponsorship of the Atlantic Refining Company through its agency, N. W. Ayer.

WPTZ did become more active in dramatic programming in 1946 and 1947. One of its first dramas was W. W. Jacobs's "The Monkey's Paw," directed by J. Paul Nickell. Soon Nickell would move to New York and become one of the principal directors for *Studio One.* "The Man from Cairo" was one drama in an hour-long, monthly series presented in 1946. A small theater used by the Germantown Theatre Guild served as the studio for WPTZ's two-camera remote pickup of "The Importance of Being Earnest," by Oscar Wilde, which was telecast the following year.

KTSL, Los Angeles

Pioneer television broadcasting on the West Coast began in 1930 at W6XAO, an experimental station owned by the Don Lee Broadcasting System. Using equipment developed by Harry R. Lubcke, the station had started telecasting programs by 23 December 1931. Recognizing the advantage of being in the center of the motion picture industry, a typical program in 1932 consisted of interviews with such stars as Tom Mix; Jean Harlow; and Ann Nichols, whose 1922 comedy, *Abie's Irish Rose,* about a marriage of a Jewish boy and an Irish girl, ran for 2,327 performances.

Using a film process, the station broadcast for three consecutive days coverage of an earthquake in the vicinity of Long Beach and Compton on 19 March 1933. The image was a crude 60 lines when the station began showing feature films from Pathé and Paramount, including *The Crooked Circle,* C. B. DeMille's *This Day and Age,* and Gary Cooper in *The Texan.* Programs were 9:00 to 11:00 Monday, Wednesday, and Friday mornings and 7:00 to 9:00 evenings. During the first three and a half years of operation, Lubcke, Don Lee's director of television, estimated that six million feet of motion picture film were transmitted from W6XAO and W6XS.

In connection with its *Hollywood on the Air* radio broadcast, RKO presented celebrity interviews on W6XAO from its Los Angeles Hillstreet Theatre in 1934. RKO stars included Ann Harding, Richard Dix, Irene Dunne, Victor McLaglen, Delores Del Rio, Bruce Cabot, Ginger Rogers, and Boris Karloff.

The Don Lee Broadcasting System was the Pacific Coast outlet for CBS television experiments until 1936. By May 1938 the Don Lee station had

Scene from "The Monkey's Paw," WPTZ, Philadelphia, 1947. (*New York Public Library*)

announced that it was ready, pending FCC approval, to produce a regular program schedule. Within the year, W6XAO was telecasting four dramatic sketches a week, including the first televised serial, *Vine Street*. This series, consisting of fifty-two weekly episodes, was a comic drama about Hollywood life, from the poverty in the community to the riches of the motion picture studios. It was written by Maurice Ashley and Wilfred Pettitt and starred Shirley Thomas and John Barkeley.[41]

By 1940 W6XAO had telecast more than 2,600 programs to an estimated 400 receivers within a thirty-mile radius of the station, which occasionally could be seen in a "highly successful" manner as far away as San Francisco.[42] As authors John Porterfield and Kay Reynolds observed, "More than 6,000 scheduled program hours have already been broadcast, which is believed to exceed the activity of any other television broadcaster in the nation."[43] According to *The Great Television Race*, further developments were as follows:

> At the same time, work was begun on moving W6XAO from its original location on the eighth floor of the Don Lee Building, at Seventh and Bixel streets in Los Angeles, to a new location, pur-

chased from the Mack Sennett estate. At this new site, now renamed Mt. Lee, located between Hollywood and Burbank, a two-story building was erected to house the modern transmitter and large sound stage, the sound stage modeled after those of motion-picture studios. In October the new facility was inaugurated by the mayor of Los Angeles, Fletcher Bowron. The station's transmitter remained at Mt. Lee over a decade, well into the era of commercial telecasting.[44]

Talent appearing on W6XAO was mostly voluntary as late as 1944. On 28 June 1944 RKO presented "The Stuffed Cat" over the Don Lee Station. The script was by the Blue Network's Carroll Coleman, and the director was Lillian Albertson. Charles Smith was the production supervisor. The cast provided a creditable job by muffing few lines. Don Owen, a reviewer for *The Billboard,* wrote:

> Those who argue that films are a better entertainment bet than live shows, as far as drama is concerned on television, claim that RKO's initial video offering over the Don Lee station more than substantiates their viewpoint. However, half hour telecasting of a so-called hair raiser, *The Stuffed Cat,* shows conclusively that if lighting and camera technique is at its best, live shows of this type will develop into first-class entertainment.[45]

In December 1944 Hal March and Bob Sweeney wrote and produced a comedy sketch on W6XAO as one of the station's semimonthly programs.

By fall 1945—a year later—the schedule at W6XAO still relied heavily on film, and the few live shows were mostly of the variety type. A live skit called "Dream," written for television by Mal Boyd, Republic Pictures radio director, and directed by Harry R. Lubcke, served as a framework for the production of several acts. The story concerned a female reporter who, though outscooped in real life, is successful in her dreams. Viewers demand "heavier drama or something that packs more punch," complained one reviewer.[46] Another sketch, "Cops Don't Get Married," by Paul Franklin, was presented in September. The script involved a policeman and a thief who find out they were once friends in school. The thief begs to be arrested, though the police officer at first refuses to do so. The idea was timeworn, yet it served as a good vehicle for video. Occasionally, radio performers, in addition to film actors, such as Jimmy Scribner, star of the Mutual Broadcasting System (MBS) radio series *The Johnson Family,* originating in 1936, tried to bring comedy-drama to television. He played all of the characters in a story of a Negro family by

changing his voice. The technique, appropriate to radio, proved to be confusing and unsuccessful on television.

By late 1945, war contracts still limited W6XAO's programming schedule and "the bans have not been entirely lifted yet."[47] In view of its curtailed activities, the station had not set any rates for sponsors. However, program experimentation for the advancement of video techniques was available to sponsors and agencies. To take advantage of its two studios and an outdoor swimming pool for televising aquatic events, W6XAO was planning more hours on the air as soon as its government contract allowed.

In the spring of 1946, W6XAO announced that it would change its call letters to KTSL, involving the initials of its owner, Thomas S. Lee. Like other stations, it drew upon the theatrical resources of community groups, drama schools, and speech teachers by encouraging them to "package" plays, a term coming into frequent use. It began to depend heavily on the Pasadena Community Playhouse for restaging many of its dramas for television. "Johnny Came Home," produced in February 1946, was a comedy about an ex-GI who finds that home does not quite live up to the expectations he dreamed about in his foxhole. The station's first full-length drama, lasting an hour and fifteen minutes, was telecast that spring. "Not Since Eve" is about an idyllic second marriage that is threatened by the first wife. John Richard Kerr and Jack Woodford directed actors at the Pasadena Community Playhouse for ten hours before rehearsing them for three more hours on two orthicon cameras in the studio. KTSL had two studios: one was 100 feet by 60 feet by 30 feet; the other was 40 feet by 26 feet by 18 feet.

Working also with the University of California extension service and army hospitals, KTSL produced "Mother Be Good," a one-act comedy about a young girl who is afraid her returning soldier-boyfriend will not approve of her mother's modern ways.

On 22 May 1946 the Pasadena Community Playhouse presented "Hedda Gabler" for FCC officials. Director Thomas B. Armistead received complaints for merely switching cameras and not dollying to vary his shots. But *The Billboard* contended, "On the credit side, producers [Jack Stewart] introduced recorded background music near play's end, highlighting suspense, and building the climax."[48]

For the most part, KTSL's future was not destined to include drama to any extent. As *Television* pointed out, "While the station has experimented with every phase of theatrical, film and radio techniques, particular emphasis will be given to educational demonstrations and a policy of 'living room education'—a program of providing visual how-to-do in-

struction in most fields of endeavor—has been developed."[49] This policy was highly noticeable in the late summer of 1946, when Lee Zhito commented:

> Don Lee's W6XAO uses canned stuff, but won't brag about it. Its weekly programs alternate between live scanner (sandwiched in between film shorts) and an all-film evening. Films used by station, however, aren't of the type usually considered in the Hollywood motion picture category, but are for the most part home movies, classroom films and commercial shorts.[50]

In December 1946 KTSL produced an original Christmas play penned by radio writer Truman Boardman. The plot dramatized the faith of a small blind girl who dreams of the miraculous restoration of her sight. The idea was appropriate to the spirit of Christmas, and Boardman, who directed the story himself, did not become sentimental. "Blessed Are They" lasted half an hour and required fifteen hours of rehearsal by actors Hall Ross, Alice Baccus, Stanley Frazer, Don Diamond, and Jim McKee, all of whom had completed a television acting refresher course conducted by the American Federation of Radio Artists (AFRA). Boardman's children—True Ann and Penelope—performed with the same high caliber as the AFRA group. *The Billboard* offered praise: "Without question, this was the best Don Lee production of the year, and from what oldsters hint, the top W6XAO offering of the past several seasons. Production sparkled with a polished touch from start to finish."[51]

KTLA, LOS ANGELES

Another Los Angeles experimental station attempting dramatic production was Paramount's W6XYZ. It was established on the company lot in 1942. Although the program schedule was minimal in the early years, Paramount did gain some production insight by restaging scenes from such feature-film successes as *This Gun for Hire,* starring Alan Ladd and Veronica Lake. These efforts were rare at W6XYZ, however.

Fearful that television could not support feature-film costs of one to two million dollars a film, various people advanced suggestions: develop new stars, new production techniques, and new stories; distribute to remote locations; and eliminate illness, accidents, and other such production incidents. In the *Televiser,* two movie and television veterans claimed: "With the unnecessary costs eliminated, television productions on film are entirely feasible, and in the opinion of many persons they are the best way to present television."[52]

Scene from "Hedda Gabler," W6XAO, Los Angeles, 1946. (*New York Public Library*)

Because W6XYZ was partially owned by DuMont, its cameras and transmitters were built by that company, but its special electronic equipment was designed and built by Television Production, Inc., another owner. During the first half of 1946, the station was off the air while a new transmitter was constructed atop Mount Wilson. The station went back on the air on 9 May 1946. In the fall, Lee Zhito complained that it did not even own a film projector: "W6XYZ has yet to use a single motion picture during the entire time it has been on the air, altho station is owned by Paramount Pictures."[53] Klaus Landsberg, who was West Coast director and manager of W6XYZ, refuted the complaint by asking: Why take up air time with something we already know how to use? The station on 22 January 1947 emerged from experimental status and changed its call letters to KTLA.

WBKB, Chicago

Chicago station WBKB (W9XBK), the Balaban and Katz subsidiary, offered a variety schedule and opened its facilities to sponsors and advertising agencies as well as educational and community groups. Most pro-

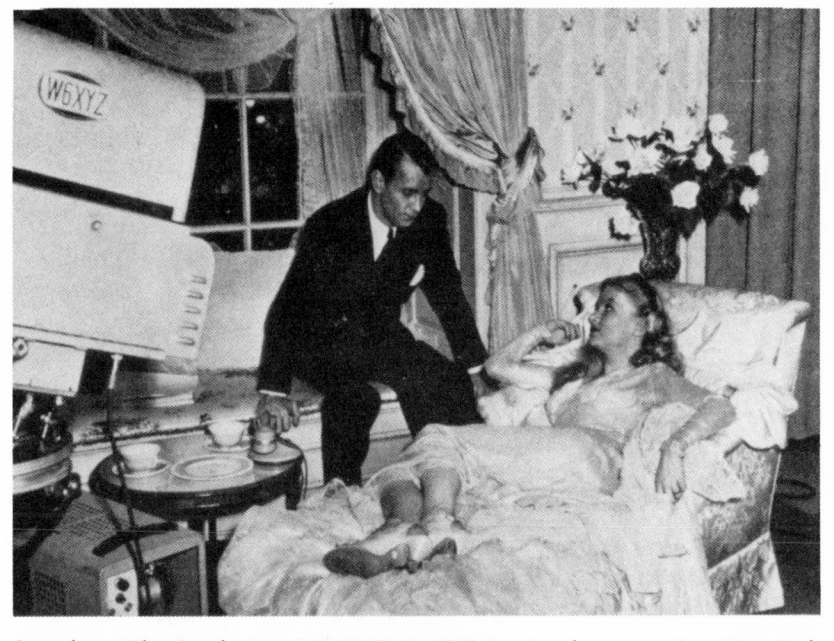

Scene from "This Gun for Hire," W6XWY-W6XYZ, Los Angeles, spring 1945. (*New York Public Library*)

grams of the mid-forties were sustaining. The staff—many were women—experimented with uneven success. One original television drama, "Willie Buys a Bond," telecast in 1944, told of the visit of a film actress to a friend's house at the time of a bond rally. During her stay, a little boy—Willie, who was planning to buy a radio with $18.75 (the price of a U.S. War Bond) he had saved—decides to buy a bond instead. "In 20 minutes WBKB set television programming back 10 years," complained *The Billboard*.[54]

Another original drama, "Now and Then," written and directed by Gladys Dalstrom, concerned a small-town teacher who tries to sell to the War Department a plan for winning the war. This production was described as "a nice try but a dismal failure."[55] It used two scenes and a cast of four. William Mogle, writer and narrator, presented a drama for the Cook County Chapter of the National Foundation for Infantile Paralysis. But, suffering from a lack of rehearsal, it was not favorably received.

Part of the problem in 1944 was limited facilities. Because the 30-by-40-foot studio had only two cameras, considerable ingenuity was required to bring productions up to minimum expectations, as illustrated in a "far from top-notch" production of "Hänsel and Gretel," adapted

and directed by Pauline Bobrov, who worked with a cast from the Chicago College of Music. She was more successful with her adaptation and direction of Arthur Miller's "That They May Live," whose cast numbered five. The opening shot pictured a girl entering a theater and sitting down. As she reads her program, a camera dollies in to reveal credits, followed by a dissolve to scene one. The story involves a returning soldier who tries to find his place in society. At the climax, in frustration he complains that his wife is suffering because of a complacent American public. A loud masculine voice is heard shouting, in essence, "You don't know what you're talking about." The camera turns at once to the audience, and a conversation between the actor and the audience ensues. After a last shot of the cast and a falling curtain, the evening ended. Twelve hours of rehearsal and realistic scenery painted on paper backgrounds contributed to this low-budget show.[56]

Fran Harris, who attempted several programs at WBKB, wrote and directed "Bright Star Shining." It depicted the emotional strain a woman goes through while trying to decide whether she should divorce her husband, who is stationed with the army overseas. She wants to marry a civilian who loves her. Using minimum dialogue and many silent close-ups, the technique ran into difficulty when facial expressions could not adequately convey meaning on the small television screen. On a more positive note, Harris directed an adaptation of "Perfect Ending," a one-act play. The cast rehearsed seven and a half hours. Cy Wagner claimed that the drama was "almost as artistically satisfying as anything Hollywood could offer."[57]

In another drama about a soldier, the WBKB staff used a kaleidoscope, for what it believed to be the first time, as a flashback bridge. Further imagination was exemplified in "Judy's Prayer," which was written and directed for television by Jerry Walker:

> Show opened with a shot of couple kneeling at an altar. Then Walker's voice began a narration giving story behind their being there. Following was flashback to a family scene at which a mother, father and daughter (Judy) were talking about a son and brother who was in the army overseas. Following this was a flashback to this soldier reading his Bible on a lonely outpost.
>
> It was then that Walker used his most imaginative device, the one that showed what could be done with video religious programming. As the soldier watched three trees, there was a dissolve in which the place of the trees was taken by three girl dancers, dressed in long black gowns. As an off-stage chorus chanted a Biblical passage in a

definite rhythm, the three danced to the chant and depicted perfectly a visual interpretation of the mood of the words.[58]

A horror series called *X Marks the Spot,* written by producer Bill Vance and directed by Helen Carson, became a live, biweekly series in July 1945. The stories were based on authentic murder cases and adapted for television. The initial program concerned England's Jack the Ripper. *The Billboard* claimed that the "use of live talent was a 1,000 percent improvement in entertainment content."[59] The live cast caused problems, however, for actor Carl Kroenke swallowed formaldehyde from the studio darkroom instead of the turpentine the script called for; he was rushed to the hospital and recovered. In August the cast, which performed without pay on the series, begged off at the last minute so that it could work for pay on a radio program. Another series appealing to the bizarre, *They Had Their Hour,* written and produced by Jack Gibney, was directed by Gladys Lundberg. Weird stories with eerie overtones included one yarn about Wamba, king of the Visigoths, who in 1680 was compelled to become a monk against his will. The series claimed historical accuracy for its productions.

WBKB was off the air in early 1946 for a change of frequencies, and returned on 20 March to present an hour and fifteen minutes of afternoon programming, including an eight-minute dramatic "sample" of "excellent video material" entitled "Goodnight."

Benefiting from the services of William C. Eddy, formerly lighting and video effects engineer for WNBT, as director of television, WBKB scheduled various series. Northwestern University was to present six hour-long dramas a year, premiering on 4 April 1946. Restaging television versions of "The Far Off Hills," Chekhov's "The Marriage Proposal," and George Jennings's "The Ring" fell to Beulah Zachary. Keeping the dramas inexpensive meant little rehearsal, unpaid actors, few scenes, and scenery painted on brown wrapping paper.

Two other series involved original video scripts by Chicago writers, most of them from radio. One radio adaptation was "The Dark Cellar," by Herb Bailey. The half-hour drama on 2 May 1946 proved to be "good tele fare," but Zachary's shots were too far from the action and thus lost their effect.[60] She also directed "The Zebra Derby" that May. It was based on Max Schulman's best-selling novel that told of Asa Hearthrug coming home from war to face a changed world. "Adam and Eve," presented on 13 August 1946, was a comedy consisting of three brief sketches. In the first, a husband and wife are smoking in bed; in the second, they are arguing about placing a bet at a racetrack; and in the third, they are fixing a water pump and getting drenched.

By 1947 dramatic activity at WBKB had heightened substantially. Zachary directed a ninety-minute version of *The Importance of Being Earnest,* by Oscar Wilde. Poe's "The Tell-Tale Heart," DeMaupassant's "The Diamond Necklace," passages from Shakespeare's *Macbeth,* and Wilde's "Sir Arthur Sauile's Dilemma" were offered in thirty- to forty-minute adaptations bimonthly. These dramas were frequently adapted by Bill Vance and directed by Helen Carson. In alternate weeks, a series of case histories on the lives of juvenile delinquents entitled *Jailbait* was presented. Perhaps the most ambitious attempt at WBKB during these early years was a remote pickup of "Night Without End" from the Eighth Street Theatre. Although they attended stage rehearsals, producer/director Zachary and her crew were unable to rehearse for the two-camera event. According to *Television,* "It marked the first time in this country that such an experiment was attempted."[61]

5

The Curtain Rises

After a decade of engineering experiments, another ten years of programming demonstrations, and the interruption of World War II television drama was ready to expand its services to the public. By 1946 the call letters of the experimental stations had been changed: NBC's W2XBS was WNBT, CBS's W2XAB was WCBW, DuMont's W2XWV was WABD, in Los Angeles W6XAO changed to KTSL, W6XYZ became KTLA, and in Chicago W9XBK was now WBKB. Personnel that had gained experience over the previous years were hired for significant roles (see Appendix A), facilities were being expanded and improved, and the struggle for distribution through networking began after DuMont's (1946) New York City to Washington, D.C., cable hookup proved to be successful. American Telephone and Telegraph (AT&T) would not link the East and West coasts for five more years (1951), however, and major dramatic program origination would therefore remain confined to the New York area.

Numerous problems faced the television industry. Two of the more complex ones involved station allocations—a flood of requests were being made—and an acceptable color system because the RCA and CBS systems were incompatible. To grapple with these problems and others, the FCC imposed a moratorium, or freeze, on the industry:

> When the television Freeze began in September 1946 . . . , only 34 stations were telecasting from 21 cities to about one million sets. . . . The major manufacturers of television transmitters—RCA, GE, and Dumont—were running six months late when the Freeze began, and were hard pressed to meet demand when it ended. Pioneering would pay off handsomely. The 107 stations that got on the air before or during the Freeze became the major money earners of the industry for more than a decade afterwards.[1]

The freeze seemed to terminate adventurism into television drama by the feature-film industry, even though its profits had reached an all-time

high and, theoretically at least, provided the financial wherewithal to produce major dramas for video. Although no one knew when the freeze would end, either radio or film interests could have announced a major effort in the production of television dramas. The film industry, which was encountering troubles of its own, would let Justice Department litigation run its course; this resulted in the separation of filmmakers from the business side of television (1952), and major film producers did not become involved with it until this litigation was settled. In fact, several independent companies in Hollywood were working on short films, but the long prestige drama would be nurtured by radio. Radio had the formats, the advertisers, the facilities, the profits, the location, the experienced talent, and the personnel who were eager to produce live theatrical dramas for a larger audience than they had been able to reach during the experimental days.

Changing the Guard

Not surprisingly, the pioneers of the first two decades of television drama entered other phases of their careers. Many became free-lance producers, directors, and consultants—Thomas H. Hutchinson, Thomas Lyne Riley, Harvey Marlowe, Bob Emery, and Gilbert Seldes—and no longer influenced network or station decision-making in drama. For half a dozen years, Worthington Miner would be an exception at CBS. Miner and Fred Coe, a comparative newcomer at NBC, would make major contributions to television's live period. Several of those who gained experience by literally working upward from the studio floor became executives.

Continually keeping abreast of engineering improvements, on 1 March 1946 WNBT went off the air so that a new transmitter could be installed on top of the Empire State Building and the station could move to Channel 4. WNBT returned to the air with "Blythe Spirit," adapted and produced by Edward Sobol. By now he had earned and received nearly every recognition given in television drama. Reviewer Joe Koehler praised Sobol: "NBC is first in drama. That's not even open to question with Ed Sobol, rating every award that anybody could give out for producing straight legit entertainment from Broadway successes." Ernest Colling, the other senior producer/director at NBC, was especially good at handling performers, but his productions on the whole received mixed reviews. *The Billboard* claimed that "Ronald Oxford and Fred Coe aren't at their NBC best with story material and while Oxford has delivered acceptably on one or two assignments, he doesn't rate with his seniors, Colling and Sobol."[2]

The Boom in Radio and Television Advertising

During the Second World War, the government had imposed a heavy excess-profits tax on wartime industries to discourage profiteering on war contracts. Advertising was excluded from the excess-profits tax and was instead taxed at normal rates. Advertising, therefore, became a highly desirable bargain for prestige-conscious companies. Ordinarily, most advertising dollars would have gone to the print media, but the war curtailed paper products, newsprint, and supplies. As a result, advertisers turned to radio and gauged the potential of television. By the mid-1940s radio was absorbing nearly 40 percent of the national advertising dollars. Often, sponsors merely wanted to remind the public of products, such as automobiles, which were not yet on the market.

Thus, the radio business set a precedent for reaching vast numbers of consumers, who were forced to save their money during the war but would purchase new products, even expensive ones, as soon as they were available. Through their advertising agencies, wealthy sponsors sought to gain public attention by means of the visual influence of television. Manufacturers—especially television set suppliers and other companies offering a range of nationally sold products and services and who, in some cases, were experienced with television from the previous two decades—seized the leadership roles by offering the most prestigious, and in the thinking of many company executives, the most exciting programs available: the dramas.

NBC program manager Warren Wade announced plans in 1946 for a six-day weekly schedule (28 hours total), in which Sunday remained as the principal showcase for drama. NBC looked increasingly to cooperative agreements with production sources such as the Dramatists' Guild of the Authors' League of America, which had undertaken the working out of procedures to license plays to television, and the Theatre Guild—sponsored on radio by United States Steel—and to strong financial backing from sponsors and advertising agencies in dramatic program development.

One agency, J. Walter Thompson, took an interest in television as an advertising medium in the mid-thirties, when its representatives were invited to an experimental performance of W2XBS's "Romantic Interlude." Although they were already heavily committed to radio drama, they expanded their approach to television drama. Substantial experience was gained by the agency when it produced a series for a prominent food company. In the spring of 1946, Standard Brands (Lipton Tea and Chase and Sanborn Coffee) sponsored a $200,000 television variety series on WNBT, *Hour Glass*. It consisted of a fifteen-minute program on Sundays

and an hour on Thursdays. The Thursday presentation often included a sketch such as "Farewell Supper," by Arthur Schnitzler and Granville Barker; "The Jest of Hahalaba," by Lord Dunsany; "A Tooth for Paul Revere," by Stephen Vincent Benét; "Two Men on a Merry-go-round," by Arthur Purcell; "Jim Bramble and the Bank Robber," by Howard Rodman; and "Western Night," by Robert Finch and Betty Smith.

By January 1947 Sobol had introduced NBC's new image orthicon cameras in an audience-participation show for Borden called *Let's Celebrate*. The refined cameras moved even closer to the motion picture standard of quality expected of future television dramas. Frequently, the emphasis was on the integration of commercials and program content, a reminder of the 1936 efforts of Grace Bradt and Eddie Albert. For a short time, *Let's Celebrate* and *Hour Glass* ran concurrently on NBC. Then in March, after ten months on the air, *Hour Glass* was canceled because of the relatively limited audience, high cost, and belief that Standard Brands had gathered enough television experience for the present:

> J. Walter Thompson and Standard Brands have learned many things since they were on television, and this is best exemplified by the contrasts in first shows and the present shows. Lately there had been a change in backgrounds, with the locale now suggested by means of cartoons. This practice permits more money to be spent on talent which they feel is more important than background . . . it is foreground with personality, and talent is as important over television as it is in any other medium.[3]

Television's Theatrical Renaissance

Despite whatever reservations may have existed in regard to high costs or audience size, major companies, already sponsoring radio drama, would move into television. Drama in that medium, especially in a weekly or monthly anthology series, began to flourish. The notion that these presentations would appeal to the upper-income, well-educated populace still prevailed, as it had since the mid-1930s, and lent impetus to sponsorship of dramas by manufacturers of television sets; automobiles; and processed food products, including connoisseur items like MacLaren's Imperial Cheese. Such thinking was prevalent among those who worked in the television industry and lived in the New York City area. A rigid theater-oriented mentality was characteristic of television decision-makers. The big-city, East Coast television viewership made it possible for dramas to play to relatively modest-sized audiences that understood

and supported live theater rather than the enormously diverse "mass" public, which was more interested in fast action, spectacle, and escapist entertainment.

For the next twelve years, a resurgence of live Broadway theater appeared on television in what Miner called "a theatrical renaissance," similar to the one on Broadway that had followed the First World War. The initial four anthology television dramas embodied the characteristics of the live dramatic anthologies that were to follow: *Kraft Television Theater* and *Philco Television Playhouse* at NBC and *Ford Television Theater* and *Studio One* at CBS. Their origins illustrate the culmination of progress that had been made in television drama during the experimental years.

KRAFT TELEVISION THEATER

After completing *Hour Glass* for Standard Brands, the J. Walter Thompson agency turned its attention to the coordination of advertising for the Kraft Food Company and to the production of the first long dramatic anthology on television. Kraft, which had sponsored the *Kraft Music Hall* on radio since 1934, held an option on the 9:00 to 10:00 P.M. time period on Thursdays, the same night as the Standard Brands variety show. Within two months after Standard Brands dropped its series, Kraft inaugurated the *Kraft Television Theater,* on 7 May 1947.

The premiere drama, "Double Door," as might be expected, had already been produced on WNBT seven years earlier. In this 1947 production, Eleanor Wilson played Victoria, the nervous, domineering head of the Van Brett household who is transformed into a "gibbering idiot at the fade out." John Baragrey and Romola Rob seemed "ill at ease" as the romantic leads. John Stephen was the doctor; Joseph Boley, the family's lawyer; and Valerie Cossart, the spinster sister.

The Thompson agency, in the person of Stanley Quinn, handled the program. He was producer/director and Al Protzman served as his all-important technical director in the system established at NBC. One review said the play suffered from "lack of direction—parts being high-schoolish." Too many slow fade-outs were used when fast fades were indicated, and the actors seemed to move from director manipulation rather than from motivation.[4] The script was adapted by Edmond Rice, who also wrote 90- and 120-second commercials for MacLaren's Imperial Cheese that were shown between the second and third acts. Because Kraft presented a long-standing radio show on Thursdays, it avoided competing with its own program by moving the television series to Wednesday nights.

But *Variety* criticized the first performance:

The new series of Kraft-sponsored one-hour dramas got off to a faulty start over WNBT Wednesday (7) night through the unfortunate selection of a dull, overly done, melodrama that has lost whatever merit it might once have possessed through the passage of time. "Double Door," scripted by Elizabeth McFadden, enjoyed a long run on Broadway in 1933 and was filmed the following year by Paramount but, for video purposes, it was too heavy, slow-paced and outdated.[5]

Despite Kraft's effort to present relatively low-budget dramas at about $4,000 a week, the anthology attracted several major writers (Frank D. Gilroy, Rod Serling, Robert Howard Lindsey), directors (George Roy Hill, Fielder Cook), and actors over its twelve-year history.

PHILCO TELEVISION PLAYHOUSE

That same year, 1947, Owen Davis, Jr., was named as director of program preparation and procurement for NBC, in which capacity he supervised all casting, writing, and obtaining of scripts for dramatic programs. He was soon made executive producer, reporting directly to the head of television programming. Davis, Jr., had already established a fine reputation as a film actor—his last film was *Knute Rockne, All-American* (1940)—and his most recent Broadway appearance had been in *Mr. and Mrs. North*. He came from a brilliant show-business family, which included his Pulitzer-prize-winning father and his brother Donald, who was World Video's producer for *Actor's Studio*, now on ABC-TV. Owen Davis, Jr., determined what properties were suitable for television and who would star in them. Once these decisions were made, he turned the scripts over to Sobol or Coe for production. Within a week of being one of five to receive long-term contracts at NBC—so that he would not be lured to CBS in a raid—he fell from a sloop on 21 May 1949 while sailing on Long Island Sound and drowned. He was only forty-two years of age.

Unfortunately, Davis's death left only Sobol, then fifty-eight, in the later years of his distinguished career as a television pioneer, and Coe, an extremely talented and likable person, clearly on the rise, as the principal figures in drama at NBC. Coe had been Sobol's heir apparent for about two years. On the same page that the *Televiser* was less than enthusiastic about the *Kraft Television Theater* debut, it heralded Coe's production of Shakespeare's "Twelfth Night," presented ten days before (27 April 1947) for Borden and the Kenyon and Eckhardt agency. It was a note of

déjà vu for Coe, who had directed it on stage at the Nashville Community Playhouse in the summer seven years earlier.

Coe would create and produce the highly acclaimed *Philco Television Playhouse,* which made its debut on 3 October 1948. He cleverly introduced the anthology with a fine comedy by none other than George S. Kaufman and Edna Ferber, "Dinner at Eight." Coe, affectionately referred to as "Pappy" and who referred to those working with him in the same way, over the next three decades would "school" a long list of artists: writers David Shaw, Horton Foote, Paddy Chayefsky, Tad Mosel, J. P. Miller, and James Costigan; directors Delbert Mann, John Frankenheimer, Fielder Cook, Robert Mulligan, Arthur Penn, Albert McCleery, Jack Smight, and William Corrigan; and several actors.

Fittingly, at the time of his death in 1979, Coe was completing a television version of his highly successful stage production, *The Miracle Worker* (Belasco Playhouse, 1959). And, as a kind of 1981 tribute to him, Tad Mosel's "All the Way Home," the Pulitzer-prize and New York Drama Critic's Circle award-winning production that he had produced on Broadway, was telecast nationally as a live stage play and directed by his colleague and friend Delbert Mann.

FORD TELEVISION THEATER

Personnel changes in 1947 at CBS were even more sweeping than at NBC. They had begun two years earlier, when William S. Paley returned from Europe. He expected to make Paul Kesten president, sharing responsibility by being in charge of daily operation, but he learned that Kesten's severe arthritis would prevent him from accepting the position. About a year later, Paley accepted the resignation of the ailing Kesten and recommended Frank Stanton, whom Kesten had hired years earlier and groomed for the position, to the board of directors for the presidency.

As yet, the U.S. government had not made a decision about a suitable color system or new station allocations. CBS announced, in part for economic reasons, that it was abandoning its live programming for an indefinite period and that it would also curtail its color television research. Beginning on 11 May 1947, it would telecast films and remote pickups only.[6] Fifty-five staff members were dropped from the payroll, including Ben Feiner, Jr., program director, Paul Belanger, director, and Jim McNaughton, the principal set designer. The day this announcement was published in *Variety,* the competition, NBC, inaugurated the *Kraft Television Theater.*

Within several months, CBS changed its program offerings once again.

This time the result was an enormously successful variety show, *Toast of the Town,* starring Ed Sullivan, and two dramatic anthologies, *Ford Television Theater* and *Studio One,* both radio adaptations.

The *Ford Television Theater* was presented before *Studio One* and was for a while the most expensive drama on television, costing $17,500 per program. The Ford Motor Company and its agency, Kenyon and Eckhardt, were familiar with television drama through the agency's program series for the Borden Company, including the memorable production of "Twelfth Night." *Ford Theater* began as a radio series on NBC. In its second season—the fall of 1948—it found a new home on CBS radio. Meanwhile, Ford had sought to present a prestigious dramatic series on television that would embody the values of quality, sophistication, and "class" it felt its products symbolized. The result was the simultaneous broadcasting of one set of dramas called *Ford Theater* for radio and a different lineup for *Ford Television Theater.*

The initial production of the monthly *Ford Television Theater* was "Years Ago," by Ruth Gordon. Winston O'Keefe was the producer and Marc Daniels the director. *Variety* was critical: "That the initial Ford presentation failed to generate the same viewer excitement as did, for example, the Philco show a few weeks back, can be attributed largely to the play chosen for the kickoff and to the casting of the principal leads, Raymond Massey and Eva LeGallienne."[7] "Years Ago" is a biography based on the life of Ruth Gordon, a well-known actress. It had not been a strong play on Broadway. It required much warmth from the mother and father, which in the opinion of one reviewer it did not receive. Patricia Kirkland, who played the original role on stage, was "outstanding as the girl." The *Ford Television Theater* began on 17 October 1948.

Experienced in theater and just recently discharged from the military service, Daniels was teaching at the Academy of Dramatic Art and was enrolled in Harvey Marlowe's television classes, which Marlowe, now a producer/consultant, conducted in a small studio in Jamaica, Long Island. Daniels recalled the rigors of his appointment as director of the *Ford Television Theater* with some amusement:

> I was directing a popular comedy in summer stock, and among the people who saw it was a man from Kenyon and Eckhardt, Ford's advertising agency. He was impressed with it, and they were then planning to do the first *Ford Theater* in the fall of 1948. They called me in and asked if I had any television experience, and I was able to quote my experience in Jamaica, New York, with this experimental station, and they allowed as how that was more than a lot of other

people had at that point, I got the job of doing the *Ford Theater,* directing the *Ford Theater* for its first season on the air, which was one play a month, one hour show a month.

It was, of course, new to everybody. I remember that the head of the radio and television department of the agency came to see a run-through in a rehearsal hall and wanted to know where the control room was. I had to explain that we didn't have any of that here—he was used to radio—that he'd have to wait until we got into the studio. Then he could see it. We did the show at CBS in the top of Grand Central Station in Studio 41, which was being built when we did our first show. I mean there were only two walls. They were building the rest of it. So, it was rather chaotic. The control booth was a plywood box with field equipment, where the screens were about four by six inches or something. I used four cameras, because you couldn't stop. You needed to have an additional camera in order to keep one scene going while you went to another.[8]

By 1950 *Ford Television Theater* had received its share of accolades for dramatic achievement. Productions required two weeks of dry-run rehearsals, two days of camera rehearsals, and more than $20,000 per program to reach an estimated audience of 2,250,000 persons in twelve cities. By the fall of 1952, *Ford Television Theater* had abandoned its hour-long, live format and premiered a half-hour filmed drama produced by Screen Gems. *Newsweek* described the initial program as a milestone in television history: "It marked the first entrance of a big movie company (Columbia) into video film production."[9] By 1955 *Ford Television Theater* ranked fifth among the top ten shows and first among dramatic anthologies. In the midst of live television's heyday, the siren call of Hollywood could be clearly heard in videoland.

Studio One

As the first echelon of key pioneers in television drama departed, their successors were already in the New York area working and studying in various capacities. When Gilbert Seldes ended his eight-year tenure at CBS, the principal television responsibilities shifted to Worthington Miner, a devotee of drama. At long last, after waiting nearly a decade himself, the CBS Grand Central studio facility was almost complete and Miner could now exercise control. Ironically, when he assumed leadership of WCBW television production, he withdrew from directing himself and, as a result, scheduled few dramas during 1946.

The industry struggle over whether CBS or RCA possessed the superior

color system influenced Miner's new role as head of CBS production. Based on his knowledge about color television technology, he presented the views of CBS to the public, with the approval of Paul Kesten. At an important meeting of industry engineers, Miner suggested that all television move to UHF, where the band width was sufficient to accommodate all black and white and color systems. This proposal so infuriated Kesten, whose main interest was promoting radio, that Miner was given "a meaningless title of Director of Program Development," his responsibilities were assumed by others, and he was temporarily forgotten.[10]

Months later, when NBC was presenting an hour-long prestige drama, *Kraft Television Theater,* and more were on the way, William S. Paley asked Miner to establish a dramatic series along the lines of CBS's *Columbia Workshop,* a highly respected radio program. Paley believed that CBS had pioneered quality drama on radio and should do the same on television. An ambitious CBS radio series called *Studio One* had received a George Foster Peabody award in drama in 1947. Paley and Miner agreed that this was a likely television conversion. Miner said he would develop the series provided that he retained control over program content, thereby prohibiting other CBS executives from interfering with his judgment. Paley concurred; an administrative liaison was appointed to solve the few problems that arose.

Studio One made its debut on 7 November 1948 with Margaret Sullavan in "The Storm." The Miners knew Sullavan and Leland Hayward, her husband, a theatrical producer. Living nearby at the Dakota, they used to roller skate in Central Park. Sullavan's London opening in John Van Druten's *The Voice of the Turtle* was critically blasted, and so Miner's offer to star in the *Studio One* premiere was welcomed. A major problem came up during rehearsal. For the last scenes, Sullavan had to react to a prerecorded voice-over-picture sequence. She started the scene and then fell apart emotionally. Miner confirmed that she was going deaf and increased the volume of the tape recorder to her audible level.[11]

Miner was shrewd and conservative in his play selection. Nearly a fourth of the first year's productions were adaptations of plays that had been produced years before during the experimental period at NBC—from "Blind Alley," originally produced on 21 November 1941, to "Julius Caesar" in modern dress, originally aired on 15 March 1940, to "Jane Eyre," telecast on 12 October 1939. Even "Little Women," an NBC Christmas choice back in 1939 and again in 1945, was shown over two nights on *Studio One* in December 1950. Miner's mock television experiments of 1939–40 were paying dividends at long last. From the outset, he realized he needed someone to help him during the telecast. He therefore created the position of assistant director and hired Lela Swift in that

capacity. Talented, hardworking, and capable, she began her career writing radio scripts and came to television in the mid-1940s, learning everything about the business. By 1950 she directed the two-part adaptation of "Little Women."

Studio One was mentioned in *The Saturday Review of Literature* as "the first experimental TV-dramatic show."[12] Among the most successful early productions were "Battleship Bismarck," on 24 October 1949, because of its technical accomplishment, and "Julius Caesar," on 6 March 1949. Jack Gould, television critic for *The New York Times,* wrote: "Its presentation of 'Julius Caesar' in modern dress was one of the most stimulating and exciting theatrical experiences of the year, regardless of media, and the first work worthy of a place in television's permanent repertoire."[13]

During all these years of administering, producing, and directing, Miner's salary never topped $500 a week. When he asked CBS for $750 and the network refused, he turned to NBC. At the time of his departure from CBS in 1952, *Studio One* had won more awards than any other dramatic series to date.

Miner influenced the careers of several young directors and writers. *Studio One* depended on adaptations by Joseph Liss, Fielder Cook, David Shaw, and Miner himself during the early years. Significantly, the first four directors of *Studio One* joined CBS television during 1948. George Zachary had begun in 1936 as a writer for *Ellery Queen,* among other radio series. He wrote, produced, and directed the first year of *Ford Theater* on radio. His *Studio One* debut was "The Glass Key," by Dashiell Hammett.

The following week, J. Paul Nickell, who had come to the television program staff as a director in the winter of 1948, directed "Shadow and Substance," by Paul Vincent Carroll, as his initial assignment. Nickell had formerly been a director at WPTZ, where he supervised some of the few dramas the station aired. John Peyser, who would replace Zachary on *Studio One* by 1950, had joined CBS-TV as an associate director on 3 April 1948. After college, he had gone into radio (1938) and then served with the U.S. government in the Office of War Information during the years 1942–45. Franklin Schaffner came to CBS as a staff director in 1948. For nearly a year and a half, he directed news and special events before becoming involved with *Studio One.*

Miner's supervision also enhanced the careers of numerous actors and actresses, such as Anne Bancroft, Grace Kelly, Don Murray, John Cassavetes, Yul Brynner, Maria Riva, Felicia Montealegre, and Charlton Heston. "Do not become overexposed early in your career" was one piece of advice Miner gave to young Heston, who first appeared as an

extra in *Studio One's* "Julius Caesar" (1949). Looking toward Hollywood and his eventual place among movie superstars, Heston signed a seven-year contract with Hal Wallis that allowed him to return to perform on television. Years later, Heston referred to Miner and the live anthology period as a day gone by, "the like of which we'll never see again." And Miner never did. Unfortunately, he related in retrospect: "I never had one rewarding, truly happy day at NBC. The shadow of the General was crass and joyless; the shadow of Bill Paley was sprinkled with sparks."[14] Miner was replaced at CBS by Donald Davis, whose background in theater and television at NBC paralleled his own.

As the curtain rose week after week on the *Kraft Television Theater, Philco Television Playhouse, Ford Television Theater, Studio One,* and numerous other dramatic anthologies, the efforts of the experimental years during the previous two decades came to fruition in an amazing array of impressive dramas, many of which were original teleplays as well as adaptations. But this phenomenon was passé before it began—live, black and white television dramas presented only once to small, dominantly East Coast audiences—and its existence would be short.

While the pioneers fostered theater on television, most of the public sought something else; and the artists—directors, producers, performers—were attuned to broader individual expression and sought less constraints than television imposed. Many of them found fame and fortune in the movies, and others were later to fight broadcasting restrictions. Because of the emergence of videotape in the mid-1950s as well as the constant assessment of what the mass of the public would watch, determined by rating systems and increasing production costs, the dramatic *series,* featuring the same strong characters living fast-action lives in romantic locations, swept away the theatrically oriented anthologies and brought a new era to television drama.

Television drama before World War II was comparable to New York's off-Broadway or London's fringe theater. After the war, television drama gradually moved toward standards similar to those of Broadway. But the productions were still theater on television, despite the resurgence of energy displayed on television in the so-called "Golden Era." The postwar period to 1958 was, in fact, merely an extension of and elaboration upon the experimental years. Television drama would not break from its theater roots until the impact of the mass public, financial stringencies, advertising, relocation in Hollywood, and emerging electronic technology was felt and a new generation of television executives and artistic leaders assumed strategic roles in the industry.

Summary and Conclusions

Benchmarks for the first two decades of American television drama began with "The Queen's Messenger," presented by General Electric in 1928, and ended with the debut of the *Kraft Television Theater*, the first sustained dramatic anthology, in 1947. Two principal trends occurred during the period: first, an improving technical capability for distributing sound and picture to a limited, mostly urban, public; and, second, a programming concept theorizing that the viewing public would be an affluent group, composed of those who appreciated theater, were well read, and supported the fine arts. Certainly those people invited by station executives to watch early demonstrations in the mid-1930s were from leadership areas of government, advertising, engineering, business, education, and the arts.

Up until the spring of 1939, a limited audience of less than 100,000 people saw television programming in the United States, primarily in New York, along the East Coast, and in Chicago and Los Angeles. In England, primarily in London, a similar number viewed programs on 23,000 receivers. The general public saw few demonstrations of any kind in the United States until NBC initiated public programming at the New York World's Fair that year, even though the press kept alive the notion that television would soon be in the home.

The main concern during the first six years was the substantial problem of converting from mechanical to electronic television. This much-debated conversion was slow, frustrating, and discouraging for administrators, engineers, programmers, and the public. Charles F. Jenkins, E. F. W. Alexanderson, John L. Baird, and many other inventors made significant individual contributions to the technology, but the collective strength and patience of American business at General Electric, Westinghouse, and, most of all, the Radio Corporation of America were required to conduct the many experiments that perfected stable and recognizable television images. While Vladimir Zworykin was encouraged and supported by David Sarnoff, the "televiser," as it was called in those days, improved to the point some people believed this new medium eventually would replace the movie house, the established place for displaying feature films. While the motion picture industry was at the same time boasting superior picture quality and a sound system, admittedly favoring high frequencies but quickly being refined, film executives capitalized on their advantages to build an empire rich in wealth and strong in social impact.

Another advantage enjoyed by the film industry was two decades of experience in production—bracketing the turn of the century. Several silent films were receiving major public approval artistically, thematically, and technically. These achievements emerged from highly sophisticated and fully equipped production studios as well as the efforts of a substantial cadre of trained artists and craftsmen. The motion picture industry was so proud of its accomplishments that it shrewdly initiated a brilliant form of self-promotion and recognition through the Academy of Motion Picture Arts and Sciences by awarding the Oscars. The film industry's disadvantage was the guesswork required to divine whether or not a motion picture would appeal to the public sufficiently to make money.

In 1939 the film industry could have taken over television drama by releasing motion pictures in quantity to the new medium, which would have discouraged live production. A tendency prevailed to show feature films on television, especially in England. However, the war, U.S. government litigation against the film industry as a monopoly, and industry reluctance to encourage the growth of another new mass medium in addition to film and radio delayed the film takeover of television drama for more than two decades, when made-for-television movies became popular.

By contrast, radio, a relatively inexpensive advertising medium, had quickly amassed during the 1930s an enormous public by programming dramatic anthologies, series, serials, and specials. These programs furnished advertisers with great wealth and provided the administrative effectiveness that enabled television to coexist with radio for awhile. It could thereby absorb those aspects of radio that would enable it to take on a character of its own and, as soon as technology permitted, become a major American *business* rather than a major American *art form*, as many motion picture enthusiasts claim to this day.

While television executives were preoccupied with technical and marketing concerns, the American television drama developed simply as one of many formats in the variety programming schedule of experiments in studios and at remote locations. Drama was not favored over sports, music, talk, or other programs. In fact, during this period, drama was at the bottom of CBS priorities. Even at NBC, it was given a minimal place in experiments until 1936, which consisted largely of makeup and lighting demonstrations. For five years thereafter, NBC telecast modest productions to illustrate feasibility, especially at low cost; as a programming enticement for viewers; and, consequently, as a sales medium for sponsors.

Despite numerous experiments with little or no scenery, paper scenery, reduced actor fees, and adaptations of materials no longer in copyright,

television drama always proved to be expensive compared with many other kinds of programming. To telecast dramas, station executive and sponsor commitment had to exceed monetary considerations. In the United States, NBC-New York was the center of dramatic activity. Efforts in Schenectady, Philadelphia, Chicago, and Los Angeles were minimal largely because these stations did not achieve sufficient technical quality until the 1940s. Only the BBC, in London, rivaled, and even surpassed, NBC's dramatic output in quantity and quality before 1940.

Until sharp, clear, stable video and sound quality was assured, television drama was continuously haunted by the superior image produced by motion pictures. An ominous foreboding in these early years was that television drama would never really compete successfully with feature films. To enable engineers to schedule one or two sketches or dramas a week at NBC, the production facilities that were familiar in Hollywood needed to be developed. Located in New York, NBC turned to theater space—at the New Amsterdam—and radio space within Rockefeller Center. The outside supporting groups and individuals, largely from theater, branched into the new medium.

Theater is infectious, and its artists and craftsmen possess the genius to take very little and maximize it. Whether it is studio space, lighting, scenery, or properties, they have a penchant for collecting, improvising, displaying, and thereby magnifying an illusion. These attributes, central to their creative thrust, were brought to television drama through the talents of the production heads, producer/directors, writers, performers, and other staff people, most of whom were identified with the theater. Many performers came from radio, too, and participated in television mainly because it was in the same building. Frequently, casting was expedient. The variety of capable actors already at the radio stations and working in local theater was plentiful, though many of them showed little aptitude for television acting.

For theater talents, money was not a big problem. Little of it was available, but they were used to that. Once a production department was established at NBC, CBS, BBC, General Electric, or elsewhere, television dramas were staged virtually with only pocket money. At most U.S. stations, even NBC, a few hundred dollars was a big budget. In England, the budgets were more generous, and some dramas were costing a few thousand pounds by 1938. Paper, paint, and clever, simple designs— usually for one or two interior settings—were all part of the illusion that Broadway talent created night after night. Television drama in the 1930s was somewhat equivalent to off-Broadway or London fringe theater, where bare necessities are sufficient even today. Then, too, production people as a group tend to become absorbed in what they conceive to be

the importance of their work, a main driving force toward excellence that often overcomes ordinary obstacles. Staging feats for such productions as "The Farmer Takes a Wife," "Julius Caesar," and, after the war, "The Battleship Bismarck," would seem incredible even to their directors and participants in retrospect.

The production department at NBC was supervised by John F. Royal, a vice-president from the early thirties until his retirement in 1951; and a combination of Gilbert Seldes and Worthington Miner administered the dramatic work at CBS until Miner left in 1952, about six years after Seldes. During this period, theatrically oriented dramas prevailed. Royal, whose background was in radio, left much of the decision-making to Max Gordon, a theatrical producer, and his producer/director colleagues: Edward Sobol, Thomas Lyne Riley, Warren Wade, and others. Although supervising the entire production operation, Seldes at CBS demonstrated less personal interest in stage fiction than in dramatic situations arising from real life. He and Miner, a theater and film producer/director, were an effective combination, though they were hampered by the lack of administrative support for drama until near the end of World War II. Before then, they mostly experimented in theory. CBS had constructed a major studio in the Grand Central Terminal Building by the mid-forties, but was forced to depend on its rival in programming, RCA/NBC, for technical leadership.

Early prognosticators were right in many ways. A limited audience, enchanted by novelty and New York theater, did want to see television drama, and this public of urban sophisticates created a viewership for adapting available theater to television right after the war. The dramatic stage—both comedy and serious drama—was telecast during the experimental years. Appearing regularly were television *specials,* single dramas complete within a single production, among them "Susan and God" (W2XBS, 1938) and "When We Are Married" (W2XBS, 1940); *anthologies,* collections of unrelated stories, such as *"The Television Ghost"* (W2XAB, 1931) or plays, such as the *NBC Television Theatre* (WNBT, 1946); *series,* such as *Casey, Crime Photographer* (WCBW, 1945), an anthology of unrelated stories in which the same principal characters figured regularly; *miniseries,* which told the same story over several nights, including the telecast of the novel *The Black Angel* (WNBT, 1945); and *serials,* the incomplete dramatization of the lives of continuing characters, featuring television's first soap operas, *Vine Street* (W6XAO, 1939) and *Faraway Hill* (WABD, 1946). As yet, serious drama and comedy were not categorized into, say, "westerns" or "medical" series, primarily because not enough of them—about three each—had been produced. "Crime" was the most consistently recognizable catego-

ry. The first one was the near-crime "The Queen's Messenger" (WGY, 1928), and later the more typical dastardly deeds in "The Three Garridebs" and "The Mysterious Mummy Case" (both W2XBS, 1938).

Following the rigid dictates of the radio business rather than the financial roller-coaster ride of the film art, nearly every drama, unsurprisingly, was a specific experiment or feasibility study in itself: to experiment with makeup and lighting ("Television Inaugural Broadcast," W2XAB, 1931); to try a new format ("Their Television Honeymoon," musical comedy, W9XAO/WIBO, 1931, or "House of Connelly," theater projection, Broadway Theatre, 1931); to present a Broadway play ("House Beautiful," GE, 1931); to impress user groups ("A Balanced Meal," for General Foods, W2XBS, 1936); to integrate film and live segments ("The Three Garridebs," W2XBS, 1938); to feature a star ("Susan and God," W2XBS, 1938); to initiate artists' contracts ("Speaking To Father," W2XBS, 1938); to promote a program contributor ("Dark Eyes Mean Danger," W2XBS, 1939); to try an adaptation from another medium ("On a Note of Triumph," from radio, WCBW, 1945); to sell a product ("Big Sister," for Rinso, WCBW, 1945); and, rarely, to present an "original" television play that was seldom written for television and almost never took the audience into consideration, such as by surveying material it might prefer.

No one seemed to be opposed to original material; a few far-sighted individuals even advocated it. The theatrically literate wanted to try stage plays on television because they were readily available, existed in sufficient quantity, had established audience appeal (on stage), and were comfortable to produce. On those rare occasions when an original play was attempted, it was often unbelievably bad ("Experience," WABD, 1946). Consequently, original television drama did not rise to any importance during the experimental years in the United States or England. If anything, it frequently discouraged other attempts. Yet, stage plays that were adapted for the prestigious anthologies after the Second World War illustrated within half a dozen years that theater on television, unless brilliantly adapted, was dreadfully dull, and certainly no more successful than theater adapted for movies. In any case, theater is not drama for the masses, as a rule; it is drama for a limited appreciative public. In recent years, it has been relegated to public broadcasting.

The brief period of successful original drama finally arrived in the early 1950s. By then, however, this type of drama—which resembled theater in style and was often personally introspective in content—was part of a larger transition that occurred apart from the theater, away from New York, and was based on the preference of a *limited* public for broader, more exciting themes treated in film, in Hollywood, and on marketing

concepts derived from surveying the views of the *mass* public. This was no "Golden Age" for television drama. Some sensitive and lovely original dramas were written in the early 1950s, but they were experiments conducted during the latter years of live drama and, like most experiments, they did not really work, and have not, with few exceptions, enjoyed longevity.

Fast-moving technology in production would soon give television the flexibility that film already enjoyed, and for the most part the public would ignore the television screen size—still the biggest deterrent to dramas of scope. The young replacements of television drama pioneers were less allied to theater and in a better position to think in transitional live-theater-to-film terms, while using the fast production techniques of television and the infusion of Madison Avenue marketing values that favored providing the kind of dramas that, according to audience research, the public desired. The newcomers who were attuned to the demands of the mass public went on to become important figures in both television and film drama.

Power, fame, wealth, sex, youth, adventure, and, to an extent, immortality were among the themes anthropomorphic heroes and heroines would struggle for, often violently, in future specials, anthologies, series, and serials. The introspective self-concerns that had been probed briefly in original dramas of the 1950s and the two decades of earlier experimental dramas staged largely in theatrical settings appeared, as the Age of Aquarius approached, to be pale and passé.

APPENDIXES

Appendix A

Production Personnel at Commercial Television Companies in 1946*

American Broadcasting Company
Television Department
(temporarily used WABD and WRGB facilities)
33 W. 42d St.
New York, New York
    Manager: Paul B. Mowrey
    Manager of Operations: Richard B. Rawls
    Executive Producer: Harvey Marlowe
    Director: Barbara Henry
    Lighting Consultant: Cheney Johnston
    Writer: Charles Speer
    Writer/Director: Richard Goggin
    Press: Bert Schwartz
    Salesmen: Jack Brook, Ken Farnsworth

KTLA-Television Productions, Inc.
Paramount Studio Lot: 5451 Marathon St.
Hollywood, California
    President: Paul Raibourn
    West Coast Director/Station Manager: Klaus Landsberg
    Sales Manager/Chief Announcer: Keith Hetherington
    Musical Director: Rex Kepple
    Engineering Supervisor: Raymond M. Moore

KTSL-Don Lee Broadcasting System
5515 Melrose Ave.; 3800 Mount Lee Drive
Los Angeles, California
    President: Thomas S. Lee
    Executive Vice-President and General Manager: Lewis Allen Weiss
    Executive Vice-President and Assistant General Manager: Willet
       H. Brown
    Director of Television: Harry B. Lubcke

*Principal sources: *Televiser,* May–June 1946; *1947 Radio Annual.*

Program Director: Jack Stewart
Production Manager: Ed Kemble
Publicity Relations Director: Mark Finley
Chief Announcer: Herb Twiss
Stage Director: Ted Driscoll
Chief Engineer: Harold Jury
Record MC: John Courcier
Film Director: Marjorie Campbell

WABD-Allen B. DuMont Laboratories, Inc.
515 Madison Ave.; John Wanamaker Studios, 9th St. and Broadway
New York, New York
President: Dr. Allen B. DuMont
General Manager of Television Division: Ernest A. Mark
Station Manager: Samuel H. Cuff
Director of Television Operations: Louis A. Sposa
Manager of Station Program Department: Bob Emery
Assistant: Richard Lockard
Program Coordinator: Edwin Woodruff
Art Director: Robert Bright
Scenic Artists: William Finley, Rudolph Lucek
Production Assistant: John B. Murphy
Studio Manager: Frank Bunetta
Studio Assistants: Florence Monroe, Irene Petroff, Barry Shear, Ina
    May Tomadelli, Eulia Turner
Chief Announcer: Dennis James
Publicity Director: John McKay
Guest Relations: Lari Wolfe
Chief Engineer: Dr. T. T. Goldsmith, Jr.

WBKB-Balaban & Katz Corp.
190 North State St.
Chicago, Illinois
Director of Television: William C. Eddy
Promotion Manager: Reginald Werrenrath
Purchasing Agent: George W. Thomas
Program Manager: A. Warren Jones
Production Manager: Lewis D. Gomavitz
Operations: David M. Crandell
Directors: Pauline Bobrov, Helen Carson, Lorraine Larson, Gladys
    Lundberg, Loretto Pagels, Beulah Zachary
Chief Announcer: Jack Gibney
Musical Director: Jeanette Levin

Personnel: Margaret Durnal
Chief Engineer: A. H. Brolly

WCBW-Columbia Broadcasting System
15 Vanderbilt Ave.
New York, New York
  President: William S. Paley
  Vice-President in Charge of Television: Lawrence W. Lowman
  Director of Television: Worthington C. Miner
  Director of Plans Division: Leonard Hole
  Commercial Manager: George L. Moskovics
  Acting Director of Television Programs: Benjamin F. Feiner, Jr.
  Director of Operations: Merritt H. Coleman
  Manager of Technical Operations: Paul Wittlig
  Manager of Production: Charles Holden
  Directors: Paul Belanger, Bob Bendick, Frances Buss, Leo
    Horwitz, Cledge Roberts
  Assistant Directors: Jerry Faust, Lucille Hudiburg, Fred Rickey
  Script Editor: Lela Swift
  Film Editor and Cutter: Rudy Bretz
  Film Assistants: John Sewall, Mortina Wilbur
  Art Director: James McNaughton
  Artists: Tom Naegele, George Olden
  Painter: Lester Vermilyea
  Assistant Casting Director: Florence Green
  News Director: Leo Hurwitz
  News Editor: Henry Cassirer
  Animation: Chester Berger, Dorothya Claras
  Manager of Press Information: James J. Kane
  Director of Sports: Robert R. Edge

WNBT-National Broadcasting Company
30 Rockefeller Plaza
New York, New York
  President: Neil Trammell
  Vice-President in Charge of Television: John F. Royal
  Vice-President and Chief Engineer: O. B. Hanson
  Manager of Television Department: Noran E. Kersta
  Executive Producer: Warren Wade
  Directors: Paul Alley, Peter Barker, Fred Coe, Ernest Colling,
    Burke Crotty, Herbert Graf, Edward Sobol, Ronald Oxford
  Program Assistants: Howard Cordery, Beulah Jarvis, Garry
    Simpson, Ira Skutch

Director of Special Features: J. Harrison Hartley
Manager, Program Production Facilities: N. Ray Kelly
Staging Coordinator: Robert Brunton
Art Director: Robert Wade
Assistant Art Director: Elwell
Titleist: Jack Rose
Makeup: Richard Smith
Director of Scripts and Library Rights: Owen Davis, Jr.
Assistant Director of Scripts: Stockton Helffrich
Manager, Television Promotion: Charlotte F. Stern
Manager, Press Department: Sydney H. Elges
Television Press Editor: Allan H. Kalmus
Eastern Sales Manager: Reynold R. Kraft

WOR-Bamberger Broadcasting Service
(temporarily used WRGB facilities. Its radio staff participated in
    television production.)
1440 Broadway
New York, New York
    President: T. C. Streibert
    Vice-President and Chief Engineer: J. R. Poppele
    Program Director: Norman S. Livingston
    Directors: Roger Bower, Ed Brainard, Dave Driscoll, Dan
        Ehrenreich, Gene King, Jock MacGregor, Tom Moore, Keith
        Thompson
    Production Supervisor: Bob Emery
    Assistant Chief Engineer: Charles Singer
    Acoustical Engineer: Edward J. Content
    Television Engineer: Joseph Waldschmidt

WPTZ-Philco Television Broadcasting Corp.
1800 Architects Bldg., 17th and Sampson Sts.
Philadelphia, Pennsylvania
    Vice-President and General Manager: E. B. Loveman
    Business Manager: Rolland V. Tooke
    Program Director: Ernest Walling
    Film: Al Mann
    Art Director: William Craig Smith
    Assistant Artist: Howard Fisher
    Chief Engineer: Raymond J. Bowley

WRGB-General Electric Company
60 Washington Ave.
Schenectady, New York
    Vice-President and Manager of Broadcasting: R. S. Peare

Assistant Manager of Broadcasting: B. J. Rowan
Station Manager: G. E. Markham
Assistant to the Station Manager: R.W. Welpott
Supervisor of Production: Helen T. Rhodes
Production Staff: Larry R. Algeo, C. Jones, Edith W. Kelly, John
    Seagle, M. H. Spinelli, Robert B. Stone
Script Editor: Ted Beebe
Art Staff: J. D. Fisk, Charles B. McGarrahan
Floor Services: E. A. Dawes, O. P. Kidder, C. P. King
Supervisor of Station Sales and Promotion: A. G. McDonald
Supervisor of Music: A. O. Coggeshall
Supervisor of News: W. T. Meenam
Engineer: W. J. Purcell

Appendix B

BBC Television Dramas Relevant to American Television, 1936–1946*

1930 (benchmark date)

14 July 1930   "The Man with the Flower in His Mouth," by Luigi Pirandello. Producer: Lance Sieveking. Settings: C. R. W. Nevinson. Cast: Gladys Young, Lionel Millard, Earle Gray. Running time: thirty minutes. First BBC television drama.

1936–1946

BBC Television Service, Alexandra Palace, London

26 August 1936
4:39:58p   Direct on-air sound and visual tuning signals.
"Cover to Cover," a Paul Rotha documentary film. Director: Alexander Shaw. Distributor: Associated British Film Distributors.

5:31:23p   Helen McKay sings live.
"As You Like It," film excerpt. Director: Paul C. Zinner. Cast: Elizabeth Bergner, Laurence Olivier, Distributor: 20th Century Fox Films Distributors.

Other film excerpts.

---

*This list, in addition to a few benchmark dates, includes only those dramas that were produced on British and American television. The list—which covers only the electronic period, 1936–47, because a list of dramas produced during the earlier mechanical period is not available—is mainly intended to be compared with NBC drama, beginning in 1936.

Principal source: BBC *Programmes as Broadcast*.

5 October 1936
3:33–4:05:35p · "The Two Bouquets," by Eleanor and Herbert Farjson. Act I.

19 October 1936
3:41:45–4:18:45p · "Murder in the Cathedral," by T. S. Eliot.

26 October 1936
3:06:50–3:11p · "Whiteoaks." Act I.

2 November 1936 · Opening of BBC Television Service using the John Baird system. Programming includes speeches, film, and variety.

4:00:06p · Opening of the BBC Television Service using the Marconi-EMI System. Same program.

3 November 1936
3:46:51p · *Starlight,* a variety program, includes a sketch written by Ben Lyon, "Thanks a Million." Cast: Ben Lyon, Bebe Daniels, Sydney King.

6 November 1936
3:27:30–3:36:10p · "Marigold," by L. Allen Harker and F. R. Short. [Most television plays for the next several months were shown between 3:00 and 3:30 in the afternoon and again at 9:30 at night on the same day.]

11 February 1937
3:01:25–3:09:05p · "Julius Caesar," by William Shakespeare. Presentation by George More O'Ferrall. Cast: Henry Oscar as Mark Antony.

20 February 1937
9:02:04–9:14:49p · "Twelfth Night," by William Shakespeare. Act II, Scene III. Producer: Stephen Thomas. Cast: Robert Atkins as Sir Toby Belch, Henry Hewitt as Sir Andrew Aguecheek, Nadine March as Maria, Esme Percy as Feste, Ion Swinley as Malvolio.

8 March 1937
3:43:51–4:22-37p · "Jane Eyre" by Charlotte Brontë. Excerpts from Athole Stewart's Aldwych Theatre production by arrangement with Fives Ltd. and Barry Jackson. Presentation by George More O'Ferrall. Cast: Reginald Tate as Edward Rochester, Curigwen

Lewis as Jane Eyre, Dorothy Hamilton as
Maniac, Florence Marriot-Watson as
Grace Poole, Susan Richmond as Mrs.
Fairfax, Phyllis Shand as Leah.

25 March 1937
3:41:32–4:15:29p
1 April 1937
3:01:53–3:13:06p

"Macbeth," by William Shakespeare.

"Julius Caesar," repeat. Presented for tele-
vision by Stephen Thomas with Peter
Creswell's Sound Programme production.
Cast: Malcolm Keen as Brutus, Robert
Holmes as Cassius, Mary Hinton as Portia.

9:02:58–9:16:41p

"The Merchant of Venice," by William
Shakespeare.

6 April 1937
3:01:55–3:33:00p

"The Proposal," by Anton Chekhov.
Translation by Constance Garnett. Producer: Eric Crozier. Cast: William Devlin
as Tchubov, Janet Bruce as Natasha,
Rudolph Brandt as Lomov.

20 April 1937
3:30:20–3:38p

"April Showers," by Nino Bartholomew, a
comedy in one act. Producer: Eric Crozier.
Cast: Fred O'Donovan as Oliver Gold-
smith, Cicely Paget-Bowman as Lady
Northumberland, Harry Hutchinson as
Lord Northumberland, John Abbott as
Lord Nugent, John Rudling as Butler.
First performance of a BBC play specially
written for television.

29 April 1937
9:36:00–9:58p

"Alice in Wonderland," by Lewis Carroll.
Adapter: Royston Morley. Producer:
George More O'Ferrall. Cast: Ursula
Hanray as Alice, Alban Blakelock as
White Rabbit, Molly Hamley Clifford as
Duchess, Campbell Logan as Cook and
Cheshire Cat, Walter Tobias as March
Hare, Earle Grey as Mad Hatter, Patricia
Hayes as Dormouse, Fred O'Donovan as
King of Hearts, Mary Hallatt as Queen of
Hearts.

6 May 1937
3:35:57–4:06:48p

"Abraham Lincoln," by John Drinkwater. Producer: Stephen Thomas. Cast: Malcolm Keen as Abraham Lincoln; Neil Porter as Hook and General Lee; Norman Shelley as Seward and General Grant; J. Adrian Byrne as Cameron and Meade; Desmond Davis as Blair, Dennis, and John Wilkes Booth; Geoffrey Keen as Slaney; Jack Allen as Messenger and Malins; Harding Steerman as Stanton; and extras.

25 June 1937
4:26:05–4:48:50p

"The Happy Journey to Trenton and Camden," by Thornton Wilder. Producer: Eric Crozier. Music composed by Dr. George Knepler. Cast: Joan Miller as Mrs. Kirby, Guy Glover as Mr. Kirby, Margaret Brereton as Caroline, Skelton Knaggs as Arthur, Elaine Wodson as Beulah, Jack Webb as Garage Hand.

20 July 1937
3:22:30–3:43:47p

"The Man with the Flower in His Mouth," by Luigi Pirandello. First presentation on electronic television.

9:08:30–9:28:50p

"The Man with the Flower in His Mouth," repeat.

16 August 1937
3:44:10–4:10:28p

"Romeo and Juliet," by William Shakespeare. Producer: Royston Morley. Cast: Jean Forbes-Robertson as Juliet, Michael Redgrave as Romeo, John Wyse as Friar Laurence, Mario Francelli as Balthasar.

1 November 1937
3:26:42–3:52:24p

"Red Peppers," by Noel Coward. An interlude with music in three scenes. Producer: Reginald Smith. Cast: Richard Murdoch as George Pepper, Marjorie Sandford as Lily Pepper, Gerald Nodin as Mr. Edwards, George Benson as Bert Bentley, Jean Moncrieff as Mabel Grace, Charles Wade as Alf.

2 November 1937
3:20:55–4:12:10p

"The Importance of Being Earnest," by Oscar Wilde. Producer: J. Royston Morley. Cast: Yvette Pienne as Gwendolen Fairfax, Agnes Lauchlan as Lady Bracknell, Sylvia Coleridge as Cecily Cardew, Dora Gregory as Miss Prism, John Abbott as John Worthing, Francis James as Algernon Moncrieff, Mario Francelli as Dr. Chasuble, Alan Wheatley as Lane, Geoffrey Clarke as Merriman.

9:33:18–10:04:36p

"Three Epic Dramas," by Stephen Leacock. The three were: "Forging the Fifteenth Amendment," a drama of the American Civil War; "Mettawamkeag," an Indian tragedy; and "Des Deux Choses L'Une," a drama of the First Empire.

11 November 1937
9:00:55–10:25p

"Journey's End," by R. C. Sherriff. Producer: George More O'Ferrall. Cast: Reginald Smith as Captain Hardy, Alexander Field as Private Mason, Basil Gill as Lieutenant Osborne, Alban Blakelock as Lance-Corporal Broughton, Wallace Douglas as Second Lieutenant Raleigh, Reginald Tate as Captain Stanhope, Norman Pierce as Second Lieutenant Trotter, Brian Oulton as Second Lieutenant Hibbert, R. Brooks Turner as Company Sergeant-Major, J. Neil More as Colonel, Olaf Olsen as Young German Soldier, John Darwin as Private Soldier, Reg Lever and Jerry Fly as Mouth-Organ Players.

6 December 1937
3:04:09–4:38:43p

"Once in a Lifetime," by Moss Hart and George S. Kaufman. Adapter: Eric Crozier. Producer: Crozier. Cast: Joan Miller as May, Charles Farrell as George, Guy Glover as Jerry, Elaine Wodson as Helen Hobart, Kay Lewis as Susan Walker, Jos Greenspun as Herman Glogauer, Oscar Ebelsbacher as Kammerling, Han-

nah Johns as Phyllis, Janet Norton as Florabel, Chris Castor as Miss Leighton, Frank Henderson as Lawrence Vail, Arthur Powell as Policeman and Bishop, Douglas Seale as Page Boy and Flick, David Denbigh as Porter, Edmund Gray as Second Page Boy and Bridegroom. With orchestra. First Kaufman play on BBC.

23 December 1937
9:24:01–10:21p

"Hänsel and Gretel," a masque to the music by Engelbert Humperdinck. Condensed score: Ernest Irving. Television Adapter: Alfred Reynolds. Producer: Stephen Thomas. Choreography and Costumes: Andrée Howard. Cast (actors): Jean Haynes as Hänsel, Muriel Pavlow as Gretel, Lilla Healing as Mother, Alured Weigall as Father, H. D. C. Pepler as Witch, Therese Langfield as Sandman, Charlotte Landor as Dew Fairy. With singers, dancers, chorus, and orchestra.

7 January 1938
10:07–10:43:20p

"The Monkey's Paw," by W. W. Jacobs. Adapter: Louis N. Parker. Producer: Moultrie R. Kelsall. Cast: Muriel George as Mrs. White, John Ruddock as Mr. White, Peter Osborn as Herbert White, Gordon James as Sergeant-Major Morris, Campbell Logan as Mr. Sampson.

20 January 1938
9:39–10:03:40p

"Comic Strip," a program of American humor. Consists of: "If Grant Had Been Drinking at Appomattox," by James Thurber; "Mantle of Whistler," by Dorothy Parker"; and "Mr. Kaplan's Hobo," by Leonard G. Ross.

24 January 1938
3:01:09–4:03:06p

"Tristan und Isolde," by Richard Wagner. Act II. English translator: Frederick Jameson. Producer: Dallas Bower. Mime arranged by Anthony Tudor. Decor: Peter Bax. Cast: Basil Bartlett as Tristan

(Mime), Walter Widdop as Tristan (Singer), Oriel Ross as Isolde (Mime), Isobel Baillie as Isolde (Singer), Mary Alexander as Brangane (Mime), Gladys Garside as Brangane (Singer), Paul Jones as King Marke (Mime), Robert Easton as King Marke (Singer), Hugh Laing as Melot (Mime), George Baker as Melot (Singer), Anthony Hyndman as Kurwenal (Mime), George Baker as Kurwenal (Singer), F. H. Grisewood as Announcer. With chorus and orchestra.

13 April 1938
9:39:58–9:58:42p

"The Maker of Dreams," by Oliphant Down. Adapter: Patrick Campbell. Producer: Lanham Titchener. Cast: Dinah Sheridan as Pierrette, Robert Helpmann as Pierrot, Quinton McPherson as Manufacturer.

24 July 1938
9:05:07–10:46:30p

"Julius Caesar," by William Shakespeare. Performed in modern dress. Adapter: Dallas Bower. Producer: Bower. Special Scenic Effects: Malcolm Baker-Smith. Incidental Music: James Hartley. Cast: Ernest Milton as Julius Caesar, Douglas Matthews as Octavius Caesar, D. A. Clarke-Smith as Marcus Antonius, David Keir as M. Aemilius Lepidus, A. Harding Steerman as Publius and Third Citizen, Douglas Stewart as Popilius Lena and Fourth Citizen, Sebastian Shaw as Marcus Brutus, Anthony Ireland as Cassius, Lawrence Hanray as Casca, Dennis Price as Trebonius and Volumnius, John Turnbull as Decius Brutus and Messala, Stuart Latham as Metallus Cimber, Erik Chitty as Cinna, Charles Lefeaux as Flavius, Second Guard, and Messenger, Jack Lambert as Marullus and First Guard, Colin Gent as Soothsayer, Patrick Ludlow as Cinna (a poet) and Pindarus, J. Ireland Wood as

Lucilius, Alan Wheatley as Titinius, Charles Paton as Varro and Commoner, Robin Wentworth as Clitus and Third Guard, Phil H. Thomas as Claudius and Second Commoner, Jack Vyvyan as Strato and First Citizen, Robin Maule as Lucius (boy), Kenneth Eaves as Dardanius and Second Citizen, Van Courtland as Caius Ligarius, Laura Cowie as Calpurnia, Carol Goodner as Portia, Will Leighton as Servant, Alan Aldridge as Waiter.

10 August 1938
3:31:36–3:45:27p

Telecrime, No. 1. "The Back-Stage Murder," by Mileson Horton and H. T. Hopkinson.

5 October 1938
9:19:35–10:25:46p

"I Pagliacci," an opera by Ruggiero Leoncavallo. English adapter: Frederic E. Weatherley. Production Director: Vladimir Rosing. Producer: D. H. Munro. Cast: The Covent Garden English Opera Company, including Hella Toros as Nedda (Columbine in the play), Frank Sale as Canio (Punchinello in the play), Dennis Noble as Tonio the Clown (Taddeo in the play), John Fullard as Peppe (Harlequin in the play), Morgan Davies as Silvio; and a chorus of eight men and eight women.

24 October 1938
9:01:44–9:20:50p

Telecrime. "Poetic Justice," by Arthur Phillips.

16 November 1938
8:33:01–10:57:32p

"When We Are Married," by J. B. Priestley. Direct from the stage of the St. Martins Theatre. Producer: Basil Dean. Presentation for Television: Philip H. Dorté. Cast: Patricia Hayes as Ruby Birtle, Richard Warner as Gerald Forbes, Beatrice Varley as Mrs. Northrop, Muriel George as Maria Helliwell, Lloyd Pearson as Alderman Joseph Helliwell, Betty Fleetwood as Nancy Holmes, Alexander

Grandison as Fred Dyson, George Carney as Henry Ormonroyd, Raymond Huntley as Councillor Albert Parker, Ernest Butcher as Herbert Soppitt, Ethel Coleridge as Clara Soppitt, Helena Pickard as Annie Parker, Mai Bacon as Lottie Grady, Norman Wooland as Rev. Clement Mercer, B. Marsh Dunn as Mayor of Clecklewyke. Dean and Priestley appeared briefly during the production.

25 December 1938
9:11:50–10:50:45p

"Hay Fever," by Noel Coward. Producer: Reginald Smith. Cast: Kitty De Legh as Judith Bliss, Maurice Denham as David Bliss, Olga Edwardes as Sorel Bliss, Guy Verney as Simon Bliss, Fabia Drake as Myra Arundel, Noel Howlett as Richard Greatham, Doreen Oscar as Jackie Coryton, John Byron as Sandy Tyrrell, Veronica Brady as Clara.

2 January 1939
8:30:10p

"Twelfth Night," by William Shakespeare. This is the first full-length production. Presented direct from the Phoenix Theatre by Bronson Albery and Michel St. Denis. Television Producer: Dallas Bower. Cast: Esmond Knight as Orsino, Basil C. Langton as Sebastian, William Devlin as Antonio, John Rae as Sea Captain, James Donald as Valentine, Peter Whitehead as Curio, George DeVine as Sir Toby Belch, Michael Redgrave as Sir Andrew Aguecheek, George Hayes as Malvolio, Thomas Heathcote as Fabian, Warren Jenkins as Feste, Alastair Bannerman as Priest, Pierre LeFevre as First Officer, John Earle as Second Officer, Vera Lindsay as Olivia, Peggy Ashcroft as Viola, Lucille Lisle as Maria, and eleven extras.

4 January 1939
3:39:18–4:07:55p

"The Tell-Tale Heart," by Edgar Allan Poe. Adapter: Michael Hogan. Decor: Edmund Hogan. Producer: Dallas Bower.

Cast: Ernest Milton as Madman, Basil Cunard as Policeman, Stuart Latham as Policeman, Olaf Olsen as Policeman and Madman, Harding Steerman as Old Man, Esme Percy as Narrator.

14 January 1939
21:23:45–22:20:05p

"Hänsel and Gretel," a masque to the music of Engelbert Humperdinck, repeat. Adapters: Ernest Irving (music), Alfred Reynolds, Stephen Thomas (story). Producer: Stephen Thomas. Choreographer: Andrée Howard. Assistant Stage Manager: Douglas Allen. Cast: Jane Vowles as Gretel (Singer), Muriel Pavlow as Gretel (Mime), Charlotte Leigh as Hänsel (Singer), Roberta Berek as Hänsel (Mime), Edith Coates as Mother (Singer), Lilla Healing as Mother (Mime), Redvers Llewellyn as Father (Singer), Al Weigall as Father (Mime), Constance Willis as Witch (Singer), H. D. C. Pepler as Witch (Mime), Betty Hutchings as Sandman (Singer), Therese Langfield as Sandman (Mime), Molly Lake as Dew Fairy (Singer), Charlotte Bidmead as Dew Fairy (Mime). With eight Angel Voices and fourteen Angels and Witches. Orchestra.

13 February 1939
3:00:16–4:16p

"The Royal Family of Broadway," by Edna Ferber and George S. Kaufman. Producer: George More O'Ferrall. Cast: Dame May Whitty as Fanny Cavendish, Beatrix Thompson as Julie Cavendish, Robert Douglas as Tony Cavendish, Dorothy Hyson as Gwen Cavendish, D. A. Clarke-Smith as Herbert Dean, Grizelda Hervey as Kitty Dean, Finlay Currie as Oscar Wolfe, Wallace Douglas as Perry Stewart, Basil Radford as Gilbert Marshall, Betty Romaine as Della, John Lothar as Jo, Renee Blakelock as Miss Peake, Peter Herschel as Hall-Boy, Benjamin Denso as Gunga.

2 March 1939
3:01:16–3:26:16p   *Telecrime.* "The Fletcher Case," by
                          Mileson Horton.

15 April 1939
10:05:10p   *Telecrime.* "The Almost Perfect Murder,"
                          by Mileson Horton.

1 September 1939   BBC Television goes on the air as usual
                          with sound and vision tuning signals. A
                          variety bill follows.

12:05:05p   "Mickey's Gala Premiere" (a film cartoon)
                          begins and then fades out. This program
                          concludes BBC telecasting until after
                          World War II.

1946

BBC-TV, Alexandra Palace, London

7 June 1946
2:30p   Official reopening of the BBC London
                          Television Service. Programming includes
                          music, ballet, variety, films, and dramas.

4:19:50p   "The Dark Lady of the Sonnets," repeat.
8:43:23–10:10:42p   "The Importance of Being Earnest,"
                          repeat.

11 June 1946
8:30:30p   "Dangerous Corner," by J. B. Priestley.
                          Cast: Lydia Sherwood as Freda Caplan,
                          Judy Campbell as Olwen Peel, Joy Shelton
                          as Betty Whitehouse, Martita Hunt as
                          Miss Mockridge, Ivan Sampson as Robert
                          Caplan, D. A. Clarke-Smith as Charles
                          Stanton, Geoffrey Keen as Gordon
                          Whitehouse.

27 September 1946
8:30:50–10:01:08p   "Jane Eyre," by Charlotte Brontë. Adapter
                          for Stage: Helen Jerome. Director: An-
                          thony Hawtrey. Cast: Embassy Theatre
                          Company. Excerpts had originally been
                          telecast by BBC on 8 March 1937.

23 October 1946
9:52:55p

Telecrimes, No. 1. "The Concert Hall Murder Case" and "Death of a Golfer," continuation of series by Mileson Horton.

28 October 1946
8:31:22p

Telecrimes, No. 2. "The Stolen Tiara" and "Death of an Aunt," by Mileson Horton.

5 November 1946
9:27:36–9:42:08p

Telecrimes, No. 3. "The Case of the Drunken Skipper" and "Death of a Scientist," by Mileson Horton.

12 November 1946
8:59:50–9:13:10p

Telecrimes, No. 4. "Poison in Pimlico" and "Case of the Gentle Accomplice," by Mileson Horton.

25 December 1946

The Queen's Christmas message, choirs, and music.

Appendix C

CBS Television Dramas, 1931–1946*

1931–1933

W2XAB, 485 Madison Ave., New York

21 June 1931	Tests: call letters, silhouettes, persons, photograph, clock.
21 July 1931 10:10–11:00p	"Television Inaugural Broadcast." No drama.
22 July 1931 9:15–9:30p 10:00–10:15p	Afternoon makeup tests. "Tele Musical," first CBS musical. Drama, first CBS drama.
23 July 1931 8:00–10:59p	Programming includes "A Night at Sea," believed to be a cartoon and the first motion picture shown by CBS.
1 [?] August 1931 2:00–10:00p	Programming includes *Half Hour on Broadway*, first CBS musical variety series. [This series was continued, but subsequent shows are not listed below.]
18 August 1931 9:00–9:15p	"Punch and Judy," first CBS puppet show.
26 August 1931 8:15–8:30p	"Sam the Taximan," believed to be the first CBS comedy monologue. Schudt, announcer; Wallace, engineer.
27 August 1931 9:00–9:30p	*Musical Miniature Comedy.* [This series was continued, but subsequent shows are not listed below.] Beuchler, announcer; Spears, engineer.

*This list includes all known dramas and dramatic-related programs through 1946, though two later benchmark dates are listed.

Principal source: CBS *Television Master Control Log.*

9:30–9:45

The Television Ghost, television's first dramatic narrative anthology series. Dean, announcer; Briean, engineer.

1 September 1931
9:00–9:15p

Drama. Roberts, announcer; Briean, engineer.

3 September 1931
8:15–8:30p

"Experimental Television Drama." Von Zell, announcer; Spears, engineer.

9:32–9:45p

The Television Ghost. Judson, announcer; Briean, engineer.

8 September 1931
8:45–9:00p

Pantomime, first CBS pantomime. Schudt, announcer; Sachs, engineer.

10 September 1931
9:30–9:45p

The Television Ghost. Judson, announcer; Spears, engineer.

17 September 1931
9:30–9:45p

The Television Ghost. Schudt, announcer; Sachs, engineer.

24 September 1931
8:15–8:30p

Drama. Cast: Henderson. Christian, announcer; Spears, engineer.

9:48–10:05p

The Television Ghost. Christian, announcer; Spears, engineer.

1 October 1931
8:15–8:30p

Drama. Cast: Henderson. Christian, announcer; Spears, engineer.

9:30–9:45p

The Television Ghost. Christian, announcer; Spears, engineer.

7 October 1931
8:45–9:15p

Television Cameos, a musical. Judson, announcer; Sachs, engineer.

8 October 1931
9:30–9:45p

The Television Ghost. Cast: A. Dickson. Knight, announcer; Spears, engineer.

13 October 1931
9:00–9:15p

The Television Ghost. Schudt, announcer; Weber, engineer.

18 October 1931
9:00–9:30p

Programming includes "Broadway Panorama," believed to be a musical. Judson, announcer; Weber, engineer.

20 October 1931 9:00–9:15p	*The Television Ghost.* Schudt, announcer; Weber, engineer.
21 October 1931 8:30–9:00p	*Television Cameos.* Judson, announcer; Sachs, engineer.
27 October 1931 9:00–9:13p	*The Television Ghost.* Schudt, announcer; Spears, engineer.
3 November 1931 9:00–9:15p	*The Television Ghost.* Schudt, announcer; Spears, engineer.
17 November 1931 9:00–9:15p	*The Television Ghost.* Schudt, announcer; Spears, engineer.
24 November 1931 9:00–9:11p	*The Television Ghost.* Schudt, announcer; Spears, engineer.
1 December 1931 9:00–9:15p	*The Television Ghost.* Schudt, announcer; Weber, engineer.
5 December 1931 9:00–10:00p	Makeup tests. Judson, announcer; Briean, engineer.
8 December 1931 9:00–9:17p	*The Television Ghost.* Schudt, announcer; Spears, engineer.
15 December 1931 9:00–9:15p	*The Television Ghost.* Schudt, announcer; Spears, engineer.
22 December 1931 9:00–9:15p	*The Television Ghost.* Schudt, announcer; Spears, engineer.
25 December 1931	Christmas card greetings.
29 December 1931 9:00–9:15p	*The Television Ghost.* Schudt, announcer; Spears, engineer.
1 January 1932 to 31 May 1932	[CBS *Television Master Control Log* is missing.]
1 June 1932 8:05–8:25p	Makeup tests. Schudt, announcer; Spears, engineer.

9:30–10:00p   Pantomimes. Cast: Estelle Sydney. Schudt,
                               announcer; Spears, engineer.

2 June 1932
8:30–9:00p   *The Silent Drama.* Cast: John Hewitt.
                               Schudt, announcer; Spears, engineer.
9:30–9:45p   Pantomimes. Cast: Lilyan Crossman.
                               Schudt, announcer; Spears, engineer.

7 June 1932
9:00–9:30p   Pantomimes. Cast: Grace Voss. Schudt,
                               announcer; Spears, engineer.

8 June 1932
9:15–9:30p   *Character Slants.* Cast: Bob Davis.
                               Schudt, announcer; Spears, engineer.
9:30–10:00p   Pantomimes. Cast: Estelle Sydney. Schudt,
                               announcer; Spears, engineer.

9 June 1932
8:30–9:15p   *The Silent Drama.* Cast: John Hewitt.
                               Schudt, announcer; Spears, engineer.
9:30–9:55p   "Dramatic Pantomime." Cast: Lilyan
                               Crossman. Schudt, announcer; Spears,
                               engineer.

10 June 1932
9:15–9:45p   Makeup tests. Schudt, announcer; Spears,
                               engineer.

15 June 1932
9:15–9:30p   *Character Slants.* Cast: Bob Davis.
                               Schudt, announcer; Spears, engineer.

16 June 1932
8:30–9:15p   *The Silent Drama.* Cast: John Hewitt.
                               Schudt, announcer; Spears, engineer.
9:40–10:00p   Pantomimes. Cast: Lilyan Crossman.
                               Schudt, announcer; Spears, engineer.

22 June 1932
9:30–10:00p   Pantomimes. Cast: Estelle Sydney. Schudt,
                               announcer; Spears, engineer.

23 June 1932
8:30–9:15p   *The Silent Drama.* Cast: John Hewitt.
                               Schudt, announcer; Spears, engineer.
9:30–9:45p   Pantomimes. Cast: Lilyan Crossman.
                               Schudt, announcer; Spears, engineer.

29 June 1932
9:30–10:00p   Pantomimes. Cast: Estelle Sydney. Schudt,
                               announcer; Spears, engineer.

30 June 1932
8:30–9:15p   *The Silent Drama*. Cast: John Hewitt. Schudt, announcer; Spears, engineer.

1 July 1932
8:30–8:45p   Sketches [probably drawings]. Cast: George Kelting. Schudt, announcer; Spears, engineer.

28 July 1932
8:25–9:00p   Sketch. Cast: Hewitt Players. Schudt, announcer; Bowman, engineer.

3 August 1932
9:30–9:45p   Pantomimes. Cast: Lilyan Crossman. Schudt, announcer; Spears, engineer.

4 August 1932
8:30–9:00p   Drama. Cast: Hewitt Players. Schudt, announcer; Spears, engineer.

8 August 1932
8:10–8:20p   *The Television Ghost*. Cast: A. Dickson. Schudt, announcer; Spears, engineer.

10 August 1932
8:01–8:15p   Monologues. Cast: Sophia Goff. Schudt, announcer; Spears, engineer.

11 August 1932
8:30–9:00p   CBS *Tele-Talkie*. Cast: Hewitt Players. Schudt, announcer; Spears, engineer.

15 August 1932
8:01–8:15p   *The Television Ghost*. Cast: A. Dickson. Schudt, announcer; Spears, engineer.

17 August 1932
8:30–9:45p   Pantomimes. Cast: Estelle Sydney. Schudt, announcer; Spears, engineer.

18 August 1932
8:30–9:00p   Sketch. Cast: Hewitt Players. Schudt, announcer; Spears, engineer.

22 August 1932
8:01–8:15p   *The Television Ghost*. Schudt, announcer; Spears, engineer.

23 August 1932
8:45–9:00p   Pantomimes. Cast: Lilyan Crossman. Schudt, announcer; Spears, engineer.

24 August 1932
9:30–9:45p   Pantomimes. Cast: Lilyan Crossman. Schudt, announcer; Spears, engineer.

25 August 1932
8:30–9:00p   CBS *Tele-Talkie*. Schudt, announcer;
                               Spears, engineer.

29 August 1932
8:01–8:15p   *The Television Ghost*. Schudt, announcer;
                               Spears, engineer.
8:15–8:30p   Pantomimes. Cast: Grace Voss. Schudt,
                               announcer; Spears, engineer.

30 August 1932
8:45–9:00p   Pantomimes. Cast: Lilyan Crossman.
                               Schudt, announcer; Spears, engineer.

31 August 1932
9:30–9:45p   Pantomimes. Cast: Estelle Sydney. Schudt,
                               announcer; Spears, engineer.

1 September 1932
8:30–9:00p   CBS *Tele-Talkie*. Schudt, announcer;
                               Spears, engineer.

6 September 1932
8:45–9:00p   Pantomimes. Cast: Lilyan Crossman.
                               Schudt, announcer; Spears, engineer.

7 September 1932
8:15–8:30p   Monologue Plays. Cast: Grace Voss.
                               Schudt, announcer; Spears, engineer.
9:30–9:45p   Pantomimes. Cast: Estelle Sydney. Schudt,
                               announcer; Spears, engineer.

12 September 1932
8:00–8:15p   *The Television Ghost*. Schudt, announcer;
                               Spears, engineer.

13 September 1932
9:30–9:45p   Pantomimes. Cast: Lilyan Crossman.
                               Schudt, announcer; Spears, engineer.

14 September 1932
8:15–8:30p   Pantomimes. Cast: Grace Voss. Schudt,
                               announcer; Spears, engineer.
9:30–9:45p   Pantomimes. Cast: Estelle Sydney. Schudt,
                               announcer; Spears, engineer.

15 September 1932
8:30–8:45p   Sketch. Cast: Hewitt Players. Schudt, an-
                               nouncer; Spears, engineer.

19 September 1932
8:01–8:15p   *The Television Ghost*. Schudt, announcer;
                               Spears, engineer.

8:15–8:30p   Monologues. Cast: Grace Voss. Schudt, announcer; Spears, engineer.

8:45–9:00p   Comedy Skit. Cast: "Senator Numb." Schudt, announcer; Spears, engineer.

21 September 1932
9:30–9:45p   Pantomimes. Cast: Estelle Sydney. Schudt, announcer; Spears, engineer.

22 September 1932
8:30–8:45p   CBS *Tele-Talkie*. Cast: John Hewitt. Schudt, announcer; Spears, engineer.

26 September 1932
8:01–8:15p   *The Television Ghost*. Schudt, announcer; Spears, engineer.

8:15–8:30p   Pantomimes. Cast: Grace Voss. Schudt, announcer; Spears, engineer.

9:30–9:45p   Pantomimes. Cast: Estelle Sydney. Schudt, announcer; Spears, engineer.

3 October 1932
8:01–8:15p   *The Television Ghost*. Peterson, announcer; Spears, engineer.

5 October 1932
8:15–8:30p   Pantomimes. Cast: Grace Voss. Schudt, announcer; Spears, engineer.

9:30–9:45p   Pantomimes. Cast: Estelle Sydney. Schudt, announcer; Spears, engineer.

11 October 1932
8:15–8:30p   Monologue Plays. Cast: Grace Voss. Schudt, announcer; Spears, engineer.

8:45–9:00p   Comedy. Cast: "Senator Numb." Schudt, announcer; Spears, engineer.

9:30–9:45p   Pantomimes. Cast: Estelle Sydney. Schudt, announcer; Spears, engineer.

13 October 1932
8:15–8:45p   Sketch. Cast: Hewitt Players. Schudt, announcer; Spears, engineer.

14 October 1932
8:45–9:00p   Comedy. Cast: Spaghett and Ravioli. Schudt, announcer; Spears, engineer.

17 October 1932
8:01–8:15p   *The Television Ghost*. Schudt, announcer; Spears, engineer.

19 October 1932
8:15–8:30p   Pantomimes. Cast: Grace Voss. Schudt, announcer; Spears, engineer.

20 October 1932

8:15–8:30p — *Character Slants*. Cast: Bob Davis. Schudt, announcer; Spears, engineer.

8:30–8:45p — Sketch. Cast: Hewitt Players. Schudt, announcer; Spears, engineer.

24 October 1932

8:01–8:15p — *The Television Ghost [Stalks]*. Schudt, announcer; Spears, engineer.

26 October 1932

8:15–8:30p — Pantomimes. Cast: Grace Voss. Schudt, announcer; Spears, engineer.

9:30–9:45p — Pantomimes. Cast: Estelle Sydney. Schudt, announcer; Spears, engineer.

27 October 1932

8:30–8:50p — Sketch. Cast: Hewitt Players. Schudt, announcer; Spears, engineer.

31 October 1932

8:01–8:15p — *The Television Ghost*. Cast: George Kelting. Schudt, announcer; Spears, engineer.

1 November 1932

8:01–8:15p — Sketch. Cast: Sally and Gene [last names unknown]. Schudt, announcer; Spears, engineer.

2 November 1932

8:15–8:30p — Pantomimes. Cast: Grace Voss. Schudt, announcer; Spears, engineer.

3 November 1932

8:15–8:30p — *Character Slants*. Cast: Bob Davis. Schudt, announcer; Spears, engineer.

8:45–9:00p — CBS *Tele-Talkie*. Cast: John Hewitt. Schudt, announcer; Spears, engineer.

4 November 1932

8:15–8:30p — *This and That*, a sketch. Schudt, announcer; Spears, engineer.

7 November 1932

8:01–8:15p — *The Television Ghost*. Cast: George Kelting. Schudt, announcer; Spears, engineer.

9 November 1932

8:15–8:30p — Pantomimes. Cast: Grace Voss. Schudt, announcer; Spears, engineer.

10 November 1932

8:45–9:00p — Sketch. Cast: Hewitt Players. Schudt, announcer; Spears, engineer.

11 November 1932
8:15–8:30p

This and That. Cast: Charlotte Wernick. Schudt, announcer; Spears, engineer.

14 November 1932
9:30–9:45p

The Television Ghost. Cast: George Kelting. Schudt, announcer; Spears, engineer.

15 November 1932
8:01–8:15p

Sketch. Cast: Sally and Gene. Schudt, announcer; Spears, engineer.

16 November 1932
9:15–9:30p

"Just Snapshots," a sketch. Schudt, announcer; Spears, engineer.

17 November 1932
8:15–8:30p

Character Slants. Cast: Bob Davis. Schudt, announcer; Spears, engineer.

8:45–9:00p

Sketch. Cast: Hewitt Players. Schudt, announcer; Spears, engineer.

18 November 1932
9:25–9:45p

Pantomimes. Cast: Charlotte Wernick. Schudt, announcer; Spears, engineer.

21 November 1932
9:45–10:00p

Comedy. Cast: George Kelting. Schudt, announcer; Spears, engineer.

22 November 1932
8:01–8:15p

Sketch. Cast: Sally and Gene. Schudt, announcer; Spears, engineer.

23 November 1932
8:15–8:30p

Pantomimes. Cast: Grace Voss. Schudt, announcer; Spears, engineer.

25 November 1932
8:15–8:30p

Monologues. Cast: Pat Garnell. Schudt, announcer; Spears, engineer.

9:30–9:45p

Character Slants. Cast: Bob Davis. Schudt, announcer; Spears, engineer.

28 November 1932
8:30–8:45p

Pantomimes. Cast: Charlotte Wernick. Schudt, announcer; Spears, engineer.

29 November 1932
8:01–8:15p

Sketch. Cast: Sally and Gene. Schudt, announcer; Spears, engineer.

30 November 1932
8:15–8:30p

Pantomimes. Cast: Grace Voss. Schudt, announcer; Spears, engineer.

1 December 1932
8:45–9:15p   Sketch. Cast: Hewitt Players. Schudt, an-
                           nouncer; Spears, engineer.

2 December 1932
8:15–8:30p   Pantomimes. Cast: Pat Garnell. Schudt,
                           announcer; Spears, engineer.

5 December 1932
9:30–9:45p   Pantomimes. Cast: Charlotte Wernick.
                           Schudt, announcer; Spears, engineer.

6 December 1932
8:01–8:15p   Sketch. Cast: Sally and Gene. Schudt, an-
                           nouncer; Spears, engineer.

7 December 1932
8:15–8:45p   Pantomimes. Cast: Grace Voss. Schudt,
                           announcer; Spears, engineer.

8 December 1932
8:15–8:30p   *Character Slants.* Cast: Bob Davis.
                           Schudt, announcer; Spears, engineer.
8:45–9:00p   Sketch. Cast: Hewitt Players. Schudt, an-
                           nouncer; Spears, engineer.

9 December 1932
8:01–8:15p   Pantomimes. Cast: Pat Garnell. Schudt,
                           announcer; Spears, engineer.

12 December 1932
9:30–9:45p   Pantomimes. Cast: Charlotte Wernick.
                           Schudt, announcer; Spears, engineer.

13 December 1932
8:01–8:15p   Sketch. Cast: Sally and Gene. Schudt, an-
                           nouncer; Spears, engineer.

14 December 1932
8:15–8:30p   Pantomimes. Cast: Grace Voss. Schudt,
                           announcer; Spears, engineer.

15 December 1932
8:45–9:00p   Sketch. Cast: Hewitt Players. Schudt, an-
                           nouncer; Spears, engineer.

16 December 1932
8:15–8:30p   Pantomimes. Cast: Pat Garnell. Schudt,
                           announcer; Spears, engineer.
8:45–9:00p   Dramatic Sketch. Cast: Bert Hilliard.
                           Schudt, announcer; Spears, engineer.

19 December 1932
9:15–9:30p   Dramatic Pantomimes. Cast: Lebeth. Pe-
                           terson, announcer; Spears, engineer.

20 December 1932
8:01–8:15p   Musical Drama. Cast: Sally and Gene.
                           Peterson, announcer; Spears, engineer.

21 December 1932
8:15–8:45p   Pantomimes. Cast: Grace Voss. Schudt,
                           announcer; Spears, engineer.

9:30–9:45p   "Wise Guy," a skit. Schudt, announcer;
                           Spears, engineer.

22 December 1932
8:15–8:30p   *Character Slants*. Cast: Bob Davis.
                           Schudt, announcer; Spears, engineer.

8:45–9:00p   Sketch. Cast: Hewitt Players. Schudt, an-
                           nouncer; Spears, engineer.

28 December 1932
8:15–8:45p   Pantomimes. Cast: Grace Voss. Schudt,
                           announcer; Spears, engineer.

9:30–9:45p   *Dramatic Moments*. Cast: Bert Hilliard.
                           Schudt, announcer; Spears, engineer.

29 December 1932
8:45–9:00p   Sketch. Cast: Hewitt Players. Schudt, an-
                           nouncer; Spears, engineer.

30 December 1932
8:15–8:30p   Dramatic Readings. Cast: Pat Garnell.
                           Schudt, announcer; Spears, engineer.

3 January 1933
8:01–8:15p   Songs. Cast: Sally and Gene. Schudt, an-
                           nouncer; Spears, engineer.

4 January 1933
8:01–8:15p   Comedy. Cast: George Kelting. Schudt,
                           announcer; Spears, engineer.

8:15–8:30p   Pantomimes. Cast: Grace Voss. Schudt,
                           announcer; Spears, engineer.

8:45–9:00p   Sketch. Cast: Clarence [last name un-
                           known]. Schudt, announcer; Spears,
                           engineer.

9:30–9:45p   *Dramatic Moments*. Cast: Bert Hilliard.
                           Schudt, announcer; Spears, engineer.

5 January 1933
8:15–8:30p   *Character Slants*. Cast: Bob Davis.
                           Schudt, announcer; Spears, engineer.

8:45–9:00p   Sketch. Cast: Hewitt Players. Schudt, an-
                           nouncer; Spears, engineer.

6 January 1933
8:30–8:45p

Pantomimes. Cast: Pat Garnell. Schudt, announcer; Spears, engineer.

10 January 1933
8:30–8:45p

Pantomimes. Cast: Sally and Gene. Schudt, announcer; Spears, engineer.

11 January 1933
8:01–8:30p

Comedy. Cast: George Kelting. Schudt, announcer; Spears, engineer.

9:30–9:45p

Dramatic Moments. Cast: Bert Hilliard. Schudt, announcer; Spears, engineer.

12 January 1933
8:45–9:00p

Sketch. Cast: Hewitt Players. Schudt, announcer; Spears, engineer.

13 January 1933
9:30–9:45p

Pantomimes. Cast: Pat Garnell. Schudt, announcer; Spears, engineer.

16 January 1933
9:30–9:45p

Characters. Cast: Charlotte Wernick. Schudt, announcer; Spears, engineer.

17 January 1933
8:01–8:15p

Sketch. Cast: Sally and Gene. Schudt, announcer; Spears, engineer.

18 January 1933
8:01–8:15p

The Television Ghost. Cast: George Kelting. Schudt, announcer; Spears, engineer.

8:20–8:45p

Pantomimes. Cast: Grace Voss. Schudt, announcer; Spears, engineer.

9:30–9:45p

Dramatic Moments. Cast: Bert Hilliard. Schudt, announcer; Spears, engineer.

9:45–10:00p

Sketches [probably drawings]. Cast: George Kelting. Schudt, announcer; Spears, engineer.

19 January 1933
8:15–8:30p

Character Slants. Cast: Bob Davis. Schudt, announcer; Spears,engineer.

8:45–9:00p

Sketch. Cast: Hewitt Players. Schudt, announcer; Spears, engineer.

20 January 1933
9:30–9:45p

Pantomimes. Cast: Pat Garnell. Schudt, announcer; Spears, engineer.

23 January 1933
8:45–9:00p

9:30–9:45p

24 January 1933
8:01–8:15p

25 January 1933
8:01–8:15p

8:15–8:30p

8:30–8:45p

8:45–9:00p

9:30–9:45p

26 January 1933
8:45–9:00p

27 January 1933
9:30–9:45p

30[?] January 1933
8:45–9:00p

9:30–9:45p

9:45–10:00p

31 January 1933
8:01–8:15p

1 February 1933
8:01–8:15p

2 February 1933
8:01–8:15p

8:45–9:00p

Characters. Cast: Isadora Newman.
Schudt, announcer; Spears, engineer.
Pantomimes. Cast: Charlotte Wernick.
Schudt, announcer; Spears, engineer.

"Talkie Short." Cast: Sally and Gene.
Schudt, announcer; Spears, engineer.

Comedy. Cast: George Kelting. Schudt,
announcer; Spears, engineer.
Pantomimes. Cast: Grace Voss. Schudt,
announcer; Spears, engineer.
Sketch. Cast: "Senator Numb." Schudt,
announcer; Spears, engineer.
"Wise Guy," repeat. Schudt, announcer;
Spears, engineer.
Dramatic Moments. Cast: Bert Hilliard.
Schudt, announcer; Spears, engineer.

Sketch. Cast: Hewitt Players. Schudt, announcer; Spears, engineer.

Pantomimes. Cast: Pat Garnell. Schudt,
announcer; Spears, engineer.

Characters. Cast: Isadora Newman. Peterson, announcer; Spears, engineer.
This and That. Cast: Pat Garnell. Peterson, announcer; Spears, engineer.
"Lonely Sailor." Cast: Jack Peterson. Peterson, announcer; Spears, engineer.

Sketch. Cast: Sally and Gene. Peterson,
announcer; Spears, engineer.

Comedy. Cast: George Kelting. Peterson,
announcer; Spears, engineer.

Character Slants. Cast: Bob Davis. Peterson, announcer; Spears, engineer.
Sketch. Cast: Hewitt Players. Peterson, announcer; Spears, engineer.

3 February 1933
8:45–9:00p   Comedy. Cast: Spaghett and Ravioli.
                             Schudt, announcer; Spears, engineer.
9:30–9:45p   Pantomimes. Cast: Pat Garnell. Schudt,
                             announcer; Spears, engineer.
6 February 1933
8:30–8:45p   *Dramatic Moments*. Cast: Bert Hilliard.
                             Schudt, announcer; Spears, engineer.
8:45–9:00p   Pantomimes. Cast: Isadora Newman.
                             Schudt, announcer; Spears, engineer.
9:30–9:45p   Dramatics. Cast: Charlotte Wernick.
                             Schudt, announcer; Spears, engineer.
7 February 1933
8:01–8:15p   Sketch. Cast: Sally and Gene. Schudt, an-
                             nouncer; Spears, engineer.
8 February 1933
8:01–8:15p   *The Television Ghost*. Cast: George Kelt-
                             ing. Schudt, announcer; Spears, engineer.
8:15–8:30p   Pantomimes. Cast: Grace Voss. Schudt,
                             announcer; Spears, engineer.
9:30–9:45p   *Dramatic Moments*. Cast: Bert Hilliard.
                             Schudt, announcer; Spears, engineer.
10 February 1933
8:30–8:45p   Pantomimes. Cast: Pat Garnell. Schudt,
                             announcer; Spears, engineer.
13 February 1933
8:30–8:45p   Characters. Cast: Charlotte Wernick.
                             Schudt, announcer; Spears, engineer.
8:45–9:00p   Pantomimes. Cast: Isadora Newman.
                             Schudt, announcer; Spears, engineer.
9:15–9:45p   *Dramatic Moments*. Cast: Bert Hilliard.
                             Schudt, announcer; Spears, engineer.
14 February 1933
8:01–8:15p   Sketch. Cast: Sally and Gene. Schudt, an-
                             nouncer; Spears, engineer.
15 February 1933
8:01–8:15p   *The Television Ghost*. Cast: George Kelt-
                             ing. Schudt, announcer; Taylor, engineer.
9:30–9:45p   *Dramatic Moments*. Cast: Bert Hilliard.
                             Schudt, announcer; Spears, engineer.
16 February 1933
8:15–8:30p   *Character Slants*. Cast: Bob Davis.
                             Schudt, announcer; Spears, engineer.

8:45–9:00p	Sketch. Cast: Hewitt Players. Schudt, announcer; Spears, engineer.
17 February 1933	
8:30–8:45p	Pantomimes. Cast: Pat Garnell. Schudt, announcer; Spears, engineer.
20 February 1933	Entire log: Schudt, announcer; Spears, engineer.
8:00–8:01p	Opening announcement.
8:01–8:30p	Muriel Asche and Kiddies.
8:30–8:45p	Characters. Cast: Charlotte Wernick.
8:45–9:00p	"Old Sailor." Cast: Jack Peterson.
9:00–9:15p	Songs. Cast: Harriet Downs.
9:15–9:30p	Cartoons. Cast: Henrietta Dunlap.
9:30–9:45p	*Dramatic Moments*. Cast: Bert Hilliard.
9:45–10:00p	Songs. Cast: Sylvia Sherry.

1937–1942

9 July 1937	CBS leases space on the second, third, and fourth floors in the Grand Central Terminal Building, 15 Vanderbilt Avenue, New York.
November 1939	Modest closed-circuit experiments follow. All studio operations are suspended.
1940	Occasional telecasts of test pattern.
23 June 1941	Pretest of program schedule begins.
1 July 1941	WCBW goes on the air as a commercial television station. A fifteen-hour-a-week program schedule includes news, dance, story, quiz, defense, and films, but no drama.
1 June 1942	WCBW initiates wartime schedule, consisting of two hours of programming Thursday nights and two on Friday nights, a total of four hours per week.
26 November 1942	WCBW goes off the air for the duration of World War II.

1944–1948

4 May 1944	WCBW's television studio in the Grand Central Terminal Building reopens.

12 May 1944	Gilbert Seldes and others begin appearing in productions.
1 June 1944 9:30–9:59p	*Backstage,* a variety series, including puppets.
30 June 1944 9:14–9:33p	"The Favor," a war-bond play by Lawrence M. Klee, is the first live drama on WCBW. Adapter: Worthington Miner. Director: Miner. Cast: Joseph Julian as Soldier, Lesley Woods as Girl.
12 July 1944 8:00–9:00p	"A GI Dreams of Home" by Irwin Shaw, for *Women in Wartime.* Producer: Gilbert Seldes. Director: Frances Buss. [This series appears throughout the year, but the programs do not always include a drama.]
13 July 1944 8:30–8:48p	"The Favor," repeat. Director: Miner.
13 October 1944	"Two Soldiers," by William Faulkner. Adapter: Gilbert Seldes. Director: Seldes.
23 November 1944 8:15–8:50p	"Amanda and the Boys."
December 1944	*Women in Wartime,* a series that includes occasional dramatic sketches. Producer: Gilbert Seldes. Directors: Frances Buss, Lucille Hudiburg. Writers: Betty Weir, Fred Rickey, Jeri Trotta, Frances Hughes. In collaboration with *Mademoiselle* magazine.
11 April 1945	"Soldiers without Uniforms," by Pierre Schaeffer and Pierre Garrgues. Adapter: Ben Feiner. Director: Feiner. Cast: Emlyn Etting.
24 May 1945	"Untitled," by Norman Corwin. Producer: Ben Feiner. Director: Feiner.
21 June 1945	"Letter from the Teens," by Lela Swift and Edward Stasheff. Director: Worthington Miner.
14 August 1945	"On a Note of Triumph," by Norman Corwin. Adapter: Ben Feiner. Producer: Feiner. Director: Feiner.

23 August 1945
8:00–9:00p

"Experiment in the Desert" by Paul Belanger and Edward Stasheff. Director: Paul Belanger.

25 September 1945
8:16–8:30p

Tales to Remember, a variety series, including some dramatic monologues. Director: Rudy Bretz.

2 October 1945
8:15–9:00p

Photocrime.

9 October 1945
8:15–8:45p

"Big Sister," a radio serial drama created by Lillian Lauferty, is the first WCBW commercial drama. Director: Worthington Miner. Cast: Mercedes McCambridge as Big Sister; also Julian Funt. Sponsor: Lever Bros. (Rinso). Agency: Ruthrauff & Ryan.

16 October 1945
8:32–8:47p

Tales to Remember.

19 October 1945
8:31–8:59p

Casey, Press Photographer, a series based on characters from *Look* magazine. Written for radio by Alonzo Deen Cole and others.

23 October 1945
8:16–8:28p

Three Houses, by Peggy Mayer and Marian Spitzer. Producer: Ben Feiner. Sets: James McNaughton.

26 October 1945
8:15–8:32p

Three Houses, continuing episode.

30 October 1945
8:27–8:42p

Tales to Remember.

2 November 1945
8:24–8:40p

Photocrime.

9 November 1945
8:27–8:58p

Casey, Press Photographer. Director: Cledge Roberts. Cast: Neil Hamilton as Casey.

13 November 1945
8:15–8:29p

Tales to Remember.

20 November 1945
8:15–8:34p

"Aunt Jenny's Real Life Stories," by

Joseph Armel Cross. Director: Worthington Miner. Cast: Edith Spencer as Aunt Jenny. Sponsor: Lever Bros. (Spry). Agency: Ruthrauff & Ryan.

23 November 1945
8:16–8:30p   *Tales to Remember.*
4 December 1945
8:15–8:30p   *Tales to Remember.*
7 December 1945
8:21–8:41p   *Three Houses,* continuing episode.
14 December 1945
8:43–8:57p   *Tales to Remember.*
25 December 1945
8:28–8:43p   *Tales to Remember.*
28 December 1945
8:30–8:59p   *Casey, Press Photographer.*
4 January 1946
8:42–9:02p   *You Be the Judge,* dramas of famous criminal cases. Cast: Edward Stasheff as Court Clerk.

8 January 1946
8:15–8:30p   *Tales to Remember.*
22 January 1946
8:10–8:31p   *Tales to Remember.*
30 January 1946
8:31–8:56p   "Sorry, Wrong Number," by Lucille Fletcher. Director: Frances Buss (originally John Houseman). Cast: Mildred Natwick as Mrs. Stevenson.

1 February 1946
8:11–8:31p   *Tales to Remember.*
5 February 1946
9:11–9:34p   *You Be the Judge.*
12 February 1946
7:55–8:00p   "Gettysburg Address," an original sketch by Sam Taylor. Cast: Raymond Massey as Abraham Lincoln, John Cromwell as John Hay.

15 February 1946
8:30–8:46p   *Tales by Hoff,* a series of bedtime stories told with drawings. [Not listed hereafter.]

21 February 1946
8:31–8:56p   *You Be the Judge.*

9 May 1946
[Unlogged]   *Tales to Remember.*
19 May 1946
8:30–8:33p   "Kaleidoscope."
8:34–9:03p   *You Be the Judge.*
26 May 1946
8:35–8:47p   *Tales to Remember.*
9 June 1946
8:30–9:00p   *You Be the Judge.*
16 June 1946
8:31–8:47p   *Tales to Remember.*
23 June 1946
8:30–9:00p   *You Be the Judge.*
4 July 1946
8:59–9:16p   "Prudence Indeed."
7 July 1946
8:32–9:00p   *You Be the Judge.*
21 July 1946
8:32–8:58p   *You Be the Judge.*
25 July 1946
8:52–9:09p   *Thornton Show,* a modeling show that
                                     includes an occasional sketch and danc-
                                     ing. [Not listed hereafter.]

4 August 1946
8:32–9:01p   *You Be the Judge.*
18 August 1946
8:31–8:54p   *Judge for Yourself,* variety/quiz. [Not list-
                                     ed hereafter.]

29 August 1946
8:46–8:58p   Improvisation.
3 October 1946
8:32–9:07p   *You Be the Judge.*
10 October 1946
8:39–8:54p   Improvisation Group.
12 December 1946
9:08–9:33p   *You Be the Judge.* [This is the first time
                                     this series is officially logged as "drama."]

17 October 1948
7:30–8:30p EST
(monthly colorcast)   *Ford Television Theater* debuts with

"Years Ago," by Ruth Gordon. Producers: Garth Montgomery, Ellis Sard. Director: Marc Daniels. Cast: Patricia Kirkland as Ruth Gordon Jones, Raymond Massey as Father, Eva Le Gallienne as Mother; and Logan Ramsey, Virginia Gorski, Jennifer Bunker, Judith Cargill, Richard Taber, Seth Arnold, Cy Feuer.

7 November 1948
7:30–8:30p EST
(bimonthly)

Studio One debuts with "The Storm," by McKnight Malmar. Producer: Worthington Miner. Director: Miner. Adapter: Miner. Cast: Margaret Sullavan.

NBC Television Dramas, 1936–1946*

1936–1941

W2XBS, 30 Rockefeller Center, New York City.

7 July 1936	First regular demonstration includes scene from "Tobacco Road," by Jack Kirkland and Erskine Caldwell. Cast: Henry Hull as Jeeter Lester. First NBC dramatic monologue.
9 September 1936	"Romeo and Juliet," by William Shakespeare. Dramatic cast.
21 September 1936	"Park Scene," sketch. Dramatic cast. "Love Nest," by Grace Bradt and Eddie Albert. Cast: Bradt and Albert, known as "The Honeymooners." First original sketch presented by NBC.
2 October 1936	"Puppets," first NBC puppet show and first NBC weekly demonstration.
6 October 1936	"Love Nest," repeat.
9 October 1936	[News, music (Southernaires), second weekly demonstration. No drama.]
16 October 1936	"A Balanced Meal," by Grace Bradt and Eddie Albert. Cast: Bradt and Albert.
28 October 1936	"A Balanced Meal," repeat. Guests: General Foods.
12 November 1936	"If Men Played Cards as Women Do," by George S. Kaufman. Cast: Mark Smith, Arthur Maitland, Alan Bunce, Max Waizman, Alvin Simmons. Guests: RCA manufacturers and station owners.

*This list includes all known dramas from the time dramatic programming began, in 1936, through 1946, though a few programming benchmark dates are also listed.

Principal sources: *W2XBS Television Master Programs; WNBT Television Master Programs.*

13 November 1936	"Just Married," by Grace Bradt and Eddie Albert. Cast: Bradt and Albert. Guests: RCA and NBC employees.
19 November 1936	"If Men Played Cards as Women Do," repeat. Guests: Sinclair Refining Company.
16 December 1936	"If Men Played Cards as Women Do," repeat. Guests: public utility employees.
January–February 1937	[The television master log is illegible.]
31 March 1937	"The Trailing Arbutus Nature Study Club," a sketch. Guests: Bureau of Foreign and Domestic Commerce.
8 April 1937	"The Maid's Night Out," a sketch. Dramatic cast. Guests: Federal Communications Commission.
3 May 1937	"Romantic Interlude" [also titled "Little Old Lady"]. Dramatic cast. "Still Alarm," by George S. Kaufman. Dramatic cast. Guests: Philip Morris Company, Sealtest, J. Walter Thompson, Philips Manufacturing Company.
5 May 1937	"Little Old Lady," repeat.
10 May 1937	"Tristan and Isolde," by Richard Wagner. Conductor: Dr. Walter Damrosch.
11 May 1937	"Little Old Lady." Cast: Helen Walpole as Girl, Lawrence Gray as Boy, Minnie Dupree as Grandma; also Grandpa, six extras. Guests: Institute of Radio Engineers, Philips Manufacturing Company.
1 July 1937 9:00p	"The Matchmaker," by Roland Jeans. Cast: James Meighan as John, John Moore as Charles, Helen Lewis as Mary, Helen Walpole as Stella. "Not Lost," by Roland Jeans. Cast: Robert Strauss, Ralph Locke, Jack MacBryde, Helen Walpole.
7 July 1937	"Not Lost," repeat. Cast: Robert Strauss, Arthur Maitland, Jack MacBryde, Helen Walpole. Guests: General Motors.

8 July 1937
12:30 and 1:00p

"Not Lost," repeat. Same cast. Guests:
Bristol Myers; Young and Rubicam.

12 July 1937
2:00p

"Not Lost," repeat. Same cast. Guests:
Batten, Barton, Durstine & Osborne.

15 July 1937
10:00p

"Midnight Murder," by Arthur Ashton.
Cast: Arthur Maitland, Neil O'Malley,
Fred Irving Lewis.

27 July 1937
3:30p

"Not Lost," repeat. Cast: Robert Strauss,
Arthur Maitland, Jack MacBryde, Helen
Lewis. Guests: *March of Time* staff.

29 July 1937
9:00p

"Midnight Murder," repeat. Guests: *Life*.

13 August 1937
1:45p

"Midnight Murder," repeat. Guests: New
York Central Railroad.

25 August 1937
1:45p

"Not Lost," repeat. Same cast. Guests:
Listerine.

26 August 1937
1:45p

"Midnight Murder," repeat. Guest: Com-
missioner Valentine.

7 September 1937
1:45p

"The Matchmaker," repeat. Cast: James
Meighan, Helen Lewis, Noel Mills, John
McGovern. Guests: Major Lenox Lohr,
General James J. Harbord.

8 September 1937
4:00p

"If Men Played Cards as Women Do,"
repeat. Guests: *The New Yorker*.

10 September 1937
1:45p

"The Matchmaker," repeat. Guests: American Legion.

22 September 1937
1:45p

"Midnight Murder," repeat. Guests:
American Association of Advertisers.

5 October 1937
7:00p

"The Services of an Expert," by Harry

Stephen Keller. Adapter: T. H. Hutchinson. Cast: Arthur Maitland as Man, Ned Wever as Intruder. Guests: Television Coordination Committee.

6 October 1937
7:00p   "Not Lost," repeat. Guests: American Public Health Association.

14 October 1937
8:00p   "Not Lost," repeat. Guests: Motion Picture Engineers.

10:00p   "Ear Muffs." Cast: Len Hollister, Leona Hollister, Hal Ford.

23 November 1937
7:00p, 8:30p, and 10:00p   "The Three Garridebs," by Arthur Conan Doyle. Adapter: T. H. Hutchinson. Director: Hutchinson. Cast: Louis Hector as Sherlock Holmes, William Podmore as Dr. Watson, Arthur Maitland as John Garrideb, Harold DeBecker as Nathan Garrideb, Violet Bosson as Mrs. Hudson, Selma Hall as Mrs. Saunders, Eustace Wyatt as Inspector Lestrade. Guests: American Radio Relay League.

24 November 1937
7:00p, 8:30p, and 10:00p   "The Three Garridebs," repeat.
30 November 1937
9:00p   "The Three Garridebs," repeat. Guests: EMG, England.

3 December 1937
11:00a, 2:00p, and 8:30p   "The Three Garridebs," repeat. Guests: FCC, William Esty & Company, Rockefeller Center.

13 December 1937
3:30p   "The Services of an Expert," repeat. Guests: *Liberty*.

17 December 1937
2:30p   "When They Play a Waltz," by Robert Wallsten. Cast: Laura Suarez, Charles LaTorre, Neil O'Malley, Burford Hampden, Jack Negley, Tom Cochran, Willie Clair, Larry Pacquin, Melda Dean,

Leah Hatch, Terry and Fran Carroll, the
Kampus Kids, Jay Meredith as Announcer.
Guests: Universal Picture Company.

January–March 1938   [*W2XBS Television Master Programs*
                         record has been lost for these months.]

— April 1938   "Stepping Out," by Dion Titneradge.
                         Cast: Harold DeBecker as Potty, Marie
                         DeBecker as Char.

19 April 1938
9:00p   "The Noble Lord." Cast: Robert Lynn as
                         He, Helen Lewis as She, Harold DeBecker
                         as Peters.

21 April 1938
9:00p   "The Valiant," by Holworthy Hall and
                         Robert Middlemass. Cast: William Daniel
                         as Warden Holt, Herman Tub as Father
                         Daly, Robert Regent as James Dyhe, Flora
                         Campbell as Josephine Paris, Neil O'Mal-
                         ley as Dan, Arthur Maitland as Governor.

26 April 1938   "Some Words in Edgewise," by Charles
                         O'Brien Kennedy. Cast: Robert Strauss as
                         Mr. Snodgrass, Elsie MacGordon as
                         Woman.

5 May 1938   "Sauce for the Gander," by Margaret
                         Freshley. Cast: Marjorie Clarke as Linda,
                         Ned Wever as Terry, William David as
                         Tom, Kay Strozzi as Luella, Julian Davis
                         as Bell Boy, Taylor Graves as Writer.

9 May 1938   "The Services of an Expert," repeat.
10 May 1938   "The Services of an Expert," repeat.
11 May 1938   "The Mysterious Mummy Case," by Tom
                         Terriss. Adapter: T. H. Hutchinson. Direc-
                         tor: Hutchinson. Cast: Tom Terriss as
                         Himself, Arthur Maitland as Dr. Harvey,
                         Dorothy McGuire as Miss Clarke, An-
                         thony Kemble Cooper as Wilson Ellis,
                         Ned Wever as Curt Picart [or Piquard],
                         William David as Edward Lawson, J. Mal-
                         colm Dunn as Colonel Murray, Harold
                         DeBecker as Gregson, Aristes [or
                         Aristides] DeLeone as Egyptian.

12 May 1938   "Confessional," by Percival Wilde.

13 May 1938	"The Mysterious Mummy Case," repeat.
16 May 1938	"The Mysterious Mummy Case," repeat.
17 May 1938	"The Mysterious Mummy Case," repeat. First television drama reviewed for *Variety*, by Robert J. Landry, which was published on the front page of the 25 May 1938 issue.
18 May 1938	"The Mysterious Mummy Case," repeat.
20 May 1938	"The Mysterious Mummy Case," repeat.
23 May 1938 8:00p	"Sauce for the Gander," repeat.
24 May 1938 8:00p	"Sauce for the Gander," repeat.
31 May 1938 8:00–9:30p	Alexander Korda's *The Return of the Scarlet Pimpernel,* the first full-length feature film shown by NBC.
9:30p	"Sauce for the Gander," repeat.
1 June 1938	"Stepping Out," repeat.
2 June 1938 8:00p	"Stepping Out," repeat.
6 June 1938	"A Game of Chess," by Kenneth Sawyer Goodman. Cast: Anthony Kemble Cooper as Alexis, Calvin Thomas as Constantine, Eugene Sigaloff as Boris, Melvin Parks as Footman.
7 June 1938 4:00p	"Susan and God," by Rachel Crothers. Producer: John Golden. Cast: Gertrude Lawrence as Susan Trexel, Paul McGrath as Barrie, Nancy Coleman as Blossom. First time a scene from a current Broadway play was telecast from a television studio.
9 June 1938	"Stepping Out," repeat.
July 1938	W2XBS goes off the air.
23 August 1938 8:00p	"Good Medicine," by Harold F. Godwin [or Jack Arnold] and Edwin Burke. Cast: Pat Lawrence as Dr. James Graves, Barbara Weeks as Mary Graves, Lily Cahill as Hetty, Elvin Field as Clerk.

24 August 1938 2:00p	"Good Medicine," repeat.
26 August 1938 8:00p	"The Nine Lives of Emily," by John Kirkpatrick. Cast: Paula McLean as Mrs. Reade, Eunice Hall as Natalie, Manart Kippen as Mr. Reade, Mildred Murray as Laura, Burford Hampden as Dr. Douglas Everett, Mona Moray as Emily, Owen Elliot as Tom Wells.
30 August 1938	"Red Carnations," by Glenn Hughes. Cast: Jack Cherry, Jack Edwards, Marifrances Carden, Helen Harvey.
2 September 1938	"Speaking to Father," by George Ade. Cast: James Spottswood as Septimus Pickering, Grace Valentine as Luella Pickering, Ronald Bennett as Edward Worthington Swinger, Robert Lyn as Professor Bliss.
6 September 1938 8:00p	"The Mayor and the Manicure," by George Ade. Cast: George Taylor as the Honorable Otis Milford, Paula MacLean as Genevieve LeClaire, Vivian Martin as Ruth Foster, Charles Long as Wallie Milford.
9 September 1938 8:00p	"The Ace Is Trumped," by H. H. Stinson. Cast: Clarence Rock as Big Ace Jacobs, Neil O'Malley as Eddie Reilly, Selena Boyle as Ella.
14 September 1938 2:00p	"Hot Lemonade."
5 October 1938 2:00p	"The Master Salesman," by William Hazlett Upson. Cast: Frank Nellis as Salesman, Patricia Murray as Stenographer, George Taylor as Zachary Taylor Allen.
7 October 1938	"The Master Salesman," repeat.
28 October 1938	"Emergency Call," by Ted Byron. Cast: Doris Light as Betty, Robert Light as Bob.
1 November 1938	"Emergency Call," repeat.

16 November 1938	"Emergency Call," repeat.
17 November 1938	"Emergency Call," repeat.
22 November 1938 to	
March 1939	[No television dramas.]
21 March 1939	
2:00–2:07p	"A Room with a View." Cast: Sue Read, Ralph Blane.
22 March 1939	"Jenny Lind" [also titled "Little Old New York"]. Cast: Terry Harris as Nicky, Burford Hampden as Dick, Mildred Murray as Lady, W. O. MacWatters as Barnum, Norman MacKay as John, Manart Kippen as Albert, Maurice Morris as Minister, Robert Haig as Genin, Ethelyne Holt as Jenny Lind, and a pianist.
23 March 1939	"The Trimmed Lamp," by O. Henry. Adapter: Edward Padula. Cast: Dana Dale as Nancy, Mavie Brown as Lou, John Cleary as Dan, Alfred Etcheverry as Wilbur Montgomery, Dillon O'Ferris as Jack Norton.
24 March 1939	
2:00p	"The Unexpected," by Aaron Hoffman. Cast: Marjorie Clarke as She, Stephen Kent as He, David More as Jenkins.
	"When the Nightingale Sang in Berkeley Square," by Michael Arlen. Adapter: Thomas Lyne Riley. Director: Riley. Cast: Anthony Kemble Cooper as Ralph Loyalty, Patricia Calvert as Joan Loyalty, John Moore as Hugo Carr, J. Malcolm Dunn as George, Bruce Evans as Austin, Neil O'Malley as Smith, S. O'Malley as Reader.
28 March 1939	"Trifles," by Susan Glaspell. Cast: Helen Westley as Mrs. Hale, Mona Hungerford as Mrs. Peters, Frank Treddell as Lewis Hale, Arthur Geary as George Henderson, Alan MacAteer as Sheriff Peters, Edmonia Nolley as Mrs. Wright.
30 March 1939	"Dark Eyes Mean Danger," by Llewellyn

Hughes. Cast: Victor Beecroft as Valet, Robert Light as Dwight Gray, Mary Mac-Cormack as Audrey Stair, Pauline Mac-Lean as Aunt Martha, James Boles as Butler, Philip Tonge as Meredith, Walter James as Lord Wollerton, Lili Valenti as Mme. Sylka Brovnikov, Grant Gordon as Robert Tilton. First television promotional credit, for evening wrap and furs from Russek's Fifth Avenue.

3 April 1939 "May Eve," by Helen M. Clark. Adapter: John Eugene Hasty. Director: Thomas Lyne Riley. Cast: Hencey Castle as Shiela MacCrea, Sydney Smith as Fergus Roy, Arthur Maitland as Dr. Larkin, Earle Larrimore as Emery MacCrea, John Porterfield as Donald MacCrea, Florence Edney as Mary, William Thornton as Dennis.

11 April 1939 "The Trimmed Lamp," repeat.

13 April 1939 "A Spot of Philanthropy," by Everett Rhodes Castle. Cast: John James as Boy, Gloria Bean as Girl, George Taylor as Colonel Humphrey Flack, Frank Nellis as Porterfield, Anthony Blair as Mack, Michael Drake as Mr. Garvey, Ralph Jewell as Brudner, Elsie Hunt as Page, Jack Davis [?] as Hotel Manager.

15 April 1939 "A Spot of Philanthropy," repeat.

20 April 1939 "The Nagger," by Jack Norworth.

21 April 1939 "The Nagger," repeat.

5 May 1939 "The Unexpected," repeat. Director: Thomas Lyne Riley. Cast: Earle Larrimore as He, David More as Jenkins, Marjorie Clarke as She.

8:00p "The Choir Rehearsal," by Clare.

10 May 1939

8:00p "The Faker," by Edwin Burke. Producer: Edward Sobol. Director: Edward Padula. Cast: Walter Greaza as Faker, Edwin Phillips as Ralph, Maxine Stewart as Ruth, Patricia Palmer as Woman, six extras.

	"A Room with a View," repeat.
12 May 1939	"The Red Hat," by Elaine Sterne Carrington. Cast: Jack Cherry as Phil, Boyd Crawford as Ted, Jean Muir as Jean, Blanche Gladstone as Another Woman.
17 May 1939	"The Smart Thing," by Frank Conlan. Cast: Martha Sleeper as Jean, Ned Wever as Mark, Burford Hampden as George.
19 May 1939	"Any Family," by Harry Delf. Cast: Grant Irvin as Father, Anne Athey [?] as Mother, Phyllis Welch [?] as Louise, Harry Richards as Charles Grant, Charles Hart [?] as Willie.
24 May 1939	"Likes and Dislikes," by Edwin Burke. Producer: Edward Sobol. Director: Thomas Lyne Riley. Cast: Margaret Callahan as Mildred, Alan Bunce as Bobbie, John Baruff as George, Patricia Palmer as Maid.
26 May 1939	"A Game of Chess," repeat. Producer: Warren Wade. Director: Edward Padula.
31 May 1939 8:30p	"Afterwards," by Geraldine McGaughan. Cast: students from Bogota High School, New Jersey: Robert Baren as Boy, Doris Young as Girl, John McEllen and Walter Rosemier as Workmen, Marjorie Palmissano and Martha Abrams as Bodies.
2 June 1939 8:30–9:30p	"Jenny Lind," repeat. Producer: Warren Wade.
14 June 1939	"Mamba's Daughters," by Dorothy Heyward and Dubose Heyward. Cast: Georgette Harvey as Mamba, Ethel Waters as Hagar, Ollie Barber as Mr. Saint.
16 June 1939	"Family Honor," by William E. Shea. Cast: William E. Shea as Joshua, Paul Ballantine as Enoch, Helen Soulby [?] as Phyllis.
17 June 1939	"The Valiant," repeat.
22 June 1939	"The Honeymooner," by Aaron Hoffman.
24 June 1939	"The Pirates of Penzance," by W. S. Gilbert and Arthur Sullivan.

25 June 1939	"Moonshine," by Arthur Hopkins. Cast: James Bell as Revenue, Theodore Newton as Luke.
29 June 1939 8:30p	"The Donovan Affair," by Owen Davis. Cast: William Harrigan, Laura Baxter, Henry Wadsworth, Matt Briggs, Horace Braham.
4 July 1939	"The Marriage of Little Eva," by Kenyon Nicholson. Producer: Warren Wade. Cast: John Boyd as Uncle Tom, Josephine Huston as Eva, Paula MacLean as Eliza, Winfield Hoeny as Simon Legree, David Mallow as Manager, Bambi Lynn as Oriole, Roberts and Martin as Dancers, Southernaires as Male Quartet, Dr. Whipple on the organ piano.
6 July 1939	"The Services of an Expert," repeat. Cast: Ethelyn Mateson, Alfred Alderdice, Maxine Rosco, Lew Daily.
11 July 1939	"Confessional" [also titled "Hour of Truth"], repeat. Cast: Wilmer Walter as Robert Baldwin, Edmonia Nolley as Martha, Cliff Carpenter as John, Helen Harvey as Evie, James Spottswood as Marshall, Earle Larrimore as Gresham.
18 July 1939	"Missouri Legend," by E. B. Ginty. Cast: Dean Jagger, Mildred Natwick, Richard Bishop, Mary Cornell, Sam Byrd, Norman Lloyd, Frank Twedell, Harry M. Cooke, G. Pat Collins, Hans Robert, Herman Lieb.
20 July 1939 8:30p	"Box and Cox," by Arthur Sullivan. Cast: Colin O'Moore, Steele Jamison, Walter Preston.
24 July 1939 8:30p	"Topsy and Eva," a sketch from *Uncle Tom's Cabin*, by Harriet Beecher Stowe. Cast: The Diamond sisters as Topsy and Eva, Winfield Hoeny as Simon Legree.

27 July 1939
8:30p   "Hay Fever," by Noel Coward. Director
                                 Edward Sobol. Cast: Isobel Elson as Judi-
                                 th Bliss, Dennis Hoey as David Bliss, Vir-
                                 ginia Campbell as Sorel Bliss,
                                 Montgomery Clift as Simon Bliss; also
                                 Wesley Addy, Lowell Gilmore, Barbara
                                 Leeds, Carl Harbord, Florence Edney,
                                 Nancy Sheridan.
28 July 1939   W2XBS closes to improve facilities.
29 August 1939   "Dulcy," by George S. Kaufman and Marc
                                 Connelly. Director: Edward Padula. Cast:
                                 Tom Powers as Husband, Helen Claire as
                                 Dulcy, also Katherine Stevens.
31 August 1939   "The Streets of New York," by Dion
                                 Boucicault. Director: Anton Bundsmann.
                                 Cast: Joyce Arling as Lucy Fairweather,
                                 Derek Fairman as Mark Livingston, Nor-
                                 man Lloyd as Badger, George Coulouris
                                 as Gideon Bloodgood, Sheila Trent as Al-
                                 ida Bloodgood, Molly Pearson as Mrs.
                                 Puffy, Tom Gorman as Paul Fairweather,
                                 Whitford Kane as Captain Fairweather,
                                 Fredrica Selmons as Mrs. Fairweather,
                                 John Call as Dan Puffy, Robert Lindsey as
                                 Daniels.
5 September 1939   "H.M.S. Pinafore," by W. S. Gilbert and
                                 Arthur Sullivan. Director: Thomas Lyne
                                 Riley. Cast: Ray Heatherton, John Cherry,
                                 Colin O'Moore.
7 September 1939   "Brother Rat," by John Monks and Fred
                                 F. Finklehoffe. Director: Edward Sobol.
                                 Cast: Juliet Forbes as Joyce Winfree, Anna
                                 Franklin as Jenny, Marjorie Davies as
                                 Claire Hamm, James Corner as Harley
                                 Harrington, Lyle Bettger as Bing Edwards,
                                 Edwin Phillips as Billy Randolph, Mary
                                 Cheffey as Kate Rice, Tom Ewell as Dan
                                 Crawford, Brammer Binder as A. Furman
                                 Townsend, Jr., Frederic DeWilde as "Mis-
                                 tole" Bottoms, Owen Martin as Slim,

Frank Camp as Colonel Hamm, Sanford McCauley as Captain Rogers, Bob Walker as Guard.

14 September 1939

"Art and Mrs. Bottle," by Benn W. Levy. Director: Donald Davis. Cast: Tom Speidel as Michael Bottle, Katherine Emery as Judy Bottle, Dorothy Mathews as Sonia Tippert, Helen Wynn as Parlormaid, Jabez Gray as George Bottle, Ann Revere as Celia Bottle, Carl Gose as Charles Davis, Shepperd Strudwick as Max Lightly.

28 September 1939
8:30p

"When the Nightingale Sang in Berkeley Square," repeat. Director: Thomas Lyne Riley. Cast: Same as on 24 March 1939 except for Matthew Smith as Ralph Loyalty, Lionel Glemster as Smith.

"Dr. Abernathy." Director: Thomas Lyne Riley. Cast: William Podmore, Robin Craven, Naomi Campbell, St. Clair Bayfield, John Carmody, Florence Fair, Richard Waring.

3 October 1939
8:30p

"The Butter and Egg Man," by George S. Kaufman. Producer: Reginald Hammerstein. Cast: Florence Sundstrom as Jane Weston, Helen Twelvetrees as Mary Marlin, Zella Russell as Fanny Lehman, Theodore Leavitt as Peter Jones, Anthony Blair as Joe Lehman, Jim Swift as Jack MacClure, Bob Pitkin as Patterson, Al Dowling as Waiter, Lew Mence as Benham, Neil Moore as Sampson, Arthur Lipson as Fritchie.

5 October 1939

"The Night Cap," by Max Marcin and Guy Bolton. Cast: Richard Rauber as Charles, Arthur Sachs as Policeman, Percy Kilbride as Jerry Hammond, Holbert Brown as Colonel James Constance, Harry Bannister as Lester Knowles, Doris Dalton

as Mrs. Lester Knowles, Claudia Morgan as Anne Maynard, Robert Light as Fred Hammond, Douglas Gilmore as Robert Andrews, Alfred Kappeler as the Reverend Forbes, George Lesoir as Coroner Watrous, Frank Nellis as Detective Selden.

12 October 1939
8:30–9:30p

"Jane Eyre," by Charlotte Brontë. Adapter: Helen Jerome. Producer/director: Anton Bundsmann. Cast: Flora Campbell as Jane Eyre, Dennis Hoey as Edward Rochester, John Clarke as Lord Ingram, Effie Shannon as Mrs. Fairfax, Naomi Campbell as Leah, Eleanor Pittis as Adele. Lorna Elliott as Lady Ingram, Philip Tonge as Solicitor, Lillian Tonge as Hannah, Ruth Matteson as Blanche Ingram, Irving Morrow as Mason, Olive Deering as Madwoman, Daisy Belmore as Grace Poole, Bryan Russell as Minister, Mary Newnham Davis as Diana, Carl Harbord as St. John.

18 October 1939
8:30–10:07p

"The Dover Road," by A. A. Milne. Producer/director: Thomas Lyne Riley. Cast: Charles Webster as Mr. Latimer, Marjorie Clarke as Anne, Maurice Wells as Leonard, Marie Carroll as Eustasia, Richard Janaver as Nicholas, William Thornton as Dominic, Judson Langill and William Robertson as Butlers, Jane Abbott and Rosalie Bishop as Maids.

20 October 1939
8:30p

"The Milky Way," by Lynn Root and Harry Clarke. Director: Edward Sobol. Cast: Ross Hertz as Spider, James Corner as Speed McFarlane, Claudia Morgan as Anne Westley, Alexander Cross as Gabby Sloan, Fred Stewart as Burleigh Sullivan, Jane Blosson as Mae Sullivan, Paul Porter as Eddie, Benson Greene as Willards, Lowell Gillmore as Wilbur Austin.

27 October 1939
8:30–9:30p

"The Fortune Hunter," by Winchell Smith. Producer: Warren Wade. Cast: Douglas Gilmore as Nat Duncan, Walter Jones as Mr. Lockwood, Percy Kilbridge as Sam Graham, Maurice Burke as Henry Kellogg, Gloria Blondell as Betty Graves, Theadora Peck as Josie Lockwood, Patricia Fitzgerald as Angie, Robert Carver as Trace, Clarke Chesney as Roland, James Swift as Mr. Burnham, Bonnie Donahue as Secretary, Maxie Stover as Mrs. Carpenter, Joseph Garry as Sheriff, John Hewitt as Sign Painter.

4 November 1939
8:30–9:30p

"Treasure Island," by Robert Louis Stevenson. Adapters: Owen Davis, Donald Davis. Producer: Donald Davis. Cast: Billy Redfield as Jim Hawkins, Harvey Young as Ben Gunn, Harry Cooke as Black Dog, Dennis Hoey as Long John Silver, William Balfour as Captain Billy Bones, William Podmore as Squire Trelawney, Robert Allen as Dr. Livesy, Alan MacAteer as Blindman, Edwin Cooper as Captain Smollett, William Barry as Will Smiley, Irving Morrow as Tom Morgan, Leslie Hunt as Anderson, Florence Edney as Mrs. Hawkins, Jabez Gray as George Merry, St. Clair Bayfield as Redruth, Simon Clayton as Pirate.

10 November 1939
8:30p

"The Farmer Takes a Wife," by Frank S. Eiser and Mark Connelly, based on the novel *Rome Haul,* by William D. Edmonds. Director: Thomas Lyne Riley. Cast: Mary Hutchinson as Molly, Wylie Adams as Dan, George Taylor as Sam Weaver, William Kent as Fortune, Francis Pieriot as Sol Tinker, Donna Earl as Lucy, George Spaulding as J. L. Fisher, Alexander Cross as Klore, Lida Kane as Gam-

	my, Douglas McMullen as Luke, Judson Langill as Conductor, William Thornton as Narrator.
12 November 1939	"The Happy Journey," by Thornton Wilder. Producer: Edward Padula. Cast: John Forsht as Stage Manager, Jane Rose as Ma Kirby, Poland Wood as Pa Kirby, Perry Wilson as Arthur, Elizabeth Goddard as Caroline, Bettina Prescott as Beulah.
17 November 1939	"Criminal at Large," by Edgar Wallace. Producer: Anton Bundsmann. Cast: Charles Gerard as Dr. Lester Amersham, Derek Fairman as Sgt. Ferraby, Charles Jordan as Sgt. Totty, Dennis Hoey as Chief Detective Inspector Tanner, Carl Harbord as Lord Lebanon, Perry Norman as Kelver, Harry M. Cooke as Gilder, Scott Moore as Brooks, Nance O'Neil as Lady Lebanon, Frances Reid as Isla.
24 November 1939 8:30p	"Three Men on a Horse," by John Cecil Holm and George Abbott. Producer: Reginald Hammerstein. Cast: Joyce Arling as Audrey Trowbridge, Jack Sheehan as Erwin Trowbridge. Sidney Stone as Patsy, Loretta Sayers as Mabel, Ben Laughlin as Charlie, Ross Hertz as Frankie, John James as Delivery Boy, William Foram as Harry, Hugh Rennie as Clarence.
1 December 1939	"Roosty," by Martin Berkeley. Cast: Peter Lewis as Dip, Clancy Cooper as Alec, Anthony Ross as Stuff Nelson, Andy Donnelly as Roosty Nelson, Robert Haig as Sgt. Pryor, Judson Fairgill as Judge Marlow, Theresa Dale as Mrs. Adams, Russell Hardie as Ed Schuster, Kate Warrener as Kate Grant, Helen Rory as Martha Schuster.
6 December 1939	"Jane Eyre," repeat. Cast: same as on 12 October 1939 except for Leslie Bingham as Mrs. Fairfax, Theresa Dale as Grace Poole, Roland Bottomsley as Lord Ingram,

Jacqueline DeWit as Blanche Ingram, Bryon Russell as Solicitor.

8 December 1939   "Another Language," by Rosen Franken. Producer: Edward Sobol. Cast: Anne Revere as Mrs. Hallam, Jabez Gray as Mr. Hallam, Robert Allen as Harry Hallam, Jane Rose as Grace Hallam, Herbert Duffy as Paul Hallam, Ben Smith as Victor Hallam, Dorothy Mathews as Stella Hallam, Jerry Clark as Jerry Hallam.

17 December 1939
8:30p   "Stage Door," by George S. Kaufman and Edna Ferber. Producer: Warren Wade. Cast: Elizabeth Paige as Mattie, Janet Fox as Bernice Miemeyer, Eleanor Kilgallen as Madeline Vauclain, Lee Patrick as Judith Canfield, Frances Fuller as Kaye Hamilton, Sydna Scott as Jean Maitland, Blanche Gladstone as Pat Devine, Margaret Curtis as Terry Randall, Cora Witherspoon as Mrs. Orcutt, Edmund Dorsay as Lou Milhouser, Michael Whalen as David Kingsley, Richard Kendricks as Keith Burgess, Halbert Brown as Dr. Randall, Larry Westcott as David Orrick, Ralph Locke as Adolph Gretzi.

22 December 1939   "Little Women," by Louisa May Alcott. Adapter: Marian DeForest. Cast: Robert Conness as Mr. March, Molly Pearson as Mrs. March, Joanna Post as Meg, Flora Campbell as Jo, Francis Reid as Beth, Joyce Arling as Amy, Charles Bryant as Theodore Lawrence, Wilton Graff as Professor Bhaer, Lida Kane as Hannah Mullert.

29 December 1939
8:30–9:52p   "Post Road," by Wilbur D. Steele and Norma Mitchell. Director: Thomas Lyne Riley. Cast: Edith Shayne as Emily, Marjorie Clarke as Girl, J. W. Austin as Cartwright, Alexander Campbell as Spencer, Ruth Cates as May, Percy Kilbride as

George, Dorothy Blackburn as Nurse, Lucia Segar as Mrs. Cashler, Madeline Pierce as Baby Cries.

5 January 1940
8:30–9:51p

"Ethan Frome," by Edith Wharton. Adapters: Owen and Donald Davis. Cast: Robert Allen as Ethan Frome, Dorothy Mathews as Mattie Silver, Edwin Redding as Jotham, Dana Hardwick as Denis Eady, Ann Revere as Zenobia Frome.

12 January 1940
8:30–9:36p

"Meet the Wife," by Lynn Sterling. Director: Edward Sobol. Cast: Phyllis Povah as Gertrude Lennox, William J. Kelly as Harvey Lennox, Margaret Ledbetter as Doris Bellamy, Staats Cottsworth as Victor Staunton, James Corner as Gregory Brown, J. W. Austin as Phillip Lord, Lucille Fanton as Alice.

19 January 1940

"The Gorilla," by Robert Spence. Cast: Olvester Polk as Jefferson Lee, Ralph Kellard as Cyrus Stevens, Victoria Cummings as Alice Denby, Robert Shayne as Arthur Marsden, Tom Tully as Mr. Mulligan, Percy Kilbride as Mr. Garrity, Jack Cherry as Simmons, Hugh Rennie as Stranger, Ben Laughlin as Sailor, A. C. Van Horn as Poe.

26 January 1940
8:30–9:44p

"The Impossible Mr. Clancy." Cast: Ralph Cullinan as Tom Clancy, Margot Ann Deighton as Mary Clancy, George Spaulding as Timothy Murphy, Effie Afton as Kate, Ross Hertz as Johnnie, Bill Johnson as Danny, George Lawrence as Shifty Blaney, Alfred Webster as Mr. Donovan, Robert J. Mulligan as Mulligan.

1 February 1940
1:45p

"The Happy Journey," repeat. Cast: same as on 12 November 1939 except for Virginia Palmer as Beulah.

2 February 1940

"June Moon," by Ring Lardner and

George S. Kaufman. Cast: Richard Quine as Fred Stevens, Julie Grant as Edna Baxter, James Spottswood as Paul Sears, Ann Seymour as Lucille, Viki Cummings as Eileen, Ray Mayer as Maxie, Ross Hertz as Goldie, Ben Laughlin as Window Cleaner, Sidney Stone as Benny Fox, Hugh Rennie as Mr. Hart.

4 February 1940 "The Long Christmas Dinner," by Thornton Wilder. Producer: Edward Padula. Cast: Lorraine Stewart as Lucia, William Hare as Roderick, Jane Rose as Mother Bayard, Nollin Bauer as Cousin Brandon, Joseph Anthony as Charles, Lucy Land as Genevieve, Mary V. Palmer as Leonora, Perry Wilson as Ermengrade, John Forsht as Sam, Elizabeth Goddard as Lucia II, Selwyn Myers as Roderick II, Patricia Coates as Nurse and Gertrude.

9 February 1940 "Charlotte Corday," by Helen Jerome. Cast: Ruth McDevitt as Contesse de Bretteville, Frances Reid as Charlotte Corday, Jose Ruban as Marat, Carl Harbord as DePerret, Naomi Campbell as Alex De-Forbin, Lewis Dayton as Montane, Robert Ober as Fouquier, Jeanette Chinlay as Simonne Evrad, Teresa Dale as Louise Grollier, Ross Hertz as Feuillard, Elaine Perry as Felice, Henry Sherwood as Jean-Jacques, Cledge Roberts as Hairdresser.

16 February 1940 8:30p

"The Perfect Alibi," by A. A. Milne. Producer: Thomas Lyne Riley. Cast: Agnes Doyle as Susan, William Mowry as Jimmy, Oswald Marshall as Ludgrove, J. W. Austin as Carter, Edgar Kent as Mullet, Edward Broadley as Adams, Katherine Meskill as Jane, William Thornton as Laverick, Maurice Wells as Sergeant.

— February 1940 "Tickets Please," by Felix Fair. Cast: Virginia Palmer as Mrs. Edward Wilson, Jane Rose as Mrs. Robert Boag, Phyllis Carver

23 February 1940
8:30–9:48p

3 March 1940
8:30p

8 March 1940

10 March 1940
15 March 1940
8:30p

22 March 1940

as Molly Allison, John Forsht as Jimmy Purdie, Elizabeth Goddard as Announcer.

"Prologue To Glory," by E. P. Conkle. Director: Anton Bundsmann. Cast: Stephen Courtleigh as Abraham Lincoln, Frances Reid as Ann Rutledge.

"When We Are Married," by J. B. Priestley. Telecast from the Lyceum Theatre. Producer: Robert Henderson. Director: Thomas Lyne Riley. Cast: Estelle Winwood, Alison Skipworth, J. C. Nugent, Tom Powers, Ann Andrews, Sally O'Neil, A. P. Kaye.

"Dangerous Corner," by J. B. Priestley. Cast: Kathleen Comegys [?] as Maud Mockridge, Helen Craig as Olwen Pell, Ruth Weston as Freda Chatfield, Helen Brooks as Betty Whitehouse, Barry Thompson as Charles Stanton, Henry Richards as Gordon Whitehouse, Alexander Kirkland as Robert Chatfield.

"Pagliacci," by Ruggiero Leoncavallo.

"Julius Caesar," by William Shakespeare. Adapter: Warren Wade. Cast: Judson Laire as Julius Caesar, Patrick Ludlow as Cassius, Eric Mansfield as Casca, Stephen Courtleigh as Brutus, Douglas Gilmore as Antonius, Muriel Hutchinson as Portia, Evelyn Allen as Calpurnia, Arthur Anderson as Lucius, Stephen Schnabel as Metellus Cimber, Grant Gordon as Cinna, Richard Coogan as Decius, Leslie Austin as Titinius and Marullus, Francis Cleveland as Messala, Jack Parsons as Pindarus.

"Passing of the Third Floor Back," by Jerome K. Jerome. Cast: Nat Burns as Joey Wright, Cameron Mitchell as Christopher Penny, Jabez Gray as Major

Tompkins, Zolya Talma as Mrs.
Tompkins, Arden Young as Vivian,
Mildred Natwick as Miss Kite, Muriel
Starr as Mrs. Percivalde Hooley, Sylvia
Field as Stasia, Jane Rose as Mrs. Sharp,
Charles Bryant as Stranger.

29 March 1940   "A Fine Place to Visit," by Kane Camp-
bell. Adapter: Thomas Lyne Riley. Direc-
tor: Riley. Cast: Marjorie Clarke as
Elizabeth, Henry Buckler as John, Wylie
Adams as Henry, George Sturgeon as
John, age 12, George Spaulding as
Adolph, Katherine Meskill as Mary, Elsa
Beamish as Jenny, William Mowry as
Arthur, Edith Shayne as Woman and
Voice of the Rocking Chair, Marie Carroll
as Voices of Boy and Girl, William Thorn-
ton as Voice of New York.

3 April 1940   "The Marriage Proposal," by Anton
Chekhov. Adapted in English by Hilmar
Baukhage and Barrett H. Clark. Cast: Ja-
bez Gray as Stephan S. Tschubikov, Frieda
Allen as Natalia Stephanovna, Robert Al-
len as Ivan V. Lamov.

5 April 1940   "Ode to Liberty," by Marcel Duran.
Adapter: Sidney Howard.

19 April 1940   "Burlesque," by George Manker Watters
and Arthur Hopkins. Cast: Audrey
Christie, Edwin Muchael, Bette Harmon,
Robert Allen.

— April 1940   "Hospital Scene," by Lawrence Dugan.

28 April 1940   "My Heart's in the Highlands," by
William Saroyan. Cast: Russell Hardie,
Ann Brody, Winfield Hoeny, Peter Miner.

1 May 1940   "House of Glass," by Gertrude Berg. Cast:
Berg. For "Milestone in Television," the
first anniversary production of NBC's initiation of public programming.

5 May 1940   "Three Wise Fools," by Austin Strong.
Director: Warren Wade. Cast: Percy Kil-
bride as Finley, Stephen Courtleigh as
Judge, Judson Laire as Doctor, John Cra-

ven as Gordon, Eydne Scott as Sidney, Edith Gresham as Saunders, James Swift as Gray, Margaret Williams as Mary, W. O. MacWatters as Poole, Joe Sailey as Clancy, Eric Mansfield as Benny.

8 May 1940
"Joe and Mary's Place," by Carl Dreher. Cast: New Jersey College for Women.

12 May 1940
8:30–10:01p
"Miss Moonlight," by Benn W. Levy. Cast: Dennis Hoey as Tom Moonlight, Frieda Altman as Minnie, Eleanor Audley as Edith Jones, Frances Reid as Sarah Moonlight, Tom Speidel as Percy Middling, Barbara Robbins as Jane Moonlight, Robert Allen as Willie Ragg, Horton Heath, Jr., as Peter.

19 May 1940
"We'll Take the High Road," by Leslie MacLeod. Cast: William Podmore as Mr. Campbell of Argyle, George Sturgeon as Angus MacNeil, Frances Fuller as Marion MacNeil, William Hollenbeck as John Campbell, Edgar Kent as Dr. Andy MacIan, Maurice Wells as Reverend William MacIntosh, Paul Zenge [?] as Peter MacDonald.

23 May 1940
9:00–10:08p
"The Old Book Shop" [perhaps titled "The Old Back Door"], from *The Simpson Boys of Sprucehead Bay*. Adapter: Warren Wade. Cast: Parker Fennelly as Mark Simpson, Charles Dow Clark as Harvey Medhurst, Herbert Duffy as Sheriff, Maurice Morris as Judge, Joan Hardy as French Lesson, Vivian della Chiese and Captain Charles Glavin as Singers.

25 May 1940
9:00–10:00p
"The Barker," by J. Kenyon Nicholson. Cast: Ross Hertz as Hap Spissell, Robert J. Mulligan as Pop Morgan, Sidney Stone as Doc Rice, Seth Arnold as Hick, Josephine Brown as May [?] Benson, Len Doyle as Sailor West and Nifty Miller,

Ann Thomas as Carrie, Judy Parish as
Lou, John Craven as Chris Miller, Effie
Afton as Cleo, Harry Anters as Colonel
Gowdy.

28 May 1940

"Overtones," by Alice Gerstenberg. Cast:
Betty Cooper, Louise Nontez, Louise
Bowne, Helen Stein.

9:00p

"The Rescuing Angel," by Clare Cummer.
Adapter: T. H. Hutchinson. Cast: Sally
O'Neil, Robert Allen, Eric Dressler.

4 June 1940
9:00–10:00p

"Dr. Jekyll and Mr. Hyde," by Robert
Louis Stevenson. Adapted from a play by
Luella Forepaugh and George F. Fish by
Warren Wade. In the *Magnolia Floating
Theatre* series. Director: Wade. Cast: Jud-
son Laire as Utterson, Winfield Hoeny as
Henry Jekyll and Hyde, Paula Stone as
Alice, Jack Cherry as Vicar and Detective,
W. O. MacWatters as Lanyon, William
Cantwell as Poole, Dan Cavanaugh as Po-
liceman, Anne Crosby as Prima Donna.

6 June 1940
9:00–10:25p

"Double Door," by Elizabeth McFadden.
Producer: Edward Padula. Cast: Mary
Morris as Victoria Van Brett, Kay Strozzi
as Caroline Van Brett, Richard Kendrick
as Rip Van Brett, Claire Niesen as Anne
Darrow, Judson Laire as Dr. John Sully,
Mortimer Neff as A. J. Herbert, Alice
Fleming as Avery, Fothringham Lysons as
Telson, William Hansen as Mr. Chase,
William Foran as Lambert, Edward Franz
as Minister.

13 June 1940

"Jack Rabbit Plays," by Alladine Bell.
Cast: Ethel Remey as Belle Hardwicke,
Tom Seidel as Darley Haskin, Edwin Mis
as Jeff Lethsote, Robert Allen as Bilker
Hardwicke, Kendell Clark as Billy
Whitaker, Dorothy Mathews as Olive Tre-
mellan, Jabez Gray as George Jackson,

Harry M. Cooke as Joe Tripp, Barbara
Robbins as Rose Tremellan.

20 June 1940
9:00–10:05p

"The Last Warning," by Thomas R. Fall-
on. Producer: Warren Wade. Cast: Paula
MacLean as Dolly, Judson Laire as
Quaile, Maurice Morris as Jonah, Mar-
jorie Brown as Gene, Mitchell Harris as
Carlton, James Swift as Tommy, W. O.
MacWatters as McHugh, Alice Buchanan
as Evelynde, John Boyd as Williams, Will
Davis as Policeman, Jack Cherry as Mike,
Hene Damur as Barbara, Horton Heath,
Jr., as Jeffery, Frederic Tozare as Robert.

2 July 1940

"The Neighbors," by Zona Gale. Cast:
American Actors Company.

31 July 1940
9:00p

"The Drums of Oude," by Austin Strong.
Cast: Maurice Wells as Captain Hector
McGregor, Carl Harbord as Lieutenant
Alan Hartley, W. O. MacWatters as Sgt.
McDougal, James Swift as Stewart, Pa-
tricia Calvert as Mrs. Jack Clayton, Jack
Cherry as Private.

August 1940 to January
1941

[Presentations include New York World's
Fair, Republican and Democratic conventions, elections, sports events, and feature
films.]

24 January 1941
12:00–1:00p

"The Aldrich Family," by Clifford Goldsmith. Adapter: T. H. Hutchinson. Director: Warren Wade.

9 May 1941

"The Parker Family," created by Don
Becker. Director: Warren Wade. Cast: Taylor Holmes as Mr. Parker, Violet Heming
as Mrs. Parker, William Lynn as Mr. Den-
nison, Helen Claire as Mrs. Jennings,
Leon Janney as Richard Parker.

24 June 1941
2:25p

"The Minuet," by Louis Parker.

1941–1946

WNBT, 30 Rockefeller Plaza, New York City.

1 July 1941	WNBT goes on the air as a commercial television station. Programming includes films (Monogram), civil defense, sports, opera workshops, and variety.
31 July 1941 2:30p	"The Puritans," by J. Raymond Hutchinson, in the *The Chronicles of America Photoplay* series. Producer: Yale University Press Film Service. The first dramatized documentary filmed series.
1 August 1941	"Prince Gabby," by Jane Murfin, based on "The Talkative Burglar," by Edgar Wallace. Director: Warren Wade.
5 August 1941 2:30p	"Peter Stuyvesant," by J. Raymond Hutchinson, in *The Chronicles of America Photoplay* series.
14 August 1941	"Gateway to the West," in *The Chronicles of America Photoplay* series.
15 August 1941	"Shanghai," by W. Stuckes.
26 August 1941 2:30p	"Wolfe and Montcalm," in *The Chronicles of America Photoplay* series.
4 September 1941	"The Eye of the Revolution," in *The Chronicles of America Photoplay* series.
6 September 1941	"A Cup of Tea," by Florence Ryerson. Director: Thomas Lyne Riley. Cast: Marjorie Clarke as Jane, Maurice Wells as Wilfort Wendall, Katherine Meskill as Azalea Waring, Blaine Cordner as John.
11 September 1941	"The Declaration of Independence," in *The Chronicles of America Photoplay* series. Director: Warren Wade.
18 September 1941	"Yorktown," in *The Chronicles of America Photoplay* series.
23 September 1941	"Frontiers" [?], in *The Chronicles of America Photoplay* series.

26 September 1941	"The Mikado," by W. S. Gilbert and Arthur Sullivan.
9 October 1941	"The Hundred Thousand Dollar Kiss," a sketch based on *Believe It Or Not,* by Robert L. Ripley.
16 October 1941	"The Frontier Woman," in *The Chronicles of America Photoplay* series.
17 October 1941	"Soldier Town," a musical comedy. Director: Ernest Colling.
21 October 1941	"False Witness," a mystery-quiz by Henry W. Denker and Arnold Lever. Producer: Martin Jones. Cast: Romeny Brent as Inspector, Florence Sundstrom as Mrs. Royce, E. King as Mr. Royce, Elizabeth Sifton as Edna, Austen Fairman as Malone. Sponsors: Bulova and Botany.
24 October 1941	"A Constitutional Point," by Augustus Thomas. Cast: Nedda Harrison, Ainsworth Arnold, Tom Hoier, Ann Brady, Nina MacDougall.
25 October 1941	"Soldier Town," Part II.
31 October 1941	"Laugh, Clown," a sketch based on *Believe It Or Not,* by Robert L. Ripley.
14 November 1941	"False Witness," Part II. Cast: Romeny Brent, Patricia Mallinson, Robert Ober, Chester Straton, Alan Hale, Kirk Allen, Denton Walker, Miss Winslow.
21 November 1941 8:30p	"Blind Alley," by James Warwick. Director: Thomas Lyne Riley. Cast: Charles Furcolowe, Maurice Wells, Jackson Wright, Katherine Warren, Elaine Perry, Michael Artist, Lida Kane, Kay Loring, Albert West, Richard Clark.
29 November 1941	"The Item of the Scarlet Ace," a crime adventure based on *The Bishop and the Gargoyle,* by Fred Wilson. Cast: Howard Petrie, Richard Gordon as Bishop, Kenneth Lynch as Gargoyle; also Ernie Owen, Peggy Allenby, Jane Lauren, Lotis Deviskey, Parker Fennelly, Arthur Allen, Ted Osborne, Arthur Hughes, Fred Sullivan.

12 December 1941	"False Witness," Part III [?]. Producer: Martin Jones. Cast: Russell Hardie, Florence Sundstrom, Gino Melo, Mathew Smith, William Chambers.
14 December 1941 11:15a	"The Heiress." Adapter: Emma B. C. Wells. Cast: Marjorie Clarke as Girl, Ruth Gates as Mother, Peggy Converse [?] as Puritan, Sandra Rogers as Southerner, Z. Cunningham as Northerner, Richard Clark as Boy.
21 December 1941	"Dust of the Road," by Kenneth Sawyer Goodman. Cast: Graham Velsey as Tramp, Dorothy Blackburn as Prudence, Blaine Cordner as Peter, Homer Miles as Old Man.
23 December 1941	"The Victorian Christmas Tree," by Helen Morley. A short monologue partly in Negro dialect.
4 [?] January 1942	"Farewell to Love."
12 [?] January 1942	"Fright," by James Beach. Adapter: Thomas Lyne Riley. Cast: George Spaulding as John Fairbride, Ruth Gates as Martha Fairbride, Edmon Ryan as Harris, G. Albert Smith as Howard, M. Battista as Eva.
18 January 1942	"False Witness," Part IV.
25 January 1942 8:30p	"The Thirteenth Chair," by Bayard Veiller. Cast: Hilda Vaughn as Rosalie, Barbara Brown as Helen, Nell Harrison as Mrs. Crosby, Virginia Campbell as Mrs. Trent, Richard Clark as Mr. Trent, Blaine Cordner as Wales, Warren Parker as Mason, Mary Howes as Miss Eastwood, Kathleen McLane as Miss Erskin, J. W. Austin as Butler, Beatrice Allen as Miss Standish, Richard Beach as Standish, Joseph Boland as Dunn, Maurice Wells as Donahue, Richard Janaver as Will, Graham Velsey as Mr. Crosby.
1 February 1942	"Suspect," by Edward Percy and Reginald Denham.

8 February 1942	"The Clod," by Lewis Beach. Cast: John Adair as Thaddeus Trask, Margaret Wycherly as Mary Trask, Wendell Phillips as Northern Soldier, Zachary Scott as Southern Soldier, Jack Tyler as Dick.
15 February 1942	"To the Ladies," by George S. Kaufman and Marc Connelly. Cast: Marjorie Clarke as Elsie, Maurice Wells as Leonard, Alexander Campbell as Kincaid, Susan Jackson as Mrs. Kincaid, J. Richard Jones as Chester, Walter Davis as Henrici, Charles Mendick as Baker, M. Battista as Fletcher, Jack Lambert as Truck, Angi O'Poula [?] as Bert Black.
20 February 1942	"False Witness," Part V. Cast: Romeny Brent, Gina Melo, Ernest Woodward, Davis Appleby, J. Friend.
10 April 1942	"The City Awakes," a civil-defense script that includes dramatized scenes. Director: Warren Wade. Cast: thirteen volunteer professional actors. Similar presentations, mainly nondramatic, followed: "Bombs and Fire Protection," "Gas Warfare," and "Allies in Arms." Writer/directors: Martin Jones, Thomas Lyne Riley, Warren Wade.
October through December 1942	[Few programs of any kind.]
January through December 1943	[Few programs; some air-raid warden lectures and films. No dramas.]
January through June 1944	Some feature films, such as *Gunga Din* and *That Certain Feeling;* some military films, such as *The War as It Happens.*
19 July 1944	"The Freedom Ferry," by Ruth A. Brooks.
29 July 1944	"The Barber of Seville," by Gioacchino Rossini. Excerpts.
	"La Bohème," by Giacomo Puccini. Excerpts.
30 September 1944	"Carmen," by Georges Bizet. Excerpts.
24 December 1944 8:00p	"Christmas in Alsace-Lorraine," by Hugh

	Chain, adapted from a short story entitled "Birthday," by James Hopper. Cast: Jimsey Somers as Fauvette, D. J. Thompson as Mother, Arthur Maitland as Grandfather, Lyle Bettger as Soldier, Milton Cross as Announcer.
16 January 1945	"Christmas in Alsace-Lorraine," repeated on the NBC Blue Network. The first television drama repeated on a radio network.
21 January 1945	"Conquest of Darkness," a biography based on the life of Tom Davenport. Originally produced at WRGB, Schenectady. Sponsored by General Electric.
24 January 1945	"Men in White," by Sidney S. Kingsley. Producer: Edward Sobol. Director: Ronald Oxford. Cast: Jane Middleton as Laura Hudson, Jack Coyle as Mr. Smith, Mary Michaels as Mrs. Smith, Pat Somers as Dorothy Smith, Mary Barthelmess as Student Nurse, Virginia Gahagan as Graduate Nurse, Roma Robb Smith as Graduate Nurse, Rupert LaBelle as Dr. Cunningham, Robert Rhodes as Dr. Gordon, Bob Harris as Dr. Hochberg, Jerry Thor as Dr. Vitale, Grover Burgess as Dr. McCabe, Vinton Hayworth as Dr. Ferguson, Kenneth Jesse Tobey as Shorty, Michael Road as Pete.
31 January 1945	"Dr. Death," adapted by Ernest Colling from *The Black Angel*, by Cornell Woolrich.
18 February 1945	"Playboy," Part III from *The Black Angel*.
25 February 1945	"The Last Name," Part IV from *The Black Angel*. Cast: Mary Patton as Alberta, Richard Keith as McKee, Philip Foster as Mason, Paul Conrad as Skeeter, Don Grusso as Kittens.
4 March 1945	"The Perfect Alibi," by A. A. Milne, Part I. Director: Edward Sobol. Settings: Robert Wade.

11 March 1945	"The Perfect Alibi," Part II.
24 March 1945	"Christmas in Alsace-Lorraine," repeat. Cast: Jimsey Somers as Fauvette, Francis Dee as Mother, Edwin Jerome as Grandfather, Philip Foster as Soldier, Milton Cross as Announcer.
— April 1945	"Portrait in Black," adapted from *Charm* magazine by Ernest Colling. Director: Colling.
15 April 1945 8:00p	"Abe Lincoln in Illinois," by Robert E. Sherwood, Act I. Producer: Edward Sobol. Director: Sobol with Don Darcy. Cast: Stephen Courtleigh as Abraham Lincoln, Wendel Phillips as Bill Herndon, also Vinton Hayworth, May Collins, Viola France, Lucille Fenton, Earl McDonald, Dorothy Emery, Kay Renard, Harry Bellaver.
21 April 1945 8:20p	"Nettie," by George Ade. Adapter: Don Darcy. Producer: Darcy. Cast: Mort L. Stevens, Steven Chase, Richard Maloy, Liela Ernst as Nettie, Gilbert Douglas as Waiter, Burton Mallory as Butler, Janis Thompson as Acrobatic Dancer, Shirley Conklin as Vocalist, Rich and Gibson as Tap Dancers.
24 April 1945	"The Patriots," a short drama sponsored by Gimbel's.
6 May 1945	"Winter Wheat," by Mildred Walker. Adapter: Maxine Word. Producer: Ernest Colling. Settings: Robert Wade. Cast: Lyle Sudrow as Gill, Richard Barrows as Dad, Thomas Heaphy as Nels, Michael Artist as Leslie, Mary Patton as Ellen, Philip Foster as Warren, Elnolora von Mendelssohn as Mother, and Joan Lazar, Julie Gay, Jack Andrews, Phillis Colling, Joyce Colling, Lois Volkman, Charles Muller as Extras.

13 May 1945	"The Family Upstairs," by Harry Delf.
20 May 1945	"Abe Lincoln in Illinois," Act II ("The Springfield Lawyer"), by Robert E. Sherwood.
27 May 1945	"Abe Lincoln in Illinois," Act III ("For President—Abraham Lincoln"), by Robert E. Sherwood.
3 June 1945	"The Veteran Comes Back," by Willard Waller. Director: Ernest Colling.
17 June 1945	"The Bourgeois Gentleman," by Molière. Translated by Margaret Baker. Adapter: Herbert Graf. Music by Richard Strauss.
24 June 1945	"The Copperhead," by Augustus Thomas. Adapter: Ernest Colling and Helen Morley. Cast: Mary Patton as Martha, Rand Elliott as Philip, Philip Farber [?] as Milt Shanks, Buck [?] Heath as Captain Hardy.
14 July 1945	"The Magic Ribbon," a play for children.
22 July 1945	"Blackmail," by Ernest Colling. Cast: Olive Hunter as Mr. Hayes, Ms. Letowsky as Mrs. Hayes, Fred Leary as Fat, Arthur Hunnicutt as Gardner, Alfred Linden [?] and Robert Bernard [?] as Waiters, also Lee Lanford, John Martin, Phil Kramer.
26 July 1945	"The Magic Ribbon," repeat.
2 September 1945	"Another Language," repeat. Producer: Edward Sobol. Settings: Robert Wade.
9 September 1945	"Victory," by Joseph Conrad. Adapter: Ernest Colling. Cast: Uta Hagen as Alma.
16 September 1945	"Beachhead at Louie's," by Mort Green. Cast: Joseph Marion as Shorty, Julian Scanlon [?] as Jimmy, Emily Ross as Mother, Jay Norris as Friend, Mary Barthelmess as Nurse, Bernard Hoffman as Big Boy, Ronnie Gibson as Entertainer.
30 September 1945	"Ring on Her Finger," by Charles R. Hoffman. Adapter: Fred Coe.
7 October 1945	"If Men Played Cards as Women Do," by George S. Kaufman. Producer: Ernest Colling. Cast: Leo G. Carroll, Neil Hamilton, Ralph Dumke, Sidney Blackmer.

"Air-Tight Alibi," by Walter Hackett. Cast: Ann Elster as Abby Cosgrove, Gayne Sullivan as Husband.

21 October 1945
8:15–9:45p

"Bedelia," by Vera Caspary. Adapter: Fred Coe. Director: Coe.

28 October 1945
8:35–10:10p

"Winterset," by Maxwell Anderson. Producer: Ernest Colling. Cast: Grandon Rhodes as Judge Gaunt, Peter Capell as Trock Estrella, Anatole Winogradoff as Esdras, John McQuade as Mio, Eva Langbord as Mirianna, Thomas Nello as Shadow, Ralph Ahearn as Garth, Sid Martoff as Carr, Anthony Blair as Policeman, Leonard Lonergan as Hobo.

4 November 1945   "Bedelia," repeat.
11 November 1945
8:25–9:30p

"The Front Page," by Ben Hecht and Charles MacArthur. Producer: Edward Sobol. Settings: Robert Wade. Cast: Vinton Hayworth as Hildy Johnson.

18 November 1945
8:20–10:00p

"You Can't Take It with You," by George S. Kaufman. Adapter: Ernest Colling. Producer: Colling. Settings: Robert Wade. Cast: Tom Seidel as Harvey.

25 November 1945   "Petticoat Fever," by Mark Reed. Producer: Fred Coe.

2 December 1945   "The Devil and Daniel Webster," by Stephen Vincent Benét. Adapter: Ernest Colling.

6 December 1945   "Columbus," in *The Chronicles of America* series. Adapted from *The Spanish Conquerors,* by Irving R. Richman. Director: Edwin L. Hollywood. Cast: Fred Eric as Columbus, Paul McAllister as King John II of Portugal, Howard Truesdell as Bishop of Ceuta, Loside Stoew as Perez, Robert Gaillard as King Ferdinand of Spain, Delores Cassinelli as Queen Isabella.

9 December 1945
8:00–10:35p

"The Strange Christmas Dinner," by Margaret Cousins. Adapter: Fred Coe. Cast: Grandon Rhodes as Charles Dickens, also George Mathews, Maxie Rosenbloom.

13 December 1945

"Jamestown," in *The Chronicles of America* series.

30 December 1945

"Little Women," repeat. Producer: Ernest Colling. Director: Colling. Cast: Charles Townsend as Mr. March, Frances Lee as Mrs. March, Dorothy Emery as Meg, Margaret Hoyle as Jo, Madeleine Lee as Beth, Billie Lou Watt as Amy, Ruth Master as Aunt March, John Robb as Theodore Lawrence, Tom Seidel as Laurie, Peter Preses as Professor Bhaer, Gene Blakeley as John Brooke, Gravia O'Malley as Hannah Mullert.

3 [?] January 1946

"Peter Stuyvesant," in *The Chronicles of America* series. Adapter: William Besil Courtney. Director: Frank Tuttle. Cast: William Calhoun as Peter Stuyvesant, Charles Laite as George Baxter, Dwight Wiman as King Charles II of England, Osgood Perkins as Fop, Cuyler Supples as James, Duke of York, J. Malcolm Dunn as Lord Clarendon, Frank Tweed as Nicasius DeSille, Pearl Sindelar as Mrs. Stuyvesant, Francetta Malloy as Relative of Charles II.

6 January 1946

"Dark Hammock," by Mary Orr and Reginald Denham.

13 January 1946

"The First Year," by Frank Craven.

17 January 1946

"Wolfe and Montcalm," in *The Chronicles of America* series.

20 January 1946

"Angel Street," by Patrick Hamilton. Director: Ernest Colling.

30 January 1946

"Children of Ol' Man River," by Billy Bryant. Director: Warren Wade. Settings: Robert Wade. Cast: Buddy Pepper as Billy Bryant, Lillian Cornell as Josephine.

10 February 1946

"Abe Lincoln in Illinois," Act III, repeat.

14 February 1946

"Vincennes," in *The Chronicles of America* series.

17 February 1946	"Laughter in Paris," an original television drama by Richard P. McDonagh. Producer: Fred Coe. Cast: Frank Lea Short as Henri Molinard.
21 February 1946	"The Pioneer Woman" and "Daniel Boone," in *The Chronicles of America* series.
24 February 1946 8:11–9:03p	"Knockout," by J. C. Nugent and Elliott Nugent.
28 February 1946	"Alexander Hamilton" and "Dixie," in *The Chronicles of America* series.
1 March 1946	WNBT goes off the air for the installation of a new transmitter on the Empire State Building and a change to Channel 4.
9 May 1946	*Hour Glass*, a variety series that includes some dramas, begins. Sponsor: Standard Brands.
	"Moonshine," repeat. Cast: Paul Douglas.
12 May 1946	"Blythe Spirit," by Noel Coward, in the *NBC Television Theatre* series. Adapter: Edward Sobol. Producer: Sobol. Cast: Philip Tonge as Charles Condemine, Leonora Corbett as Elvira, Carol Goodner as Ruth, Estelle Winwood as Madam Arcati, Alex Clark as Dr. Bradman, Valerie Cossart as Mrs. Bradman, Doreen Long as Edith.
19 May 1946	"Mr. and Mrs. North," by Frances and Richard Lockridge. Adapter: Owen Davis. Cast: John McQuade and Maxine Stewart as Jerry and Pamela North.
26 May 1946	"The Bad Man," based on *The Bandit*, by Porter Emerson Browne. Adapter: Ernest Colling. Cast: Peter Capell as Pancho Lopez ("The Bad Man"), Beverly Roberts as Lucia Pell, Brandon Peters as Morgan Pell, W. Black as Gilbert Jones, Tom Nello as Petro, Frank Nellis as Lano, Paul Keyes as Bradley.
2 June 1946	"The Flattering World," by George Kelly. Adapter: Edward Sobol. Cast: Edward

	Kreisler as the Reverend Loring Ridgeley, Louise Campbell as Mary, Enid Markey as Mrs. Zooker, Joyce Van Patten as Lena, Adam Handley as Eugene Tesh.
9 June 1946	"Enter Madame," by Gilda Varesi and Dolly Byrne. Cast: Carol Goodner as Mme. Della Rabbis, John Graham as Gerald Fitzgerald, Beverly Bain as Flora Preston, John Fitzgerald as Richard Maloy, Lili Valenti as Brice, Tito Vuello as Archimede, William Walton as Doctor, Vaughn Taylor as Alec.
16 June 1946	"The Strangest Feeling," by John Kirkpatrick. Adapter: Ernest Colling.
23 June 1946	"Tea," by William G. B. Carson.
30 June 1946	"First Person Singular." Episode 1 in the *Lights Out* series, created by Wyllis Cooper. Adapter: Fred Coe.
7 July 1946 8:45–10:12p	"Seven Keys to Baldpate," by George M. Cohan, based on a novel by Earl Derr Biggers. Adapter: Ernest Colling. Settings: Robert Wade. Cast: Vinton Hayworth as William Magee.
14 July 1946	"The Weak Spot," by George Kelly. Cast: Lillian Foster as Jenny, Maxine Stewart as Mrs. West, John Harvey as Mr. West.
21 July 1946 8:30	"The Home Life of a Buffalo," by Richard Harrity. Director: Fred Coe. Settings: Bob Wade. Cast: John McQuade as Eddie, Virginia Smith as Wife, Mickey Carroll as Joey; also Enid Markey, Perry Helton.
28 July 1946	"The Merry Widow," by Franz Lehar. In the *Memories with Music* series. Producer: Ernest Colling. Cast: Mae Murray.
1 August 1946	"The Finger of God," by Percival Wilde. In the *Hour Glass* series. Cast: Vinton Hayworth, Mary Shipp, Philip Clark.
4 August 1946	"The Show-Off," by George Kelly. Producer: Edward Sobol. Settings: Robert Wade.

11 August 1946
9:30–9:55p   "Something in the Wind." Episode 2 in
                                    the *Lights Out* series. Adapter: Fred Coe.
                                    Director: Coe.
18 August 1946   *Memories with Music,* a musical drama
                                    series, continues. [Not listed hereafter.]
1 September 1946   "De Mortius," by John Collier. Episode 3
                                    in the *Lights Out* series. Adapter: Fred
                                    Coe. Producer: Coe. Cast: John Loder,
                                    Haskell Coffin, Alexander Clark.
8 September 1946   "The Clod," repeat. Producer: Ernest
                                    Colling.
15 September 1946   "The Lady and the Law," by George W.
                                    Cronyn. Adapter: Edward Sobol.
22 September 1946   "Mr. Mergenthwirker's Lobblies," by
                                    Nelson Bond and David Kent. Adapters:
                                    Bond and Kent. Producer: Fred Coe. Di-
                                    rector: Coe. Cast: Vaughn Taylor as Mr.
                                    Mergenthwirker.
29 September 1946   "The Walrus and the Carpenter" [?], by
                                    Noel Langley Colling.
6 October 1946   "The Curtain Rises," by Benjamin M.
                                    Kaye. Adapter: Edward Sobol.
13 October 1946   "The Brave Man with a Cord," by Peter
                                    Strand and Rudolph Bernstein. Episode 4
                                    in the *Lights Out* series. Adapter: Fred
                                    Coe.
20 October 1946   "Black Alibi," Part I, adapted by Ernest
                                    Colling from *The Black Angel,* by Cornell
                                    Woolrich. Cast: Peter Capell, Vinton Hay-
                                    worth, Virginia Smith.
27 October 1946   "Dr. Death," Part II, from *The Black An-
                                    gel,* repeat.
10 November 1946   "The Last War," by Neil Grant.
22 December 1946   "A Poem for Christmas." Producer: Amer-
                                    ican Theatre Wing's Television Workshop.
                                    Cast: Jane Delmar as Mother, Robert
                                    Emerick as Father, Stanley Roberts as Pe-
                                    ter, Patsy Foster as Susan, Vaughn Taylor
                                    as Moore, Cy Travers as Halleck, Patsy
                                    Campbell as Emily, Dorothy Emery as
                                    Mrs. Moore, Sonny Curven as Clem,

	William Kuluva as Doctor, Marie N. Chambers as C. Rolers.
7 May 1947	*Kraft Television Theater* debuts with "Double Door," by Elizabeth McFadden. Adapter: Edmond Rice. Producer: Stanley Quinn. Directors: Quinn (agency) and Fred Coe (station). Settings: Robert Wade. Cast: Eleanor Wilson as Victoria Van Brett; also John Baragrey, Romola Rob, John Stephen, Joseph Boley, Valerie Cossart.

Summary of NBC Television Dramas

7 July 1936–1 January 1947

Experimental Period (W2XBS), 7 July 1936–29 April 1939

Television Dramas	92, eight repeated six times or more; many repeated twice; running time from 5 to over 60 minutes. Estimated cost of all programming, including dramas: $9 million.

Public Demonstrations (W2XBS), 30 April 1939–30 June 1941
First Public Dramas

30 April 1939–August 1939	24, transition to major productions, some with music.
Drama's "Best Year" 29 August 1939–31 July 1940	60, one repeated, running time from 30 to over 60 minutes.
Hiatus 1 August 1940–31 December 1940	0, period of election news, sports and films.
1 January–30 June 1941	3, two radio adaptations, one short play.

Commercial Programming (WNBT), 1 July 1941–1 January 1947
Precessation Dramas

1 July 1941–April 1942	34, few repeated, running time from 30 to over 60 minutes.

Wartime Cessation
1 March 1942–30 November
1944   0, few programs of any kind.
Postcessation Dramas
1 December 1944–1 January
1947   83, few repeated, running time
                                       from 30 to over 60 minutes.

Total dramatic productions, 7 July 1936–1 January 1947: 296

NBC's First Public Dramas
30 April 1939–August 1939

Comedies
   3 May   The Choir Rehearsal
  10 May   The Faker
  10 May   A Room with a View
  12 May   The Red Hat
  17 May   The Smart Thing
  16 June   Family Honor
  22 June   The Honeymooner
  20 July   Box and Cox
  27 July   Hay Fever

Dramas
  19 May   Any Family
  24 May   Likes and Dislikes
  31 May   Afterwards

Crime Stories
   3 May   The Unexpected
  26 May   A Game of Chess
  25 June   Moonshine
  29 June   The Donovan Affair
   6 July   The Services of an Expert
  11 July   Confessional
  18 July   Missouri Legend

Musicals
   2 June   Jenny Lind
  14 June   Mamba's Daughters
  24 June   The Pirates of Penzance
   4 July   The Marriage of Little Eva
  24 July   Topsy and Eva

Total dramatic productions: 24, including 9 comedies, 3 dramas, 7 crime stories, 5 musicals.

NBC Drama's "Best Year"
29 August 1939 through 31 July 1940

Comedies

29 August 1939	Dulcy
7 September	Brother Rat
14 September	Art and Mrs. Bottle
3 October	The Butter and Egg Man
18 October	The Dover Road
20 October	The Milky Way
27 October	The Fortune Hunter
24 November	Three Men on a Horse
17 December	Stage Door
12 January 1940	Meet the Wife
26 January	The Impossible Mr. Clancy
2 February	June Moon
— February	Tickets Please
3 March	When We Are Married
8 March	Dangerous Corner
5 April	Ode To Liberty
19 April	Burlesque
5 May	Three Wise Fools
12 May	Miss Moonlight
19 May	We'll Take the High Road
25 May	The Barker
28 May	The Rescuing Angel
2 July	The Neighbors

Dramas

28 September 1939	The Nightingale Sang in Berkeley Square
28 September	Dr. Abernathy
1 November	The Happy Journey
8 December	Another Language
29 December	Post Road
19 January 1940	The Gorilla
4 February	The Long Christmas Dinner
22 March	The Passing of the Third Floor Back
29 March	A Fine Place To Visit
— April	Hospital Scene
28 April	My Heart's in the Highlands

1 May	House of Glass
8 May	Joe and Mary's Place
23 May	The Old Book Shop
28 May	Overtones
6 June	Double Door
13 June	Jack Rabbit Plays

Crime Stories

5 October 1939	The Night Cap
17 November	Criminal at Large
1 December	Roosty
16 February 1940	The Perfect Alibi
20 June	The Last Warning
31 July	Drums of Oude

Classic Plays

31 August 1939	The Streets of New York
12 October	Jane Eyre
4 November	Treasure Island
22 December	Little Women
5 January 1940	Ethan Frome
15 March	Julius Caesar
3 April	The Marriage Proposal
4 June	Dr. Jekyll and Mr. Hyde

Historical Dramas

10 November 1939	The Farmer Takes a Wife
8 February 1940	Charlotte Corday
23 February	Prologue To Glory

Musicals

| 5 September 1939 | H.M.S. Pinafore |
| 10 March 1940 | Pagliacci |

Total dramatic productions: 60, including 23 comedies, 17 dramas, 6 crime stories, 8 classic plays, 3 historical dramas, 2 musicals, 1 repeat ("Jane Eyre").

NBC Dramas to Wartime Cessation
1 January 1941–April 1942

Comedies

24 January 1941	The Aldrich Family
9 May	The Parker Family
15 February 1942	To the Ladies

Dramas

24 June 1941	The Minuet
15 August	Shanghai
6 September	A Cup of Tea
24 October	A Constitutional Point
21 November	Blind Alley
14 December	The Heiress
21 December	Dust of the Road
23 December	The Victorian Christmas Tree
4 January 1942	Farewell to Love
8 February	The Clod
10 April	The City Awakes

Crime Stories

1 August 1941	Prince Gabby
9 October	A Hundred Thousand Dollar Kiss
21 October	False Witness (5 episodes)
31 October	Laugh Clown
29 November	The Item of the Scarlet Ace
12 January 1942	Fright
25 January	The Thirteenth Chair
1 February	Suspect

Historical Dramas

31 July 1941	The Chronicles of America Photoplay (8 episodes)

Musicals

26 September 1941	The Mikado
17 October	Soldier Town
25 October	Soldier Town, II

Total dramatic productions: 37, including 3 comedies, 11 dramas, 12 crime stories, 8 historical dramas, 3 musicals.

NBC Dramas after Wartime Cessation
1 December 1944–1 January 1947

Comedies

21 April 1945	Nettie
13 May	The Family Upstairs
17 June	The Bourgeois Gentleman
30 September	Ring on Her Finger
7 October	If Men Played Cards as Women Do

18 November	You Can't Take It with You
25 November	Petticoat Fever
24 February 1946	Knockout
12 May	Blythe Spirit
2 June	The Flattering World
9 June	Enter Madame
16 June	The Strangest Feeling
7 July	Seven Keys to Baldpate
14 July	The Weak Spot
21 July	The Home Life of a Buffalo
4 August	The Show Off
29 September	The Walrus and the Carpenter [?]
6 October	The Curtain Rises

Dramas

24 December 1944	Christmas in Alsace-Lorraine
24 January 1945	Men in White
6 May	Winter Wheat
3 June	The Veteran Comes Back
24 June	The Copperhead
2 September	Another Language
9 September	Victory
16 September	Beachhead at Louie's
2 December	The Devil and Daniel Webster
9 December	The Strange Christmas Dinner
30 December	Little Women
6 January 1946	Dark Hammock
13 January	The First Year
30 January	The Children of Ol' Man River
17 February	Laughter in Paris
23 June	Tea
1 August	The Finger of God
8 September	The Clod
10 November	The Last War
22 December	A Poem for Christmas

Crime Stories

31 January 1945	Dr. Death, II
18 February	Playboy, III
25 February	The Last Name, IV
4 March	The Perfect Alibi
11 March	The Perfect Alibi, II
— April	Portrait in Black
22 July	Blackmail

7 October	Air-Tight Alibi
21 October	Bedelia
28 October	Winterset
11 November	The Front Page
20 January 1946	Angel Street
9 May	Moonshine
19 May	Mr. and Mrs. North
26 May	The Bad Man
30 June	First Person Singular
11 August	Something in the Wind
1 September	De Mortius
15 September	The Lady and the Law
22 September	Mr. Mergenthwirker's Lobblies
13 October	The Brave Man with a Cord
20 October	Black Alibi, I

Historical Dramas

21 January 1945	Conquest of Darkness
15 April	Abe Lincoln in Illinois
24 April	The Patriots
20 May	Abe Lincoln in Illinois, II
27 May	Abe Lincoln in Illinois, III
6 December	Columbus
13 December	Jamestown
3 January 1946	Peter Stuyvesant
17 January	Wolfe and Montcalm
10 February	Abe Lincoln in Illinois, III (repeat)
15 February	Vincennes
21 February	Pioneer Woman
21 February	Daniel Boone
28 February	Alexander Hamilton
28 February	Dixie

Musicals

19 July 1944	The Freedom Ferry
29 July	La Bohème
29 July	The Barber of Seville
30 September	Carmen
28 July 1946	The Merry Widow
—	Soldier musicals

Total dramatic productions: 83, including 18 comedies, 20 dramas, 22 crime stories, 15 historical dramas, 6 musicals, 2 repeats ("Bedelia" and "Black Alibi, II").

"Firsts" in Television Drama, 1925–1947

13 June 1925	First motion picture film telecast: Charles Francis Jenkins experiment.
5 May 1928	First "Radio Movie" television transmissions in silhouette: W3XK, Washington, D.C., Jenkins experiment.
21 August 1928	First puppet drama on television: Bamberger's department store and WOR, New York.
11 September 1928	First television drama: "The Queen's Messenger," by J. Hartley Manners, WGY, Schenectady, New York.
15 December 1928	First television animal performer, a cat: in "Box and Cox," by Arthur Sullivan, John L. Baird experiment, London.
14 July 1930	First televised play produced by BBC, in England: "The Man with the Flower in His Mouth," Baird experiment, London.
7 January 1931	First musical comedy on television: "Their Television Honeymoon," W9XAO and WIBO, Chicago.
1 May 1931	First current Broadway play televised: excerpt from "House Beautiful," by Channing Pollack, General Electric experiment.
22 July 1931	First CBS television musical, "Tele Musical," and first CBS drama, W2XAB, New York.
1 [?] August 1931	First televised musical variety series: *Half Hour on Broadway,* W2XAB, New York.
18 August 1931	First CBS puppet show: "Punch and Judy," W2XAB, New York.
27 August 1931	First televised dramatic narrative anthology series: *The Television Ghost,* W2XAB, New York.
	First televised musical comedy series: *Ned Wayburn's Musical Comedy,* W2XAB, New York.

24 October 1931	First television drama projected for a theater audience: scenes from the "House of Connelly," by Paul Green, Broadway Theatre, New York.
25 February 1933	First review of a television drama ("Dramatic Moments," W2XAB, New York, 20 February) published in *The Billboard*.
7 July 1936	First dramatic monologue presented by NBC; Henry Hull in scene from "Tobacco Road." First regular NBC demonstration, W2XBS, New York.
26 August 1936	First filmed scenes from a Shakespearean play presented on television: "As You Like It," by William Shakespeare, BBC, London. Producer: Interallied Films. Director: Paul C. Zinner. Cast: Laurence Olivier, Elizabeth Bergner.
9 September 1936	First scene from a Shakespearean play believed to have been presented "live" in a television studio: W2XBS, New York.
21 September 1936	First original sketch on NBC: "Love Nest," by Grace Bradt and Eddie Albert, W2XBS, New York.
19 October 1936	First crime drama on BBC television: scenes from "Murder in the Cathedral," by T. S. Eliot, BBC, London. Producer: Mercury Theatre Production. Cast: Robert Speaight as Thomas Becket.
10 May 1937	First telecast of a scene from grand opera: "Tristan and Isolde," W2XBS, New York.
23 November 1937	First full-length dramatic production on television integrating live studio and film: "The Three Garridebs," by Arthur Conan Doyle, W2XBS, New York.
25 May 1938	First review of a television drama ("The Mysterious Mummy Case," W2XBS, New York, 17 May) published in *Variety*. Review by Robert J. Landry.
31 May 1938	First televised full-length feature film: *The Return of the Scarlet Pimpernel*, W2XBS, New York.

7 June 1938	First entire scene from current Broadway play telecast from a television studio: "Susan and God," by Rachael Crothers, W2XBS, New York. First major star in a television drama: Gertrude Lawrence.
2 September 1938	First television cast to receive artists' contract and uniform fees: "Speaking to Father," W2XBS, New York.
16 November 1938	First three-act play telecast, by BBC, London, direct from St. Martin's Theatre: "When We Are Married," by J. B. Priestley.
January 1939	First televised serial drama: *Vine Street*, W6XAO (KTSL), Los Angeles.
30 March 1939	First commercial credit for contribution to a drama: "Dark Eyes Mean Danger," by Llewellyn Hughes, Russek's Fifth Avenue for an evening wrap and furs, W2XBS, New York.
18 July 1939	First western shown on television: "Missouri Legend," by E. B. Ginty, W2XBS, New York.
20 October 1939	First flash-forward montage on film used in a television drama: "The Milky Way," by Lynn Root and Harry Clark, W2XBS, New York.
1 December 1939	First NBC full-length original television drama: "Roosty," W2XBS, New York.
3 March 1940	First current Broadway play telecast in its entirety, from a television studio: "When We Are Married," by J. B. Priestley, W2XBS, New York.
10 March 1940	First television presentation of an abridged full-length opera, "Pagliacci," W2XBS, New York.
15 March 1940	First U.S. television production of a full-length Shakespearean play: "Julius Caesar," W2XBS, New York.
31 July 1941	First filmed documentary (reenactment) series on television: *The Chronicles of America Photoplay,* W2XBS, New York.

30 June 1944	First CBS full-length drama: "The Favor," by Lawrence M. Klee, WCBW, New York.
28 September 1944	First full-length musical comedy written for television: "The Boys from Boise," WABD, New York.
January 1945	First novel-for-television miniseries presented over four nights: *The Black Angel*, by Cornell Woolrich, WNBT, New York.
4 March 1945 and 11 March 1945	First Broadway play presented in two acts on two different nights: "The Perfect Alibi," by A. A. Milne, WNBT, New York.
15 April 1945	First Broadway play presented in three acts on three different nights: "Abe Lincoln in Illinois," by Robert E. Sherwood, WNBT, New York.
21 June 1945	First television drama used as a springboard for discussion: "Letter from the Teens," by Lela Swift and Edward Stasheff, WCBW, New York.
9 October 1945	First commercial telecast of a serial drama: "Big Sister," WCBW, New York.
15 April 1946	First "network" drama shown on first network (via cable) from New York to Washington, D.C.: "Experience," by George Lowther, WABD, New York.
12 May 1946	First NBC dramatic anthology: NBC *Television Theatre*, WNBT, New York.
9 October 1946	First serial drama on commercial television: *Faraway Hill*, WABD, New York.
7 May 1947	First dramatic anthology series sponsored on television: *Kraft Television Theater*, WNBT, New York.

Notes

Chapter 1

1. Richard Griffith and Arthur Mayer, *The Movies: The Sixty-Year Story of the World of Hollywood and Its Effect on America, from Pre-Nickelodeon Days to the Present* (New York: Simon and Schuster, 1957), p. 47.
2. Benn Hall, "Television," *The Billboard*, 22 April 1933, p. 15.
3. Ibid., 15 July 1933, p. 15.
4. Frank Buxton and Bill Owen, *The Big Broadcast, 1920–1950* (New York: Viking Press, 1972), p. 137.
5. *The Billboard*, 7 March 1931, p. 3.
6. *The New York Times*, 27 February 1935, p. 21.
7. Gilbert Seldes, *The Great Audience* (New York: Viking Press, 1951), p. 105.
8. *The Billboard*, 28 November 1936, p. 10.
9. Erik Barnouw, *Handbook of Radio Production* (Boston: Houghton Mifflin Company, 1949), p. 37.
10. Ibid.
11. Griffith and Mayer, *The Movies*, p. 3.
12. E. H. Chapman, *Wireless To-Day* (London: Oxford University Press, 1936), pp. 151–158.
13. Worthington C. Miner, "A Report for the Columbia Broadcasting System on Twelve Years of Television" (typescript, 1942), Part I, p. 2.
14. Joseph H. Udelson, *The Great Television Race: A History of the American Television Industry, 1925–1941* (University, Alabama: The University of Alabama Press, 1982), p. 31.
15. Ibid., p. 50.
16. "WGY Today to Start Television Programs," *The New York Times*, 11 May 1928, p. 50.
17. "Play Is Broadcast by Voice and Acting in Radio-Television," *The New York Times*, 12 September 1928, pp. 1, 10.
18. Robert E. Sherwood, "Beyond the Talkies—Television," *Scribner's* 86 (July 1929): 1–8.
19. "Television Drama Shown with Music," *The New York Times*, 22 August 1928, p. 1:2.
20. "Television Is Actors' Hope," *The Billboard*, 31 May 1930, p. 3; "Television on the Theater Screen," *The Literary Digest* 106 (5 July 1930): 25.

21. "Theater Telly Test Is Held," *The Billboard,* 31 October 1931, p. 4. *House Beautiful* was directed by Worthington C. Miner.

22. Arthur H. Lynch and Dr. C. Francis Jenkins, "What Are the Facts about Television?" *Radio News* 11 (August 1929): 125.

23. Joe Calcaterra, "The Boston Television Party," *Radio News* 13 (May 1931): 988.

24. *Chicago Daily News,* 8 January 1931, p. 26.

25. "Television Drama Tonight," *Chicago Daily News,* 3 April 1931, p. 45; "Television's First Play," *Television News* I, no. 2 (May–June 1931): 158.

26. Patrick Robertson, *The Book of Firsts* (New York: Bramhall House, 1974), p. 182.

27. Ibid., p. 185.

28. *The New York Times,* 22 September 1929, p. 12:12.

29. "The Mad Scramble for Television Privilege Threatens Amateurs," *Radio News* 18 (October 1936): 202.

30. Robertson, *The Book of Firsts,* p. 186.

31. Gleason L. Archer, *Big Business and Radio* (New York: The American Historical Society, 1939), p. 442.

32. Marie Seton, "Television Drama: Alexandra Palace," *Theatre Arts Monthly* 22 (December 1938): 878.

33. Archer, *Big Business and Radio,* p. 182.

34. Ashley Dukes, "Television Drama So Far: The English Scene," *Theatre Arts Monthly* 22 (April 1938): 262.

35. Jack Alicoate, ed., *1947 Radio Annual* (New York: Radio Daily, 1947), p. 1021.

Chapter 2

1. *The Billboard,* 6 September 1930, p. 3.

2. Ibid., 11 January 1930, p. 6.

3. Joe Laurie, Jr., *Vaudeville: From the Honky Tonks to the Palace* (New York: Henry Holt and Company, 1953), p. 482.

4. Edwin K. Cohan, CBS technical director, quoted in "W2XAB Birthday Program," 21 July 1932.

5. William A. Schudt, Jr., CBS director of television, quoted in "W2XAB Birthday Program," 21 July 1932.

6. *Television Master Control Log,* Columbia Broadcasting System, 20 February 1933.

7. Script, "CBS Television Inaugural Broadcast," 21 July 1931.

8. *The Billboard,* 25 February 1933, p. 15.

9. Benn Hall, *The Billboard,* 26 November 1932, p. 15.

10. Ibid., 3 December 1932, p. 15.
11. "The Television Ghost—Murder Stories," *Television News* 2, no. 4 (September–October 1932): 167.
12. CBS *Production Handbook* (radio), 15 September 1933, p. 13.
13. Samuel Kaufman, "Television Progress," *Radio News* 13 (November 1931): 375.
14. "20th Anniversary of CBS Television," CBS Press Information, 10 July 1951, p. 5.
15. Interview with Worthington C. Miner, Meurice Hotel, New York, August 1982.
16. Miner, "A Report for the Columbia Broadcasting System on Twelve Years of Television," Part I, p. 15.
17. *The Billboard*, 22 May 1937, p. 9.
18. William S. Paley, *As It Happened: A Memoir* (Garden City, New York: Doubleday and Company, 1979), p. 64.
19. Miner, "A Report for the Columbia Broadcasting System on Twelve Years of Television," Part I, p. 24.
20. Interview with Miner.
21. Miner, "A Report for the Columbia Broadcasting System on Twelve Years of Television," Part I, p. 1.
22. Ibid., Part II, p. 29.
23. Ibid., Part II, p. 41.
24. Worthington Miner, "Look Back in Wonder," (typescript, 1980), p. 242.
25. Ibid., p. 238.
26. Miner wrote "A Guide to Writers" for CBS. This memo, which is believed to be lost, was based on his experiences with "Burlesque."
27. Miner, "A Report for the Columbia Broadcasting System on Twelve Years of Television," Part II, p. 27.
28. Ibid., Appendix to Part I, p. 1.
29. Ibid., Part II, p. 27.
30. Ibid.
31. Ibid., Part III, p. 19.
32. Ibid., Appendix to Part I, p. 44.
33. Ibid., Appendix to Part II, pp. 2–3.
34. Ibid., Part II, p. 38.
35. Ibid., p. 43.
36. Ibid., p. 45.
37. *CBS Program Book* (New York: Columbia Broadcasting System, 1 November 1944), p. 33.
38. CBS Television News (release), 11 July 1944.
39. Marty Schrader, *The Billboard*, 8 July 1944, p. 14.

40. CBS Television News (release), 13 July 1944.
41. Marty Schrader, *The Billboard*, 22 July 1944, p. 12.
42. Miner, "Look Back in Wonder," p. 255.
43. Richard Hubbell, "Programming," *Television* 1 (Summer 1944): 27.
44. *The Billboard*, 21 October 1944, p. 10.
45. Gilbert Seldes, "Regarding Video Experiments," *The New York Times*, 24 December 1944, p. 2:7.
46. CBS Television News (release), 6 April 1945.
47. Marty Schrader, "Who Gets What in Video," *The Billboard*, 18 November 1944, pp. 10–12.
48. The original CBS radio production of "Untitled," starring Fredric March as Hank Peters, was on *Columbia Presents Corwin* in April 1944.
49. Lou Frankel, *The Billboard*, 2 June 1945, p. 14.
50. *Variety*, 25 April 1945, p. 36.
51. Fred Hickey, "Adapting a Script for Television," *Televiser* 2 (September–October 1945): 15.
52. *The Billboard*, 6 October 1945, pp. 2, 13.
53. *Television* 3 (June 1946): 33.
54. Marty Schrader, *The Billboard*, 30 June 1943, p. 11.
55. *The Billboard*, 1 September 1945, p. 12.
56. Ibid., 25 August 1945, p. 13.
57. Marty Schrader, *The Billboard*, 20 October 1945, p. 12. In a conversation with the author of this book on 9 February 1984 (Meridan Hotel, Houston), Miss McCambridge said she was not on the telecast.
58. Marty Schrader, *The Billboard*, 1 December 1945, p. 11.
59. Ibid., 3 November 1945, p. 12.
60. Judy Dupuy, "Review of Teleshows," *Televiser* 3 (March–April 1946): 38.
61. A. H. Lass, Earle L. McGill, and Donald Axelrod, eds., *Plays from Radio* (Cambridge, Massachusetts: Houghton Mifflin Company, 1948), p. 8.
62. *The Billboard*, 10 November 1945, p. 12.
63. *Television* 3 (February 1946): 37.
64. *The Whistler* became a thirty-minute syndicated television series in 1954.

Chapter 3

1. Archer, *Big Business and Radio*, p. 439.
2. "Roof Garden for Studios," *The Billboard*, 8 March 1930, p. 37.

3. Eugene Lyons, *David Sarnoff: A Biography* (New York: Harper and Row, 1966), p. 209.

4. Albert W. Protzman, "Television Studio Technic," *Journal of the Society of Motion Picture Engineers* (July 1929). Reprinted in *RCA Review,* p. 224.

5. Ibid., p. 407.

6. Ibid., p. 411.

7. "Another Television Demonstration in N.Y.," *Variety,* 8 July 1936, p. 31.

8. A Pathé sound motion picture record was apparently made of this first demonstration and shown in the RCA Photophone Office, 411 Fifth Avenue, on 28 July 1936. The film has been lost.

9. No other references to these scenes have been found. MGM had premiered its version of *Romeo and Juliet,* starring Norma Shearer and Leslie Howard, on 20 August 1936. NBC's television scene from *Romeo and Juliet* on 9 September 1936 may be related to the film premiere.

10. *The Billboard,* 14 November 1936, p. 6.

11. Ibid., 15 July 1939, p. 8.

12. Telephone interview with Arthur Hungerford, 8 January 1983, from his home in Pennsylvania. His personal papers are in the Broadcast Pioneer Library, Washington, D.C.

13. "Shadowing the Sleuth," *The New York Times,* 28 November 1937, p. 11:12.

14. Bob Landry, "'Mummy Case,' Television's Equivalent Of 'Great Train Robbery,'" *Variety,* 25 May 1938, pp. 1, 22.

15. *The New York Times,* 22 May 1938, p. 11:10.

16. Ibid., 8 June 1938, p. 29.

17. "Susan and God," audiotape of telecast, W2XBS, 3 June 1938, Museum of Broadcasting, New York City.

18. *Time* 51 (10 May 1948): 45.

19. Interview with Hungerford.

20. "Paying for Television Acts; About $100 a Crack," *Variety,* 26 April 1939, p. 22.

21. William C. Eddy, *Television: The Eyes of Tomorrow* (New York: Prentice-Hall, 1945), pp. 4–5.

22. Ben Bodec, "Importance of Showmanship, Makeup, Clothes Point Up in NBC Telecast," *Variety,* 10 May 1939, p. 38.

23. Paul Ackerman, *The Billboard,* 20 May 1939, p. 8.

24. Ibid.

25. Paul Ackerman, *The Billboard,* 27 May 1939, p. 8.

26. *Variety,* 2 August 1939, p. 4.
27. *The Billboard,* 24 June 1939, p. 10.
28. Thomas Lyne Riley, "The Television Director," *Televiser* 1 (1944): 6. Reprinted from John Porterfield and Kay Reynolds, eds. *We Present Television* (New York: W. W. Norton, 1940), pp. 169–172.
29. *Variety,* 15 May 1940, p. 36.
30. This was the third year of the awards, but the first year "Best Actress" was honored.
31. Orrin E. Dunlap, Jr., "Televiews of Pictures," *The New York Times,* 3 September 1939, p. 9:3.
32. *Variety,* 13 September 1939, p. 24.
33. Ibid., 29 September 1939, p. 42.
34. Ibid., 25 October 1939, p. 36.
35. *The New York Times,* 18 February 1940, p. 9:12.
36. Orrin E. Dunlap, *The Future of Television* (New York: Harper and Brothers, 1942), p. 98.
37. *The New York Times,* 18 February 1940, p. 9:12.
38. *Variety,* 11 October 1939, p. 36.
39. Bernard Sobel, ed., *The Theatre Handbook and Digest of Plays* (New York: Crown Publishers, 1950), p. 836.
40. *The Billboard,* 21 October 1939, p. 6.
41. *Variety,* 18 October 1939, p. 24.
42. Two of Owen Davis's screen credits from this period were *The Great Gatsby,* an adaptation of the F. Scott Fitzgerald story in 1926, and *The Good Earth,* the Pearl Buck novel, in 1932.
43. Paul Ackerman, *The Billboard,* 17 November 1939, p. 6.
44. Mann's films include *God's Little Acre, El Cid, The Fall of the Roman Empire,* and eight films that starred James Stewart.
45. Thomas Lyne Riley, "The Television Director," in Porterfield and Reynolds, eds., *We Present Television,* pp. 169–172.
46. Edward Smith, "Television Opera Blah," *Variety,* 13 March 1940, p. 21.
47. "NBC's First Tele Year," *The Billboard,* 18 May 1940, p. 6.
48. *The New York Times,* 3 August 1941, p. 9:10.
49. Paul Denis, "War Themes Still Weak," *The Billboard,* 22 November 1941, p. 3.
50. Ibid.
51. Austin Lescarboura, "Television: The Wartime Instructor," *Radio News* 27 (May 1942): 77.
52. Giraud Chester, Garnet R. Garrison, and Edgar E. Willis, *Television and Radio* (Englewood Cliffs, New Jersey: Prentice-Hall, 1971), p. 37.
53. *Business Week* (17 June 1944): 94.

54. Porterfield and Reynolds, eds., *We Present Television*, p. 29.
55. "What's Happened to Television," *The Saturday Review of Literature* 25 (21 February 1942): 4.
56. *The Billboard*, 21 October 1944, p. 11.
57. *Television* 3 (March 1946): 26.
58. Interview with Hungerford.
59. Francis J. Griffith and Joseph Mersand, eds., *One-Act Plays for Today* (New York: Globe Book Company, 1945), p. 50.
60. Ibid.
61. Joe Koehler, *The Billboard*, 13 October 1945, p. 38.
62. Ibid., 24 November 1945, p. 44.
63. *Television* 3 (February 1946): 38.
64. *Television* 3 (May 1946): 26.
65. " 'Blythe Spirit,' NBC's Top Show: Was Much Hard Work: Sobol," *Televiser* 3 (July–August 1946): 21.
66. Joe Koehler, "Stem Shot-callers Tele-Rated," *The Billboard*, 15 June 1946, p. 19.
67. "Programming," *Television* 3 (September 1946): 29.
68. *The Billboard*, 3 August 1946, p. 14.
69. *The Billboard*, 3 February 1945, p. 11.
70. *Variety*, 9 May 1945, p. 24.
71. Marty Schrader, *The Billboard*, 8 September 1945, p. 38.
72. Joe Koehler, *The Billboard*, 17 November 1945, p. 41.
73. *The Billboard*, 9 February 1946, p. 58.
74. Judy Dupuy, "Reviews of Teleshows," *Televiser* 3 (March–April 1946): 38.
75. *Television* 4 (January 1947): 31.
76. *The Billboard*, 17 February 1945, p. 32.
77. Ibid., 10 March 1945, p. 33.
78. Ibid., 17 March 1945, p. 31.
79. "Programming," *Television* 2 (November 1945): 37.
80. Joe Koehler, *The Billboard*, 27 October 1945, p. 32.
81. *Television* 2 (November 1945): 34.
82. Joe Koehler, *The Billboard*, 3 November 1945, p. 32.
83. John Reich, "Stage Plays for Television," *Televiser* (January–February 1946): 12.
84. *Television* 3 (February 1946): 38.
85. *Television* 3 (October 1946): 31–32.
86. Ibid.
87. *Variety*, 23 May 1945, p. 34.
88. *Television* 1 (Fall 1944): 29.
89. *Television* 3 (September 1946): 32.

Chapter 4

1. "Red Carnations" was repeated with a different cast on 9 March 1944. Judy Dupuy, *Television Show Business* (Schenectady, New York: General Electric Company, 1945), p. 32.
2. Ibid., p. 25.
3. Ibid., p. 32.
4. Ibid., p. 33.
5. Ibid., p. 32. See also "2-Year Log of Outstanding WRGB Programs," *Televiser* 2 (Summer 1945): 20–21, 54.
6. *Television* 2 (November 1945): 33–34.
7. "One Camera Used on One-Set Show," *Television* 4 (May 1947): 23.
8. *The Billboard*, 5 October 1946, p. 11.
9. Wanda Marvin, *The Billboard*, 1 January 1944, p. 11.
10. *Television Daily*, 12 April 1949, p. 23.
11. Wanda Marvin, *The Billboard*, 3 June 1944, p. 7.
12. *The Billboard*, 8 July 1944, p. 4.
13. Ibid., 19 August 1944, p. 12.
14. Wanda Marvin, *The Billboard*, 30 September 1944, p. 8.
15. *The Billboard*, 7 October 1944, p. 10.
16. Joe Koehler, *The Billboard*, 21 October 1944, p. 10.
17. Tony Ferreira, "Adapting a Radio Play for Television," *Televiser* 1 (Fall 1944): 20.
18. "Touring Companies Bring Live Shows To Inde Stations," *Televiser* 3 (November–December 1946): 20.
19. Wanda Marvin, *The Billboard*, 17 February 1945, p. 32.
20. Joe Koehler, *The Billboard*, 7 April 1945, p. 13.
21. Marty Schrader, *The Billboard*, 8 January 1945, p. 12.
22. Harvey Marlowe, "Drama's Place in Television," *Television* 3 (March 1946): 17.
23. This was the larger of two WABD studios. Business and transmitter facilities were still at 515 Madison Avenue.
24. Jack Gould, "Television in Focus," *The New York Times*, 26 May 1946, p. 7:1.
25. Judy Dupuy, *Televiser* 3 (May–June 1946): 31.
26. *The New York Times*, 16 April 1946, p. 23:2.
27. Interview with Florence Monroe, University of Houston—University Park, 18 October 1983.
28. *The Billboard*, 11 May 1946, p. 16.
29. "What a N.Y. Ad Agency Learned about Its Nighttime Tele Serial," *Televiser* 4 (January–February 1947): 34.

30. *The Billboard*, 9 November 1946, p. 13.
31. Ibid., 28 December 1946, p. 13.
32. Jack Alicoate, ed., *1947 Radio Annual* (New York: Radio Daily, 1947), pp. 1026–31.
33. Bob Emery, "The Television Producer's Job," *Televiser* 3 (January–February 1946), p. 23. From an address before the "Production Panel," Television Institute, Hotel Commodore, 15 October 1945.
34. Joe Koehler, *The Billboard*, 7 April 1945, p. 13.
35. "Programming," *Television* 2 (November 1945): 23.
36. The spelling of the name varies between Emory and Emery in the trade press. "WOR Staff Training Underway at WRGB," *Television* 3 (April 1946): 24.
37. "Blue Network's Video Debut," *Televiser* 1 (Spring 1945): 30.
38. Interview with Monroe.
39. *Televiser* 3 (May–June 1946): 32. *Famous Jury Trials* would be telecast by DuMont in 1949 and syndicated in 1971.
40. Harvey Marlowe, "Drama's Place in Television," *Television* 3 (March 1946): 18.
41. Udelson, *The Great Television Race*, p. 123.
42. *The Billboard*, 9 June 1934, p. 8.
43. Porterfield and Reynolds, eds., *We Present Television*, p. 225.
44. Udelson, *The Great Television Race*, p. 123. The Don Lee regional network folded in 1967; the pioneers retired; and a new, younger staff, some without broadcasting experience, was hired.
45. Don Owen, *The Billboard*, 8 July 1944, p. 14.
46. Lee Zhito, *The Billboard*, 1 September 1945, p. 12.
47. "Advertising," *Television* 2 (November 1945): 28.
48. *The Billboard*, 1 June 1946, p. 16.
49. "Don Lee to Step Up Remote Coverage," *Television* 3 (April 1946): 24.
50. Lee Zhito, "H'Wood Slow on Pix Uptake," *The Billboard*, 7 September 1946, p. 14.
51. *The Billboard*, 4 January 1947, p. 9.
52. Arch B. Heath and J. Raymond Hutchinson, "Making Motion Pictures for Television," *Televiser* 1 (Spring 1945): 29.
53. Zhito, "H'Wood Slow on Pix Uptake," p. 14.
54. *The Billboard*, 7 October 1944, p. 10.
55. Ibid., 2 December 1944, p. 12.
56. Ibid., 23 December 1944, p. 10.
57. Cy Wagner, *The Billboard*, 4 November 1944, p. 10.
58. Ibid., 7 April 1945, p. 13.

59. Ibid., 19 July 1945, p. 14.

60. *The Billboard*, 11 May 1946, p. 16.

61. "WBKB Experiment," *Television* 4 (September 1947): 38.

Chapter 5

1. Christopher H. Sterling and John M. Kittross, *Stay Tuned* (Belmont, California: Wadsworth Publishing Company, 1978), p. 258.

2. Koehler, "Stem Shot-Callers Tele-Rated," p. 19.

3. Sidney R. Lane, "Standard Brands' 'Hour Glass' Show," *Television* 3 (October 1946): 12.

4. *Televiser* 4 (May–June 1947): 36. Fred Coe is listed in the *Televiser* review as station director.

5. *Variety*, 14 May 1948, p. 38.

6. "CBS Live Programming Ban Stirs Up Trade Queries; Effect on Smalltown Operations Seen as Hurting Industry," *Variety*, 7 May 1947, p. 46.

7. *Variety*, 20 October 1948, p. 26.

8. Interview with Marc Daniels at his home, Studio City, California, 11, 13 November 1981.

9. "Moneyed but Motley," *Newsweek* 40 (13 October 1952): 57.

10. Interview with Miner; Miner, "Look Back in Wonder," p. 275.

11. Miner, "Look Back in Wonder," pp. 296–99.

12. "Channel & Dial," *The Saturday Review of Literature* 33 (28 October 1950): 48.

13. Jack Gould, "The Honor Roll," *The New York Times*, 1 January 1950, p. 2:9.

14. Interview with Miner.

Selected Bibliography

Appleyard, Rollo. *Pioneers of Electrical Communications*. London: Macmillan, 1930.

Archer, Gleason L. *Big Business and Radio*. New York: American Historical Society, 1938. Reprinted by Arno Press, 1971.

Arlen, Michael J. *The Camera Age: Essays on Television*. New York: Farrar Strauss Giroux, 1976. These essays originally appeared in *The New Yorker*.

Barnouw, Erik. *Handbook of Radio Production*. Boston: Houghton Mifflin Company, 1949.

_____. *A Tower of Babel: A History of Broadcasting in the United States to 1933*. New York: Oxford University Press, 1966.

_____. *The Golden Web: A History of Broadcasting in the United States, 1933–1953*. New York: Oxford University Press, 1968.

The Billboard. This trade periodical is a major source of news and reviews for the entire early period of television.

Blum, Daniel. *A Pictorial History of Television*. Philadelphia: Chilton, 1959.

Briggs, Asa A. *The Golden Age of Wireless: The History of Broadcasting in the United Kingdom*. London: Oxford University Press, 1965. Covers the period 1926–39.

British Broadcasting Corporation. *Television Programmes as Broadcast* (26 August 1936–1 September 1939; 7 June 1946–1 January 1947). London: BBC, n.d. This official program log includes titles, dates, times, cast lists, and music credits. These early volumes are in the BBC Written Archives Centre, Caversham Park, Reading, England.

Broadcasting. This trade periodical contains news and features.

Brooks, Tim, and Earle Marsh. *The Complete Directory of Prime Time Network TV Shows, 1946–Present*. New York: Ballantine Books, 1979.

Brown, Les. *Encyclopedia of Television*. New York: Times Books, 1977.

Buxton, Frank, and Bill Owen. *The Big Broadcast: 1920–1950*. New York: Viking Press, 1972. A principal source for radio program descriptions and cast lists.

Campbell, Robert. *The Golden Years of Broadcasting: A Celebration of the First 50 Years of Radio and Television on NBC*. New York: Charles Scribner's Sons, 1976. Provides brief narratives in chapters on "Weekly Drama," "Soap Operas and Quiz Shows," and "Dramatic Specials." Well illustrated.

CBS Production Handbook. New York: Columbia Broadcasting System, 15 September 1933.

CBS Program Book. New York: Columbia Broadcasting System, 1938–42, 1944–45. This monthly publication is especially useful for the mid-1940s.

CBS Sponsored and Sustaining Programs. New York: Columbia Broadcasting System, 1947. Published monthly.

"CBS Television Inaugural Broadcast," 21 July 1931. Script. CBS Reference Library, New York.

CBS *Television Master Control Log.* New York: Columbia Broadcasting System, 1931–33, 1940–41. This official list of programs that are now in the archives provides dates, times, program titles, and names of engineers.

CBS *Television Program Log, WCBW, New York, 1 July 1941–1 January 1947.* New York: Columbia Broadcasting System, 1941–47.

CBS "W2XAB Birthday Program," 21 July 1932. Script. CBS Reference Library, New York.

Cerf, Bennett, and Van H. Cartmell, eds. *Thirty Famous One-Act Plays.* New York: Random House, 1943.

Chamberlain, A. B. "CBS Grand Central Television Studios." New York: CBS General Engineering Department Publications, ca. July 1948.

Chapman, E. H. *Wireless To-Day.* London: Oxford University Press, 1936.

Chase, Francis, Jr. *Sound and Fury: An Informal History of Broadcasting.* New York: Harper, 1942.

Chester, Giraud, Garnet R. Garrison, and Edgar E. Willis. *Television and Radio.* Englewood Cliffs, New Jersey: Prentice-Hall, 1971.

Chicago Daily News. Helpful for the Chicago area.

Crosby, John. *Out of the Blue: A Book about Radio and Television.* New York: Harper and Brothers, 1942.

Dunlap, Orrin E., Jr. *The Future of Television.* New York: Harper and Brothers, 1942.

———. *Radio and Television Almanac.* New York: Harper, 1951.

———. *Radio's 100 Men of Science: Biographical Narratives of Pathfinders in Electronics and Television.* New York: Harper, 1944.

Dunning, John. *Tune in Yesterday: The Ultimate Encyclopedia of Old Time Radio, 1925–1976.* Englewood Cliffs, New Jersey: Prentice-Hall, 1976.

Dupuy, Judy. *Television Show Business.* Schenectady, New York: General Electric, 1945. A principal source of information about GE's dramas during the 1940s.

Eddy, William C. *Television: The Eyes of Tomorrow.* New York: Prentice-Hall, 1945.

Edmondson, Madeleine, and David Rounds. *From Mary Noble to Mary Hartman: The Complete Soap Opera Book.* New York: Stein and Day, 1976.

Emmens, Carol A. *An Album of Television.* New York: Franklin Watts, 1980. Contains many photographs, including those pertaining to "The Queen's Messenger."

Fidell, Estelle. *Play Index, 1953–1960.* New York: H. W. Wilson Company, 1963.

Gianakos, Larry James. *Television Drama Series Programming: A Comprehensive Chronicle. Vol. I (1947–59); Vol. II (1959–75).* Metuchen, New Jersey: Scarecrow Press, 1978.

Glut, Donald F., and Jim Harmon. *The Great Television Heroes.* New York: Doubleday, 1975.

Greenfield, Jeff. *Television: The First Fifty Years.* New York: Harry N. Abrams, 1977. A highly useful overview of television history, especially drama after the mid-1940s.

Griffith, Francis J., and Joseph Mersand, eds. *One-Act Plays for Today.* New York: Globe Book Company, 1945.

Harmon, Jim. *The Great Radio Heroes.* Garden City, New York: Doubleday and Company, 1967.

Hatcher, Harlan, ed. *Modern Dramas.* New York: Harcourt, Brace, and Company, 1948.

Hawes, William K., Jr. "A History of Anthology Television Drama through 1958." Ann Arbor, Michigan: University Microfilms International, 1981.

Heath, Eric. *Writing for Television.* Los Angeles: Research Publishing Company, 1950.

Husing, Ted. *Ten Years before the Mike.* New York: Farrar and Rinehart, 1935.

Hutchinson, Thomas H. *Here Is Television: Your Window to the World.* New York: Hastings House, 1950.

Journal of Broadcasting. This scholarly quarterly, which has been published since the mid-1950s, contains a few articles on drama.

Julian, Joseph. *This Was Radio: A Personal Memoir.* New York: Viking Press, 1975.

Kemper, Stanley. *Television Encyclopedia.* New York: Fairchild, 1948.

LaGuardia, Robert. *From Ma Perkins to Mary Hartman: The Illustrated History of Soap Operas.* New York: Ballantine Books, 1977.

Landry, Robert J. *This Fascinating Radio Business.* Indianapolis: Bobbs-Merrill, 1946.

Lass, A. H., Earle L. McGill, and Donald Axelrod, eds. *Plays from Radio.* Cambridge, Massachusetts: Houghton Mifflin Company, 1948.

Laurie, Joe, Jr. *Vaudeville: From the Honky-Tonks to the Palace.* New York: Henry Holt and Company, 1953.

Lichty, Lawrence, and Malachi C. Topping. *American Broadcasting: A Source Book on the History of Radio and Television.* New York: Hastings House, 1975. Primarily discusses radio drama.

Limbacher, James L., ed. *Haven't I Seen You Somewhere Before?: Remakes, Sequels, and Series in Motion Pictures and Television, 1896–1978.* Ann Arbor, Michigan: Pierian Press, ca. 1980.

Lohr, Lenox R. *Television Broadcasting.* New York: McGraw-Hill Book Company, 1940.

Lowther, James B. *Dramatic Scenes from Athens to Broadway.* New York: Longmans, Green, and Company, 1937.

Lyons, Eugene. *David Sarnoff: A Biography.* New York: Harper and Row, 1966.

Metz, Robert. *CBS: Reflections in a Bloodshot Eye.* Chicago: Playboy Press, 1975.

Michael, Paul, and James R. Parish. *The Emmy Awards: A Pictorial History.* New York: Crown, 1970.

Miner, Worthington C. "A Report for the Columbia Broadcasting System on Twelve Years of Television." Typescript, ca. 1942. This 500-page report provides complex details on many subjects regarding early CBS history. CBS, the Miner heirs, and the author of this volume possess the few copies known to exist.

_____. "Look Back in Wonder." Typescript, ca. 1980. An autobiography written with the assistance of Franklin J. Schaffner. Most of the material in this work was included in a recently published book: *Worthington Miner Interviewed by Franklin J. Schaffner* (Metuchen, New Jersey: Scarecrow Press, 1985).

Museum of Broadcasting. *Subject Guide to the Radio and Television Collection of the Museum of Broadcasting.* New York: Museum of Broadcasting, 1979. The museum's archives contain good post-1947 audiovisual sources dealing with television.

Nadel, Norman. *A Pictorial History of the Theatre Guild.* New York: Crown Publishers, 1969.

The New York Times. A valuable source of articles that also published some reviews.

Paley, William S. *As It Happened: A Memoir.* Garden City, New York: Doubleday and Company, 1979.

Parish, James Robert. *Actors' Television Credits, 1950–1972.* Metuchen, New Jersey: Scarecrow Press, 1973. First supplement, 1978.

Perry, Jeb H. *Variety Obits: An Index to Obituaries in Variety, 1905–1978.* Metuchen, New Jersey: Scarecrow Press, 1980.

Porterfield, John, and Kay Reynolds, eds. *We Present Television.* New York: W. W. Norton, 1940. A collection of articles written by prominent participants in television drama.

Quinlan, Sterling. *Inside ABC: American Company's Rise to Power.* New York: Hastings House, 1979. Contains a few references to ABC dramas.

Radio Annual. This trade directory, which published statistics and provided an annual review of radio from 1937 to 1964, included some television information during the 1940s.

Radio News. Some of the articles during the early 1930s deal with television.

"A Remembrance of 'Pappy,' Fred Coe 1914–1979." This booklet, published ca. 1980 by his friends, especially the Delbert Manns, contains comments of his colleagues as well as photographs. The Manns and the author of this volume possess copies.

Robertson, Patrick. *The Book of Firsts.* New York: Bramhall House, 1974. Includes a section on international firsts in television.

Sarnoff, David. *The Wisdom of Sarnoff and the World of RCA.* Beverly Hills, California: Wisdom Books, 1968.

Seldes, Gilbert. *The Great Audience.* New York: Viking Press, 1951.

Settel, Irving. *A Pictorial History of Radio.* 2d. ed. New York: Gossett and Dunlap, 1967.

Settel, Irving, and William Lass. *A Pictorial History of Television.* New York: Gossett and Dunlap, 1969.

Sharp, Harold S., and Marjorie Z. Sharp. *Index to Characters in the Performing Arts, Part IV: Radio and Television.* Metuchen, New Jersey: Scarecrow Press, 1973.

Shulman, Arthur, and Roger Youman. *How Sweet It Was: Television—A Pictorial Commentary.* New York: Shorecrest, 1966.

Sobel, Bernard, ed. *The Theatre Handbook and Digest of Plays.* New York: Crown Publishers, 1950.

Stedman, Raymond. *The Serials: Suspense and Drama by Installment.* Norman, Oklahoma: University of Oklahoma Press, 1971.

Sterling, Christopher H., and John M. Kittross. *Stay Tuned: A Concise History of American Broadcasting.* Belmont, California: Wadsworth Publishing Company, 1978.

Televiser. Published excellent features and reviews of dramas during the 1940s.

Television. From 1944 to 1968, published excellent features on and reviews of dramas.

Television Factbook. A major data source and directory since it began publication in 1945.

Terrace, Vincent. *The Complete Encyclopedia of Television Programs. Vol. I (A–K); Vol. II (L–Z)*. South Brunswick and New York: A. S. Barnes and Company, 1976.

Theatre Arts Monthly. Occasional feature articles during the 1930s described television drama.

"20th Anniversary of CBS Television: An Account of the Pioneering and Progress of CBS-TV since July 21, 1931." New York: CBS Press Information, 10 July 1951.

Udelson, Joseph H. *The Great Television Race: A History of the American Television Industry, 1925–1941*. University, Alabama: The University of Alabama Press, 1982. One of the few sources that details television's early development.

Variety. A major source of news, features, and reviews after 1938.

Wade, Robert J. *Designing for Television: The Arts and Crafts in Television Production*. New York: Pellegrini and Cudahy, 1952. Contains photographs and designs of many experimental-period productions.

Wilk, Max. *The Golden Age of Television: Notes from the Survivors*. New York: Delacorte, 1976.

WNBT Television Master Programs. New York: National Broadcasting Company, 1941–47. This master log lists programs, casts, occasional scripts, and comments. Preserved on microfilm at NBC and RCA.

W2XBS Television Master Programs. New York: National Broadcasting Company, 1936–41. This master log lists programs, casts, some scripts, and comments. The typed original master program materials have been destroyed, but most of the pertinent information is on microfilm at NBC and RCA.

Index

ABOUT THE AUTHOR

William Hawes is professor in the School of Communication, University of Houston–University Park. He received his bachelor of arts degree from Eastern Michigan University, and his master of arts degree and doctorate from the University of Michigan.